W9-BRM-529

Hearts and Minds

A volume in the series *Perspectives on the Sixties*
Edited by *Barbara L. Tischler*

Hearts and Minds

Bodies, Poetry, and Resistance in the Vietnam Era

Michael Bibby

RUTGERS UNIVERSITY PRESS
New Brunswick, New Jersey

Library of Congress Cataloging-in-Publication Data

Bibby, Michael, 1957–
    Hearts and minds : bodies, poetry, and resistance in the Vietnam
era / Michael Bibby.
        p.   cm. — (Perspectives on the sixties)
    Includes bibliographical references (p.) and index.
    ISBN 0-8135-2297-8 (cloth : alk. paper). — ISBN 0-8135-2298-6
(pbk. : alk. paper)
    1. American poetry—20th century—History and criticism.
2. Vietnamese Conflict, 1961–1975—Literature and the conflict.
3. Vietnamese Conflict, 1961–1975—Protest movements.   4. Protest
poetry, American—History and criticism.   5. War poetry, American—
History and criticism.   I. Title.   II. Series.
PS310.V54B53   1996
811'.5409358—dc20   95-52261
                                                                      CIP

British Cataloging-in-Publication information available
Copyright © 1996 by Michael Bibby
All rights reserved
Published by Rutgers University Press, New Brunswick, New Jersey
Manufactured in the United States of America

for Shari

Contents

4

Fragging the Chain(s) of Command: Mutilation and GI Resistance Poetry   123

Acknowledgments

When I first entered graduate school, like many writers and critics I found explicitly political poems distasteful. My master's thesis argued strenuously in favor of a symbolist style of political address, a poetry that kept its politics quiet. But, in my admittedly limited experiences in anti-apartheid, anti-nuclear, and anti–Gulf War actions, I always admired the men and women I met who refused to keep quiet in the face of explicit abuses of power. In a writers' seminar on poetry and politics, I read poems by people in El Salvador, South Africa, Turkey, and other countries where the stakes for writing explicitly about abuses, "telling truth to power," were much higher than we in that seminar or demonstrating in American streets could adequately comprehend. These poetic testimonies—often blunt and unimaginative but always compelling—shattered the luxurious, private calm of so much imagistic, symbolist poetry I read in college. As I wrestled with the age-old conflict between poetry and politics, I began reading political poems written in the United States. Having grown up under the shadow of the Vietnam War and bearing deep memories from those turbulent years, I always felt that this period's political poetry deserved attention.

When I describe this project to interested strangers, they often ask, Did I go to the Vietnam War? Was I an activist? It seems that the Vietnam era remains, even a generation after, a period in which "being there" is paramount. It is presumed by such questions that to be interested in the 60s, one must have experienced it firsthand. I grew up in this period, but I was only thirteen when students were being murdered at Kent State and Jackson State, and I turned eighteen only days before the evacuation of the U.S. embassy in Saigon. I remember clearly the assassinations, the riots on the Ohio State University campus not far from where I lived, the fears in my white suburban enclave of an invasion by Black Panthers, the My Lai massacre, the body-count figures reported daily in the local newspaper alongside the weather reports—but, of course, anyone born earlier than 1970 can probably recall similar impressions. So it seems curious that I am asked to authenticate my interest in the activist poetry of the Vietnam era, to lay claim to this period with some direct personal experience. Why should *this* period, more than others, exert such a call for authentic experience? To paraphrase Michael Herr on the Vietnam era: we've all been there.

And yet so much has been forgotten. The more I researched the poetry of the Vietnam era, the more I was confronted by a paradoxical silence. The greatest portion of my labor in this project has been locating the out-of-print and underground poems. What I found was that *everyone* seemed to be writing and publishing poems in the Vietnam era, and most of these poems were explicitly expressive of the social turmoil and political resistance of its times. Despite this, in the space of less than twenty years, this outpouring of poetry has practically evaporated without a trace. And the literary establishment—professors, critics, the well-published and recognized poets working today—have written virtually nothing about a literature that by any measure defines American poetry of the Vietnam era. The complete absence of any critical engagement with activist poetry of the 60s astonished me as a graduate student of the late 80s. With the insistence on politics in literary and cultural theories in the academy, it seemed ironic that the only poetry of resistance accorded much attention was invariably written in the Third World. Why has the American resistance poetry of a time many critics can vividly remember not been examined with the same politically progressive and theoretical interest?

In many senses, then, this book is a work of recuperation, an attempt to combat the cultural amnesia that has settled over us about the Vietnam era. But it is also an attempt to demonstrate how the activist poetry of this period can be both recuperated and given new meaning by reading it as cultural critique, sites of political contestations, historical indices of important social conflicts. Further, by examining the expressive documents of the activists engaged in these struggles, this book means to shed new light on the historical grounds upon which our contemporary discourses of identity and resistance have largely been mapped.

Just as the poetry I discuss bears the impression of its communities, my book owes much to its community. Although this book has been long in the making, I have been very fortunate to have had the generous support and advice of colleagues, friends, and institutions. I must first thank my professors at the University of Minnesota, who oversaw this project when it was my dissertation. Maria Damon's work on poetry as cultural critique first encouraged my approach, and her erudite understanding of contemporary poetry, her careful readings of the many drafts of my manuscript, and her enthusiastic support have proved indispensable. Throughout my work on this book, Paula Rabinowitz's scholarship and personal engagement in the field of radical literature has been inspirational. Shirley Garner, David Noble, Kent Bales, and Phil Furia gave my work many thoughtful readings. And I owe a great debt to Michael Dennis Browne, whose writers' seminar on politics and poetry first sparked my interest in the field, and whose poetry workshop advice gave me the courage to follow my obsessions. And, although my interests were far removed from their own, David Wallace and Rita Copeland offered much professional advice, encouragement, and camaraderie.

My editors and reader have borne up under the burden of reading my manuscripts several times, and for their patience and commitment I am deeply grateful. My series editor, Barbara L. Tischler, saw the potential in this project, and I am greatly indebted to her enthusiasm for it, her careful editing, and her principled commitment to 60s studies. Leslie Mitchner's patience, perceptive comments, and decisive direction have helped me better realize the project. My anonymous reader helped me better understand what I wanted to say and offered many useful suggestions and incisive comments. I also thank Willa Speiser for her thorough and perceptive copyediting.

Portions of this book have been presented as papers at the following conferences: Modern Language Association Annual Meeting (1995), American Studies Association Annual Meeting (1995), the 1995 Sixties Generation Conference, Midwest Modern Language Associations Annual Meetings (1990, 1993), and popular culture associations annual meetings (1989, 1990, 1991). For their useful comments, conversation, and support, I thank my audiences and co-panelists at those sessions, especially Leah Hackelman, Maureen Heacock, Kara Provost, the late Tom Yingling, Kalí Tal, Lorrie Smith, Vince Gotera, and N. Bradley Christie. Theresa L. Brown gave me keen editorial advice on an abbreviated version of chapter 4, which appeared as "Fragging the Chains of Command: GI Resistance Poetry and Mutilation," *Journal of American Culture* 16, no. 3 (1993). For helping me track down addresses for some hard-to-find Vietnam veteran poets, I am grateful to the poet W. D. Ehrhart.

Although many friends over the years have both helped shape my thinking and given me much needed moral support, my deepest thanks here go to Patricia Briggs, for the many years of conversation and friendship. Lauren M. E. Goodlad's conversations with me about postmodernism, goth music, and postpunk subcultural style have given me welcome respite from the intensities of the present project. And for her collegial support, advice, and rides to the airport, I thank Kim van Alkemade.

A University of Minnesota College of Liberal Arts Senior Teaching Fellowship facilitated my completion of a draft of this project. A generous Summer Research Grant from the Pennsylvania State System of Higher Education helped me revise my book and conduct research at libraries in Minnesota and Wisconsin. For assistance in obtaining permissions, I thank the office of Dr. Robert Golden, dean of arts and sciences at Shippensburg University.

I owe my deepest debt, however, to Shari Horner, who has always been a compassionate comrade. Her scholarly integrity, advice, support, and enduring faith over the years have sustained me in more ways than I can ever adequately acknowledge.

The author and the publisher would like to thank the following people for permission to reproduce copyrighted material. Every effort has been made to trace ownership of all copyrighted materials and obtain permission for its use in this book.

Etel Adnan, "The Enemy's Testament," reprinted from *Where is Vietnam?: American Poets Respond*, ed. Walter Lowenfels (Garden City, N.Y.: Doubleday, Anchor, 1967), by permission of the author.

John Balaban, "Mau Than" and "After Our War," from *After Our War* by John Balaban; copyright © 1974 by John Balaban.

Amiri Baraka, "Black Art," "An Agony. As Now," and "Ka' Ba," from *The LeRoi Jones/Amiri Baraka Reader* by Amiri Baraka; copyright © 1989 by Amiri Baraka; used by permission of Thunder's Mouth Press; "Sacred Chant for the Return of Black Spirit and Power"; copyright © 1972 by Amiri Baraka; reprinted by permission of Sterling Lord Literistic, Inc.

Jan Barry, "Memorial for Man in Black Pajamas," reprinted from *Winning Hearts and Minds: War Poems by Vietnam Veterans*, ed. Larry Rottmann, Jan Barry, and Basil T. Paquet (Brooklyn: 1st Casualty Press, 1972), by permission of the author.

D. C. Berry, "The sun goes down," reprinted from *Saigon Cemetery* (Athens: University of Georgia Press, 1972), by permission of the author.

DeWitt Clinton, "Spirit of the Bayonet Fighter," reprinted from *Winning Hearts and Minds: War Poems by Vietnam Veterans*, ed. Larry Rottmann, Jan Barry, and Basil T. Paquet (Brooklyn: 1st Casualty Press, 1972), by permission of the author.

W. D. Ehrhart, "The Sniper's Mark," reprinted from *Winning Hearts and Minds: War Poems by Vietnam Veterans*, ed. Larry Rottmann, Jan Barry, and Basil T. Paquet (Brooklyn: 1st Casualty Press, 1972), by permission of the author; a revised version appears in *To Those Who Have Gone Home Tired* by W. D. Ehrhart (New York: Thunder's Mouth Press, 1984).

Patricia Giggans, "Two Poems," reprinted from *Aphra* 3, no. 3 (Summer 1972), by permission of Patricia Occhiuzzo Giggans.

Dotty LeMieux, "The war is still on somewhere," reprinted from *Women* (Fall 1970): 6, by permission of the author.

Clarence Major, "Vietnam #4," reprinted from *New Black Voices: An Anthology of Contemporary Afro-American Literature*, ed. Abraham Chapman (New York: Mentor/New American Library, 1972); copyright © 1972 by Clarence Major.

Robin Morgan, "Freaks," reprinted from *Monster* by Robin Morgan; copyright © 1972 by Robin Morgan; reprinted by permission of Edite Krohl Literary Agency.

Raymond Patterson, "What We Know" and "Black Power," reprinted from *New Black Voices: An Anthology of Contemporary Afro-American Literature*, ed. Abraham Chapman (New York: Mentor/New American Library, 1972), by permission of the author.

Basil T. Paquet, "Basket Case" and "In a Plantation," reprinted from *Winning Hearts and Minds: War Poems by Vietnam Veterans*, ed. Larry Rottmann, Jan Barry, and Basil T. Paquet (Brooklyn: 1st Casualty Press, 1972), by permission of author.

Sylvia Plath, "Lady Lazarus" from *Ariel* by Sylvia Plath; copyright © 1963 by Ted Hughes; "Tulips" from *Ariel* by Sylvia Plath; copyright © 1962 by Ted Hughes. Copyrights renewed; reprinted by permission of HarperCollins Publishers, Inc.

Stan Platke, "Gut Catcher," from *Winning Hearts and Minds: War Poems by Vietnam Veterans*, ed. Larry Rottmann, Jan Barry, and Basil T. Paquet (Brooklyn: 1st Casualty Press, 1972), by permission of the author.

Don Receveur, "night fear" and "August 17, 1970," from *Winning Hearts and Minds: War Poems by Vietnam Veterans*, ed. Larry Rottmann, Jan Barry, and Basil T. Paquet (Brooklyn: 1st Casualty Press, 1972), by permission of the author.

Adrienne Rich, "Tear Gas," reprinted from *The Fact of a Doorframe: Poems Selected and New, 1950–1984* by Adrienne Rich, by permission of the author and W. W. Norton and Company, Inc.; copyright © 1984 by Adrienne Rich; copyright © 1975, 1978 by W. W. Norton and Company, Inc.; copyright © 1981 by Adrienne Rich.

Larry Rottmann, "S.O.P.," reprinted from *Winning Hearts and Minds: War Poems by Vietnam Veterans*, ed. Larry Rottmann, Jan Barry, and Basil T. Paquet (Brooklyn: 1st Casualty Press, 1972), appears courtesy of the author.

Anne Sexton, ["I'm dreaming the My Lai soldier again"], from *Words for Dr. Y* by Anne Sexton; copyright © 1978 by Linda Gray Sexton and Loring Conant, Jr., executors of the will of Anne Sexton; reprinted by permission of Houghton Mifflin Co. All rights reserved.

A. B. Spellman, "tomorrow the heroes," reprinted from *Vietnam and Black America*, ed. Clyde Taylor (Garden City, N.Y.: Doubleday, Anchor, 1973), by permission of the author.

Hearts and Minds

Introduction

On May 4, 1965, Lyndon B. Johnson told a meeting of the Texas Electric Cooperatives, Inc.: "We must be ready to fight in Vietnam, but the ultimate victory will depend on the hearts and minds of the people who actually live out there." Coming on the heels of the first mass deployment of U.S. troops to Vietnam, this speech marks one of the earliest public uses of the phrase "hearts and minds" in relation to the Vietnam War.[1] In his speech, Johnson celebrated U.S. plans to build a dam on the Mekong River to provide electricity to the Vietnamese as part of the administration's program of "pacification." By building up the country economically, it was believed, the United States could win the allegiance of the Vietnamese people in a way that military force clearly could not.[2]

The U.S. policy of "pacification" was often referred to as "winning hearts and minds," which meant that it sought to win the emotional and political support of the rural South Vietnamese who, impoverished and disenfranchised by their U.S.-backed government, were sympathetic to and supportive of nationalist revolutionary forces. "Winning hearts and minds" was often called "the other war" by Johnson's staff. Its advocates in the White House envisioned this program as the rational alternative to the economically and politically expensive intensification of military involvement.[3] Pacification was often derided by military officials, however, who believed it jeopardized their authority over the U.S. intervention and subordinated military options to bureaucratic, civil ones. Early in the intervention, Gen. William Westmoreland strongly favored military solutions to the "problem" in Vietnam. This view ultimately prevailed, leading to major troop increases and massive munitions buildups.[4] Yet despite the military's hostility to it, pacification lingered on in U.S. policy throughout the war, resulting in what many historians have regarded as a central contradiction in the U.S. approach to the conflict. Military analysts have cited pacification theory as evidence of the kind of political bureaucratic meddling that led to the war's loss. Robert Komer and others maintain that it would have been successful if only the military had supported it.[5] Although using the term "winning hearts and minds" as a euphemism suggests the achievement of goals and the consolidation of forces, it also ironically calls forth an image of sundered body parts; as official U.S. policy in Vietnam, this euphemism has also come to signify a divided political agenda. Just as "hearts and minds" is a metaphor grounded in an image of divided body parts, the U.S. military *corps* would find itself repeatedly split over its priorities: search-and-destroy or pacification; intervention or development; military or civil.[6]

"Winning hearts and minds" has also become a key trope of the historical period from 1965 to 1975. In relation to the Vietnam War, it stands as a metaphor for the divisiveness, duplicity, and moral ambiguities of U.S. policy in Vietnam. On its face, "winning hearts and minds" appeals to a vision of moral victories and righteous intents. The hypocrisy of this was apparent to soldiers and antiwar activists who understood that, as military jargon, "winning hearts and minds" actually spoke less about victories over abstract, disembodied loyalties and more about the violent production of body counts. Indeed, this euphemism became known in the military by the acronym WHAM, and thus it was rewritten as an onomatopoeic sign of the bombing and killing that actually enforced "pacification."

As "winning hearts and minds" passed into the vernacular, it became articulated in ways that transgressed its official uses by Johnson's administration and the military. In one example, particularly relevant to the present study, a group of antiwar soldiers and veterans adopted "winning hearts and minds" as the title for their anthology of antiwar poetry. Here the phrase becomes multiply transgressive: it implicitly critiqued the "commander-in-chief" and countermanded the military ideology that antiwar soldiers were subject(ed) to, and it also traversed the often conflicting subject positions of soldier and antiwar activist.[7] "Hearts and minds" is a trope that signifies along a number of often contradictory and divergent valences in American cultural history. After the war, "hearts and minds" was used as the title to a documentary about the war, casting the war's tragedy primarily in terms of the sufferings of the Americans who fought it. The recuperation of the war into American mythography since the Reagan era further complicates the status of this trope. To invoke it now is to call up images of the sufferings of American soldiers in Vietnam and the debate over the war in American life.[8] From its use as a euphemism for foreign policy to its rearticulation as an ironic sign of the war's immorality to its recent recuperation as a metonym of American suffering in the war, "hearts and minds" captures the conflicted, fragmentary meanings of the Vietnam era.

Throughout its various deployments and articulations, "hearts and minds" has been grounded in a classic binary opposition between emotion and reason that has troubled Western thought throughout history. The "heart" in this dichotomy is associated with emotion, but also by extension with sensuality, corporeality, and matter, and—as has been demonstrated by feminist philosophy—ultimately with the female. The "mind," then, is associated with intellect and reason, rationality, thought, and the soul, and the male.[9] This binarism, reiterated in the various ways "hearts and minds" has been cited as a trope of the Vietnam era, registers the social and political conflicts over the meanings of corporeality central to the American cultural history of the Vietnam era. Throughout the years when the United States waged war in Vietnam, America found itself torn apart by oppositional activism aimed at challenging, contesting, subverting, and overthrowing long-held assumptions about society, identity, and ultimately the relationship of body and mind. Invigorated by everyday life's saturation by visual media and the concomitant spectacle the media industry made of the body, by the post–World War II expansion of commodities and consumer capital, and an emerging postmodern intellectual and artistic celebration of sensuality, the young people of the 60s who took to the streets in record numbers proclaimed with Whitmanesque exuberance the glories of the human body. The beats, radicals, hippies, and countercultural youth of the period imagined the human body as the source of an authentic being, a "natural" self. These young people rejected "head games" and "mind trips" in favor of cultivating the senses and sensory experience. The corporeal was celebrated over the intellectual, and thus, "hearts and minds" also captures this central contest in the cultural history of the Vietnam era. Yet the trope also depends on a notion of union. Contrary to this narrative of oppositions that I have suggested, the 60s is also cast as a period in which the old Cartesian boundaries between rationality and sensuality seemed to dissolve, a period when "hearts and minds," body and soul, could be unified. It was a period that mixed radical politics with bohemian hedonism, Third World liberation with sexual liberation, Marx with LSD, revolution with pop music.

I have cited this diversely signifying, contradictory trope in my title to foreground the central concerns of this book. Just as "hearts and minds" has been the site of ideological struggles over the meaning of the 60s, corporeality—the images, tropes, and symbols of human bodiliness, the means by which the human body could be thought—was itself rhetorically figured as a site of political struggle in the Vietnam era.[10] The phrase articulates both a joining and a fragmentation, suture and mutilation, consensus and division, mutual and conflictual aspects that epitomize 60s cultural history. Indeed, the trope of a body politic torn apart has become so common in portrayals of the 60s as to be cliché; and yet this cliché is rooted in the historical fact that political struggle, activism, and social contestation defined the period. Whether viewed in terms of counterculturalism, political activism, the war, race, gender, or sexuality, the years from 1965 to 1975 mark a period of widespread social conflict, a turning point in U.S. liberalism, and a crisis stage in the so-called American century. Outside of early twentieth-century radicalism, no other period in American history saw such widespread dissent against dominant ideologies. And the aftereffects of 60s oppositionalism have configured the skepticism and subversiveness of postmodernism, with its heralding of the death of grand narratives, its critique of spectacle culture, and its celebrations of fragmentation and difference.[11] The political upheavals of the period carved profound divisions that continue to motivate contemporary conflicts in U.S. culture. That the conservative Republican Speaker of the House, Newt Gingrich, can mobilize his ideological forces and manipulate mainstream media debate in 1995 by demonizing the "counterculture" and "McGoverniks" of the 60s demonstrates not only how these divisions still register in present-day debates, but also how profoundly the legacy of this period continues to shape the political maps.

Yet this book is a study of neither the Vietnam War nor exclusively antiwar poetry. By calling attention to the war's legacy, I mean to emphasize the fact that the key social and political struggles of the period from roughly 1965 to 1975 erupted in a time of war. Throughout the Vietnam era, social activists challenged authority and exclusionary practices and struggled for a more just, democratic, and liberated society. Although the specific arena of struggle varied, whether on the grounds of race, gender, the war, class, sexuality, and/or any combination of these factors, one significant thread running through the left-oriented activism of the Vietnam era and the poetry it produced was a concern with issues of self-representation, identity, and community.[12] This focus on self-representation and identity-in-community, on the personal as the political and the politics of the personal is, I believe, the paradigmatic theoretical innovation of Vietnam-era social activism. While specific agenda have changed, concepts of self-representation and identity continue to mobilize social action, political theory, and cultural critique in the contemporary scene.

I will argue that the struggles over the meanings of identity and corporeality central to social activism and oppositional politics in the 60s are significantly played out in the poetry published during the Vietnam era. When I began working on the period, my goal was to examine the canonized poetry of the 60s—poetry by professional writers and teachers, such as Robert Bly, Robert Duncan, Denise Levertov, and David Ignatow. The more I studied, however, the more I found that 60s poetry was both deeply inscribed with the social conflicts of its time and more diverse and widespread than the canon suggested. Although these canonized poets often wrote about their political activism, there remained a vast archive of poetic texts written by activists that literary history has largely ignored. Because the 60s is a period so thoroughly enmeshed in political opposition—and because poetry was so widely written, published, performed, and read in the contexts of oppositional activism—I decided to focus my attention on the key resistance literature of the Vietnam era, the poetry of activists.

Thus my book is primarily concerned with how literary texts register the social, political, and historical experiences of this ideologically conflicted era. While I focus on poetry and my approach is predominantly literary, the object of my analysis will be less the literary text per se than the discursive formations of what I have discerned as the Vietnam-era oppositional politics of corporeality. I will examine the ways images, tropes, and symbols of human bodies in activist poetry express views of corporeality, political identity, and modes of resistance as they intersect with and negotiate key ideological struggles of the period. In other words, I will view poetry as not only literary but also social, as textual constructions in which the ideologies and cultural discourses of certain social groups in specific historical contexts have been negotiated, circulated, and produced. I will focus on these poetic texts as sites of cultural contestation, as artifacts of a social history that has immeasurably shaped our present moment. As Barbara Harlow defines it, "Resistance literature calls attention to itself, and to literature in general, as a political and politicized activity. The literature of resistance sees itself further as immediately and directly involved in a struggle against ascendant or dominant forms of ideological and cultural production."[13] The activist poetry of this period was tendential, partisan, and polemical, challenging both the literary norms inherited from New Critical formalism and the socially contained role poetry had been assigned since World War II. For many poets active in oppositional movements, poetry was, as Harlow describes it, "an arena of struggle."[14] The analytics made hegemonic by New Criticism, with its preference for ambivalent, trans-historical, individualistic, ironic, linguistically and formally complex texts, will not suffice for my project; an approach engaging the cultural, social, political, and historical textures of activist poetry is called for. My overarching concern has been how political ideologies and cultural identities were articulated in the imaginative construction of human corporeality evident in activist poetry of the Vietnam era.

By "oppositional" I mean the styles, practices, and forms associated with movements organized for political and social change and opposed to ruling ideological formations; the conscious and systematic articulation of a position in opposition to dominant and dominating cultural forms. In general I will describe as "oppositional" the range of political and cultural practices in the Vietnam era loosely identified with leftist, radical, and/or countercultural perspectives. Yet my book is in no way meant to offer a comprehensive account of 60s oppositionalism. Rather I have focused on three broadly defined movements that I believe can serve as case studies of historically significant terrains of struggle over corporeality in the Vietnam era: Black Liberation, Women's Liberation, and the GI Resistance. These movements forged critical interventions in U.S. culture over the meanings of race, gender, and the war, and generated important points of resistance against what was argued to be a white, masculinist hegemony that both dominated oppressed peoples in the United States and waged a racist war of imperialism in Vietnam.

My focus on poetic texts is supported by the prominence of poetry in the oppositional cultures of the period. More poetry was published in the United States after 1960 than in any previous historical period. This is due not only to social but also to material factors, such as the move by major publishing houses into paperback printing in the late 1940s, the development of relatively inexpensive printing technologies (mimeographing, photocopying, offset printing), and— with the increased availability of printing—the proliferation of small presses, underground newspapers, and alternative printing (for example, posters and broadsides). Along with this, the pop music explosion made lyrics not only more accessible to more people than ever before, but its rhythms and styles, thoroughly inflected by and appropriative of black vernacular musical expressions and working-class social protest traditions (both viewed as inherently oppositional) also captured the spirit of youthful rebellion. By the late 1960s nearly every city and campus had at least one underground press that advocated alternative lifestyles, radical politics, and/or opposition to the war and that regularly published poems.[15] The spread of small and underground presses throughout the country meant that not only recognized writers but also movement activists and nonprofessional writers could now publish their work cheaply and distribute it widely.[16] According to publishing industry statistics, poetry publication by mainstream presses increased in each year throughout the 1960s. Poetry production during the Vietnam era reached phenomenal proportions; in many ways, American culture was being "lyricized." People caught up in the tumultuous experiences of social activism and dissent now could imagine themselves more than ever before as poets and saw poetry as an inherently anti-establishment vehicle for their political expressions. A relatively compact literary form, easily copied, memorized, and disseminated, a form that lends itself to haphazard schedules, as well as to performance, chant, and demonstration, the poem became an ideally practical genre for 60s activism.

Underground newspapers and small presses provided widely accessible forums for this poetry boom. When Len Fulton noted in his 1967 *Directory of Little Magazines and Small Presses* that "the little magazine revolution that began sometime after 1960" was "moving toward a peak," he credited this expansion to the proliferation of poetry.[17] The present analysis concerns poetic texts recovered from this vast and otherwise neglected archive of underground presses and of the movement-oriented and topical anthologies published in the time. Naturally, any attempt to offer a comprehensive account of all the poetry of the underground 60s would be futile and necessarily superficial. I have tried instead to limit my survey to those periodicals and anthologies that played significant roles in the shaping of oppositional culture, but I have also considered interesting poetic texts both from less influential sources and less movement-specific collections. Much important poetry, then, may be overlooked, but my hope is that this approach will suggest something of the breadth of oppositional poetry produced in the period and encourage further research into these neglected texts.

To begin I will address two theoretical and methodological issues both central to the present study and critical to my conception of Vietnam-era oppositional culture. Since my book discusses how bodies were figured in politically committed poetry, I open by engaging some key theoretical concepts of reading corporeality. In particular I give a brief outline of the philosophical dilemma of the body/mind split and its meaning for post–World War II culture as it entered the Vietnam era. By associating existentialist phenomenology with popular leftist discourses of the period, I argue that oppositional 60s culture perceived body and mind as essentially coextensive of each other. It was largely because the cultural and political vanguard of the early 60s began to understand the body as indissociable from the mind, the inner as the outer, the public as the private, that the personal could be seen as the political and the body as a site of ideological struggle. Further, my book makes certain claims about periodization. Although literary history has largely marginalized the Vietnam War—most notably by casting all post-1945 writing as "postwar"—I argue that literature from 1965 to 1975 should be periodized as "Vietnam era" to express more accurately the material and political conditions configuring its production. Both the war and oppositional social activism from about 1965 to 1975 need to be reconsidered in relation to each other. The war should be viewed as an objective historical condition that, in many ways, gave shape to specific political and cultural practices of such social movements as Black Liberation and Women's Liberation. The war is not, of course, the only significant condition; but its overwhelming impact on political, economic, and cultural experience in the period and its recurrence as a trope and theme in activist poetry qualifies the Vietnam War as a dominant factor in the history of this period.

The first movement I examine is the one that first brought the discourse of "liberation" and a politics of self-in-community and corporeality to bear on 60s oppositionalism and that remained throughout the period the widely acknowledged vanguard of revolutionary activism: Black Liberation. Black Liberation occupies the liminal space between a "postwar" history and a Vietnam-era history. Its roots in Civil Rights activism link it to the discourses of racial equality and justice forged in the 40s and 50s, while its articulation of theoretical and practical links to Third World liberation movements evokes associations with the Vietnam War. Through Black Liberation's invocation of the tropes of the war and nationalist liberation, the epistemological focus of revolutionary politics from around 1965 to 1975 shifts from "postwar" to a Vietnam-era perspective. I begin by comparing the Black Liberation movement's assertion of "blackness" to the postwar elision of "color" in mainstream African American culture. In Black Liberationist poetry, I argue, "blackness" is posed as the definitive presence of identity, representing not only a cultural sign but an "epidermal difference" that marks the body. Following theories of liberation prevalent in Third World movements, Black Liberationist poets seek to transfigure the image of African American bodies, to rearticulate their physical features, historically "denigrated" in U.S. culture, so that they signify power and beauty. By foregrounding and celebrating black corporeality, Black Liberationist poets seek to forge a vision of a distinctively "black" nation. Further, I demonstrate how the poetics of black corporeality in this period register Black Liberation's concerns with the Vietnam War. Citing the language of the war, its images and tropes, Black Liberationist poetry often identified African America's plight under white rule with the anticolonialist struggles of the Vietnamese.

Next I turn to feminist poetry associated with the Women's Liberation movement. As many historians have noted, Women's Liberation had important roots in Civil Rights activism and the emergence of Black Liberation. Feminist poets in this period, however, foregrounded gender, generally represented as a trans-racial, universal biological essence, as the determinant of personal and political identity. Discourses of female corporeality in Women's Liberation, I argue, often appropriate the vernacular of liberation and Third-Worldism made current by Black Liberation and the Vietnam War to represent the female body as colonized, suggesting that "women" constitute a "nation." The politics of liberation that Vietnam-era feminists often advocated reiterate Third World concepts of national self-determination. My study focuses on how corporeality in feminist poetry relates to a specific struggle central to feminist politics in the Vietnam era: the Women's Health Movement and the politics of reproductive rights. Discussing a number of poems that draw associations between medical technologies, patriarchal oppression, and militarism, I argue that the female body's interior could be viewed in this period as a site of political struggle so that the politics of access to the body's organs and internal life processes were associated with the struggle for self-determination articulated in Third World liberation. Attacking male-dominated medical professions as an insensitively rationalistic force for colonizing the interior of the female body, feminists in the Vietnam era developed a unique means of constructing their interests within the paradigms of liberationist politics.

Although much has been written on the Black Liberation and Women's Liberation movements, very little attention has been paid to the GI Resistance movement.[18] Yet this movement posed an unprecedented threat to the stability of U.S. operations in Vietnam and a challenge to normative perceptions of the soldier. No other movement of its kind can be found in American history. More significantly, activists in the GI Resistance developed a prolific subculture that included hundreds of covert newspapers and several literary collections featuring poetry as an important means of expression. Chapter 4 of this book focuses on GI Resistance poetry, antiwar and dissident poems written by both active soldiers and veterans and printed during the war. I argue that GI Resistance poetry articulates resistance through images, tropes, and poetics of mutilation in which the fragmented, dismembered, disincorporated (masculine) body signifies both the brutal incoherence of the war and the failure of dominant ideology's notion of the soldier body as an impenetrable totality. By emphasizing the mutilation of bodies, GI poems "frag"—GI slang for the assassination of an officer—the narrative chains that command militaristic ideology, foregrounding the inherent incoherence of the military "corps."

Recent critical approaches have laid the groundwork for a reassessment of politically engaged literature. Cary Nelson's recent work has recuperated the proletarian poetry of the early twentieth century in ways that call our current canonical boundaries into question.[19] Paula Rabinowitz's work on the proletarian 30s has brought a theoretically informed perspective to the long-neglected fiction of women associated with this period of radicalism.[20] Barbara Harlow has written compelling accounts of prisoner and Third World activist literatures that theorize the possibilities for reading resistance literature outside the ideological constraints of New Criticism.[21] Maria Damon has helped establish the methodological and theoretical ground for reading the neglected poetic texts of people marginalized in U.S. society as a vanguard literature in which social identities, positions, and politics are negotiated.[22] No comparable study, however, has appeared on politically engaged literature of the Vietnam era.[23] Yet the political ground upon which many of the critical projects I have cited rest was indelibly mapped out through the activism of the Vietnam era. The lack of any critical engagement with the poetry of this period marks a troubling lacuna in our current understanding of not only contemporary poetry but also cultural history.

As a white male who turned thirteen a month before Kent State, I must acknowledge that my book will be fraught with the difficulties of speaking about "others." Inevitably such work risks misrepresentation precisely because it stems from education and experiences socially sanctioned by my subject position—white, male, Euro-American, middle-class, college-educated, academically employed—a position made hegemonic in a cultural system based on the historical oppression and misrepresentation of those "others." I do not, however, seek to speak *for* and in place of African Americans, feminists, and soldiers, and thus silence their own narratives. Rather I hope to offer new ways to hear their voices and to develop new audiences for their cultural and political work in the process. Recognizing the problems he faced as a Euro-American writing about "race," Dominick LaCapra argued,

> In one sense, I do not have a viable voice or position in addressing many of the problems discussed in this volume. Still, my presence may be taken as a sign of an increasingly obvious fact: it is vitally important for all scholars and critics to listen attentively to, and even attempt to enter into a mutually provocative exchange with, the voices that sound in these pages, however difficult and problematic such an undertaking may be.[24]

My goal is, thus, to intervene in the centripetal discourses that have legitimated corporeality as an a priori site of authenticity, precisely because it has been through such a construction of corporeality that whiteness and masculinity have been implicitly secured as hegemonic. Furthermore, by demonstrating how discourses of corporeality historically mobilized as tools of oppression were rearticulated as forms of resistance by African American, feminist, and soldier activists in recent history, I hope this book recuperates and thereby honors their struggles as critical to the development of contemporary U.S. culture. My intention is not to foreclose on their voices but rather to supplement them, to join them, and to enter into conversation with them—and further, to enunciate my solidarity with the struggles against racism, sexism, and militarism that were intensified by their work as Vietnam-era activist-poets.

1

Bodies, Poetry, and Resistance in the Vietnam Era

Putting Bodies on the Line

Popular histories of the 60s often focus on images of bodies—the long hair, nudity, postures, and dress, the frank celebration of sensuality of 60s youth—to render some sense of the broad social upheavals and carnivalesque atmosphere of the period. Yet little attention has been paid to the body's status, the utility of its meanings, and its articulations in the cultural discourses of the 60s. What seems most obvious about 60s oppositionalism is often overlooked or regarded as superficial: such slogans as "black is beautiful" and "off our backs," which have become metonymic of 60s radicalism, were rooted in assumptions about the human body as a site of political struggle. Indeed, these assumptions have significantly shaped contemporary politics of identity, and the recent theoretical interest in the body is deeply inscribed with the cultural logic of 60s oppositionalism.

To use the term "discourse" today is to evoke the theories of Michel Foucault. For Foucault, discourse has the sense of not only a system of signifying, but also a unity of expressions that legitimate forms of knowledge and enact a will to power.[1] Foucault's notions of discourse are particularly apt for a study of the poetry of social activists insofar as they posit the realm of language and expressivity as a site of contest and conflict.[2] The Foucauldian theory of discourse's relations to power and the body looms large over recent cultural theories. According to this theory, the body, as it is known through politics and the modern human sciences, is the effect of power relations rather than an essence preexisting the historical and social exchange and circulation of power.[3] The ways that we know the body, understand its meanings, read its signs are intimately related to the ways society organizes, manages, and disciplines populations and subjects individuals. Individuals internalize these forms of social power as "technologies of the self." Such technologies "permit individuals to effect by their own means or with the help of others a certain number of operations on their own bodies and souls, thoughts, conduct, and way of being, *so as to transform themselves* in order to attain a certain state of happiness, purity, wisdom, perfection, or immortality."[4] "Technologies of self," transformations of identity through the re-figuration of the human body's meanings, are key to the social activism of the Vietnam era. Many black cultural nationalists argued, for example, that only African Americans whose hair was "natural," who adopted certain postures, who adhered to a Muslim diet, and who wore African-style clothing could be considered truly committed to an Afrocentric cause.[5] And some feminist groups advocated strict codes of dress and grooming.[6] Although Foucault suggests that such "technologies" are complicit with power in a negative sense, his theories also suggest that they may constitute a site of resistance.

The question of whether Foucault's theories allow for resistance has vexed discussions of his work by the left for years. Yet Foucault maintains that wherever there is power there is also resistance. He argues that "[t]hese points of resistance are present everywhere in the power network."[7] For people whose identity has been principally linked to their "bodies"—African Americans, women, or soldiers, for example—the politicization of tropes, symbols, and images of the body both served to foreground a principal locus of their oppression and helped them articulate new ways of perceiving their own bodiliness as political identity. The discursive articulations of corporeality in the poetry of Black Liberation, Women's Liberation, and the GI Resistance, then, formed critical points of resistance in radical political technologies of self.

The notion of "articulation" I mean here stems from Ernesto Laclau and Chantal Mouffe's poststructuralist reading of Antonio Gramsci.[8] In their sense of the term, articulation defines the form of an arrangement or construction of ideological and/or social elements that achieves a unity of expression in an historically specific moment.[9] This Gramscian notion of articulation is also important to the present study for the specific connotations the term bears. As Stuart Hall aptly put it:

> The term has a nice double meaning because "articulate" means to utter, to speak forth, to be articulate. It carries that sense of language-ing, of expressing, etc. But we also speak of an "articulated" lorry . . .: a lorry where the front . . . and back . . . can, but need not necessarily, be connected to one another. The two parts are connected to each other, but through a specific linkage, that can be broken.[10]

Thus, "articulation" bears this double sense of the discursive (the spoken, enunciated, textual) and the constructed (the material and instrumental, as well as the conditional). This is especially useful for a study of poetic texts, which were often considered instrumental expressions of political doctrine and tools of cultural revolution.

This emphasis on constructedness, discourse, and articulations points to another underlying concern in this book. Unlike other recent studies of the body, which have predominantly stemmed from sociological, ethnographic, and anthropological approaches that privilege organic, living bodies, my approach is concerned less with bodies as extradiscursive, "real," and "material" entities than with the poetic figurations and renderings of corporeality. In this I do not presume some inherent and extradiscursive "truth" to bodies that can be rendered or "re-presented"; rather I mean that images, tropes, and symbols of bodies and bodiliness in activist poetry of the Vietnam era express discursively constituted conceptions of self and the politics of self. Moreover this study does not concern itself with the "construction" of bodies by poetry, since such a notion also presumes a prediscursive, blank, and passive materiality to bodies that can be fashioned and/or written upon by discourse. Rather I will be interested in the *discourse* of corporeality itself, the ways "bodies" are written about, imagined, conceptualized as politico-poetic objects of oppositional cultures in the Vietnam era.

By examining corporeality in activist poetry I seek to show how bodies were imagined as "sites" of ideological struggle. Figurations of human bodies in oppositional poetry established discursive terrain within which activist poets could think "self."[11] As Elspeth Probyn has argued, an image of corporeality "enables a certain solidarity to be thought" in feminist discourses: "[H]istorically, as a concept this image of body unity was the condition of possibility for concrete political battles." Similarly, I argue that figurations of corporeality in Vietnam-era activist poetry mark key points of resistance in the sociopolitical struggles being waged at that time. By focusing on corporeality as a discourse rather than as an "authentic" materiality, I hope to resist reinvoking an androcentric tendency in much literary study focused on "the body" to privilege the living, organic body as a "truth" over and against the enunciative. Probyn concludes, "What is at stake . . . is not the body as truth but the multiple positions it may give rise to within feminist [and, as I would argue, other oppositional] enunciations. It is not the 'fact' of the body that concerns me here; rather, it is the discursive effects that it may engender."[12]

It might be countered, however, that what most defines oppositional struggle in this period is the very tangibility of the material, physical threats to living human bodies posed by racism, sexism, war, the threat of nuclear holocaust, the society of the spectacle, and so forth. By drawing attention to poetic figurations of corporeality, my intention is to underscore how the tangibility of oppositional struggle in the Vietnam era permeates discursive formations. My approach to "bodies," then, is not meant to devalue and elide the corporeal tangibility of oppositional struggle in the 60s. Quite the contrary. By examining the ways political struggles were waged at the level of discourse, by focusing on images, tropes, and symbols of bodies in activist poetry, I seek to give new life to the often clichéd yet historically compelling leftist notion of "putting bodies on the line." Just as demonstrations, riots, acts of civil disobedience, sabotage, and street theater put the living bodies of Black Liberation, Women's Liberation, and GI Resistance activists on the line against ideological domination, conformity, and complacency, the poetic texts of these activists also traced corporeality along the "ragged," uneven lines of poetry.

This attention to corporeality in 60s oppositional culture, I believe, exemplifies broader trends in cultural and intellectual history. Since the mid-twentieth century there has been an intensified interest in the body as a source of selfhood. From the classical age to modernism, the human body had been conceived of as radically other than self. In premodern Western thought, the body was likened to a housing, a fleshly structure enclosing the soul. Plato argued that "the body is the tomb of the soul." Saint Paul asserted that the "body is the temple of the Holy Spirit." As recent scholarship has suggested, early medieval English Christianity envisioned the human body as a corrupt enclosure of the soul.[13] With the Renaissance, the body became increasingly privatized and mechanized. Descartes instituted the paradigm of the body/self dichotomy, which would dominate much of Western scientific and humanist rationalism until the twentieth century. In his view, "The human body may be considered as a machine." The body is seen as secular and private, an instrument to enact the will of the self, but essentially other than that self.[14]

In the nineteenth century the materialism of Ludwig Feuerbach, Karl Marx, and Charles Darwin began to question the Cartesian dichotomy of body/self. Feuerbach stated, "The individual is an individual only in this, his corporeal life."[15] Marx envisioned the human body as becoming, under the development of capitalism, nothing more than another economic asset. Darwin disputed the Cartesian notion of the mind's superiority over body and argued that the mind was dependent on the body.[16] Friedrich Nietzsche anticipated the late twentieth-century political discourse of corporeality by stating, in *Thus Spake Zarathustra*, "Behind your thoughts and feelings, my brother, stands a mighty commander, an unknown sage—he is called Self. He lives in your body, he *is* your body."[17] Yet even in Nietzsche, a distance remains between body and self. The self is known only in terms of the body. In this sense, Nietzsche, while inverting the classic binary of body/mind, reasserts it. While the self "lives in" and "is" our body, it is also clearly different from corporeality as it is a "being" made possible only by the organic essentialism of the body.[18]

Jean-Paul Sartre's existentialist phenomenology laid an important philosophical groundwork for the concepts of corporeality that would be instrumental in Vietnam-era political discourses. Sartrean existentialism had an enormous impact on the shape of 60s oppositional thought, and Sartre was often cited by student activists as one of their most important philosophical sources.[19] Furthermore, Sartre was an important activist in oppositional struggles internationally, circulating key statements against imperialism and chairing the 1967 International War Crimes Tribunal against the Vietnam War. In *Being and Nothingness* (1943), Sartre had argued that there is essentially no difference that can be reasonably discerned between self and body: "There is nothing *behind* the body." Being is only knowable insofar as it is embodied. Sartre wrote, "The body is not a screen between things and ourselves; it manifests only the individuality and the contingency of our original relation to instrumental-things. . . . In one sense the body is what I immediately am. . . . I *am* my body to the extent that I *am*; I *am not* my body to the extent that I am not what I am."[20]

This notion that self is indissociable from body and that, further, it is the body which manifests the self's material relations to the world, presages the notions of body as a medium of political identification. If I am my body, then my body must manifest my being, my thought, my imagined relation to lived experience, my politics. If my being, as Black Liberation and Women's Liberation activists would argue, is both public and private, a self ineradicably shaped by political ideologies, then my body must also manifest these ideologies. In the sense that Sartre clings to notions of the body "manifesting" individuality, however, his existential phenomenology remains fundamentally Cartesian. Indeed, in Sartre's philosophy, consciousness, being-for-itself is construed as transcendent and prior to the materiality of the body, being-in-itself. Although Sartre blurred the boundaries between mind and body fixed by Descartes in ways that would prove crucial for the political discourses of corporeality in 60s oppositional culture, these lines remained.

Simone de Beauvoir's conception of the female body offered a possibility out of Cartesian dualism by critiquing the corporealization of the female effected by masculinist philosophy. Beauvoir's *The Second Sex* (1952), like Sartre's book, helped further the legitimacy of existential phenomenology in Vietnam-era oppositional discourse. Like Sartre, Beauvoir blurs the distinctions between mind and body, but reaffirms this duality by thinking the body as instrumental. It is the *perception* of female bodiliness that oppresses woman as "other": "Woman? Very simple, say the fanciers of simple formulas: she is a womb, an ovary; she is a female—this word is sufficient to define her. In the mouth of a man the epithet *female* has the sound of an insult." And while Sartre can assert that self is body, Beauvoir delineates a critical difference, which would occupy feminist political thought in the 60s: "Woman, like man, *is* her body; but her body is something other than herself."[21] For Beauvoir, the male has been constructed as radically incorporeal while the female has been reduced to nothing more than corporeality. As Judith Butler points out, Beauvoir posits "that the female body ought to be the situation and instrumentality of women's freedom, not a defining and limiting essence." But as Butler goes on to argue, "Beauvoir maintains the mind/body dualism, even as she proposes a synthesis of those terms."[22] Although the body, in both Beauvoir and Sartre, is the site of subjectivity, it is still construed as a passive terrain, an instrument, or a vehicle of expression, and thus, a materiality "other" than consciousness. It is precisely these notions of body as *site* of political subjectivity, however, that distinguish the oppositional politics of bodies in the 60s.

The African American body in Black Liberationist cultural politics was often viewed as an instrument of the revolution, a weapon against whiteness, its distinctive physical features an assault on white hegemony. The "transfiguration of blackness," as Stephen Henderson termed it, is articulated as an ideological program for the training, discipline, and modification of African American corporeality. But this program seeks not simply the modification of bodies as much as the modification of bodies in order to signify independence, liberation, and self-identification in relation to white hegemony. Similarly, in Women's Liberation, the female body was construed as an instrument of change; by becoming more "in tune" with female physiology, a woman could become more politically aware, less dependent on masculinist culture, and would thus further the goals of revolution. This thinking involved modification, training of one's body; consciousness-raising sessions often focused on training women to diagnose their own medical conditions; feminist sourcebooks advocated norms of hygiene and dress in accord with political ideologies. Yet clearly, such instrumentality related to seeing the body as a medium of expression. This instrumentality is mobilized in feminist and Black Liberation discourses of corporeality so as to construe bodies as ideologically expressive in ways that collapse boundaries between public and private. The reformation of radical, leftist oppositional struggle through the discourses of "the personal is the political," "black is beautiful," and "our bodies, ourselves" pivots on this erasure of difference between the body and self, private and public. Further, this politicizing of corporeality in the specific historical contexts of the U.S. war with Vietnam and the general phenomenon of decolonization metaphorizes the human body as a terrain or zone of political struggle. Rather than seeing the self as transcendent of the body, 60s corporeality posits a self that must identify with the body in the same sense that a colonized subject must identify with the imaginative ideal of the precolonial nation.

The emergence of this new paradigm of body-self takes shape in the contexts of an array of political and social upheavals during the mid-twentieth century. As Bryan Turner and other sociologists have noted, it has always been true that corporeality has been figured in tropes and signs of social, religious, political, and cultural ideologies, but it is only in recent history that we find corporeality actively invested as the source of political self-identity.[23] This is not simply a politicizing of the body, which, again, is a historically common phenomenon; but rather, what we find manifested in the post–World War II era is the increasing figuration of corporeality *itself* as a locus of ideological conflict and the source of political self-identity. In previous ages the metaphors used to describe the body's relation to self always envisioned clear separations between the body and self. This implies two related conceptions of the body that would shift by the period of late modernity. First, such views posit a body that, however related to self-identity in philosophy, can never *be* self-identity. In this sense, corporeality cannot undergo the same sorts of transformations that consciousness can. After World War II, however, it becomes more the case that one experiences political transformation as also corporeal, signaled by marked changes in grooming, postures, dress, and diet. Second, views that distinguish clearly between body and self consider the body extrapolitical, in the sense that it cannot be a subject of ideology since it cannot be self. In Marx, for example, the human body is an object, a material exploited, which confines the possibilities of the subject. A split between self and body was maintained such that the political subject has tended to be thought of as principally a self and only secondarily a body.

Leftist cultural activism of the 60s put the body on a line that had historically separated corporeality from politics and in so doing forced an intervention into the boundaries separating what could and could not be legitimately considered political. In the Black Liberation, it is not simply that adopting or affecting certain modes of appearance is a means of signifying political ideology, but rather that the movement *invested* these modes of corporeality in such a way that a black political identity could be rooted in black corporeality. In his study of the culture of black power, William Van Deburg writes that the prevailing ideological tenets of the new black consciousness held that "[t]o become conscious of one's blackness was a healthy psychosocial development. It was to make a positive statement about one's worth as a person."[24] As Stephen Henderson wrote in a 1969 essay on militancy in black poetry, "to say, 'I'm black,' in the United States is an act of resistance; to say out loud, 'I'm black and I'm proud' is an act of rebellion; to attempt systematically to move black people to act out of their beauty and their blackness in white America is to foment revolution."[25] Henderson's emphasis here is on more than "black" as a cultural trope: it underscores a prevailing belief in Black Liberationist culture that African Americans needed to reconstruct, reconceive, and rearticulate black corporeality, a corporeality that had been "denigrated" under white cultural oppression in the United States.

The paradigm of the body as political self also corresponds to notions of self in the work of social critics such as C. Wright Mills, Betty Friedan, R. D. Laing, and Herbert Marcuse, popular among the New Left, the counterculture, and radicals of the 60s. Marcuse's *Eros and Civilization* (1955) and *One-Dimensional Man* (1964) had a profound impact on the philosophical foundations of the New Left.[26] His work forged alliances between Freudianism and Marxism that circumvented the positivism and determinism of the older U.S. Marxism that many young activists felt had become too bureaucratic and stifling. Marcuse's philosophy posited an important critique of the mind-body dualism of European philosophy that had contained self-realization in consciousness and marginalized physical, sensual desires as irrelevant. This dualism, Marcuse argued, was an essentially conservative "doctrine of a beautiful and free spirit within an enslaved body [that] served to perpetuate the established economic order."[27] Marcusean radical psychology envisioned the repression of the body and sexual impulses as consistent with the exploitative social and economic orders of late capitalism. Further, although Marcuse largely rejected Sartrean existentialism, in an early critique of *Being and Nothingness,* Marcuse agreed with Sartre on the significance of corporeality as constitutive of identity. Like Sartre, Marcuse believed that it was in eros that one could get outside of the instrumentality of "one-dimensional" existence and experience self as body, being in itself.

> The *"désir sexuel"* which reveals its object as stripped of all the attitudes, gestures, and affiliations which make it a standardized instrument, reveals the "body as flesh" and thereby "as fascinating revelation of facticity." Enslavement and repression are cancelled, not in the sphere of purposeful "projective" activity, but in the "body lived as flesh," in the "web of inertia."[28]

Marcuse's call for a resexualization of the body in *Eros and Civilization* anticipated the philosophical discourses underlying the much vaunted "sexual liberation" of the Vietnam era and prefigured the counter-cultural celebration of sensuality as authenticity.

In relation to these philosophical contexts, the work of third-world national liberationists such as Frantz Fanon, Kwame Nkrumah, and Amilcar Cabral (who themselves were influenced by Sartre's existentialism) was key to the development of U.S. oppositional discourse in the Vietnam era. Many of these writers envisioned the body as a site for the construction of a politicized self-identity. In *The Wretched of the Earth* (1963), Fanon asserted that "[t]he native intellectual who takes up arms to defend his nation's legitimacy and who wants to bring proofs to bear out that legitimacy, who is willing to strip himself naked to study the history of his body, is obliged to dissect the heart of his people."[29] And his *Black Skin, White Masks* (1952) situates the dilemma of the colonized in the social construction of the colonized body.[30] For Fanon, the body racialized and colonized is a primary site of struggle. Similarly, Malcolm X in the mid-60s also emphasized the racialized body as a site of ideological struggle:

> [Whites] very skillfully make you and me hate our African identity, our African characteristics. You know yourself that we have been a people who hated our African characteristics. We hated our heads, we hated the shape of our nose, we wanted one of those long dog-like noses, you know; we hated the color of our skin, hated the blood of Africa that was in our veins. And in hating our features and our skin and our blood, why, we ended up hating ourselves. And we hated ourselves.[31]

These developments in intellectual history helped forge a new conception of corporeality as a field of political struggle. We can see this conception first emerging as political praxis among the activists involved in the Student Nonviolent Coordinating Committee (SNCC). Accounts of SNCC's style during the early 60s suggest that these activists began seeing their bodies as coextensive of their political identities. Charles Jones, remembering the 1961 SNCC summer meeting, has said that the talks delineated "a notion that separated the serious people from the not serious. The notion was, 'Where is your body?' Talking was cheap. Throw your *body* into the Movement."[32] In 1964 John Lewis noted that in SNCC, "There's been a radical change . . . since 1960; *the way they dress, the music they listen to, their natural hairdos—all of them want to go to Africa.* . . . I think people are searching for a sense of identity, and they're finding it."[33] Their gestures and dress, the way they wore their hair, the food they ate, all became a matter of political significance. In many ways this style can be seen as an early articulation of the cultural nationalism that would come to dominate Black Liberation by the late 60s.

This emphasis on the corporeal in political activism found reso-
nances in post–World War II poetry. The importance of Walt
Whitman as a literary influence on the period cannot be underesti-
mated. Whitman's glorification of the body and his radical democratic
vision of the body politic, expressed in long, oratorical free-verse
forms, were well suited to the sentiments of 60s oppositionalism. In
many ways, Whitman's understanding of the corporeal presaged that
of the Vietnam era. When Whitman asked, in "I Sing the Body Electric," "And if the body were not the soul, what is the soul?" he also
sought to dissolve the Cartesian boundary between mind and body.[34]
The open form, radical democratic vision, and celebration of physi-
cality that Whitman pioneered in American poetry characterizes
much of the poetry of activism in the 60s. Allen Ginsberg, whose
Howl (1955) has been one of the best-selling poems in U.S. history,
often acknowledged his debt to Whitman, not only in his poetry's
long, sweeping lines, but also in its catalogs, oratorical tone, and vi-
sionary style. The Whitmanesque line can also be found in Black Arts
poets, such as Lance Jeffers, Larry Neal, and David Henderson, as
well as feminist poets, such as Rochelle Owens.

Whitman's impact on American poetry of the 60s coincides with a
turn away from the intellectual and often impersonal formalism of
post–World War II New Critical poetry and toward an attention to
material and private life, sensuality, anatomy, and the body. The
"deep image" poets (such as Robert Bly) and the "primitivists" (such
as Gary Snyder) sought to ground their post-Romantic quests for self-
realization in the archetypal significance of the body. A common
thread running through the widely popular post–World War II social
criticism of C. Wright Mills, William Whyte, and David Riesman in
the 1950s, and later Herbert Marcuse, Norman O. Brown, and R. D.
Laing—writers who articulated founding ideological positions for the
New Left and the counterculture—was that social conformity was in-
authentic, an unnatural restriction, and an artificial covering that kept
humans from their true selves.[35] Such notions were manifested in a
Whitmanesque celebration of the body in much of the poetry published during the 60s.[36] Marjorie Perloff has stated that "[t]he dominant poetic of the American sixties [was a poetic] of strenuous
authenticity, the desire to present a self as natural, as organic, and as
unmediated as possible."[37] The titles of Paul Carroll's *The Poem in its
Skin* (1968) and Stephen Berg and Robert Mezey's anthology *Naked
Poetry: Recent American Poetry in Open Forms* (1969) exemplify the Vietnam-era emphasis on the corporeal as the authentic ground for aesthetics in U.S. poetry. Leftist oppositionalism in the 60s typically
couched its rhetoric and values in the countercultural obsession with
unmasking and celebrating "real," "authentic," and "naked" expres-

sion—being "in tune" with one's feelings, with one's body; sensitivity as an "authentic" register of true knowledge; poetry as "authentic" literary expression (usually over and against prose); music as "authentic" medium of expression; the whole drug culture and its appeals to opening up the emotions. These countercultural beliefs were imaginatively configured as political during the Vietnam era.

Consequently, an examination of corporeality as it operates not only in 60s poetry generally but also, and more specifically, in the poetry of oppositionalism, may elucidate the ways poetry served to articulate, mediate, and transmit cultural values and political discourses in this period. This method of analysis, I believe, will shift the focus from the narrow interests of most literary studies and toward broader concerns that question the role of poetry in culture and history. By studying how activist-poets put "bodies on the line," both in their politics and their poetics, I will examine the intersections between cultural, political, historical, and literary discourses in the recent construction of new forms of identity, the "new subjects of history" that have played a significant role in contemporary oppositional politics.

Periodizing 60s Poetry

Studies of American poetry often periodize the 60s as "postwar," meaning post–World War II. "Postwar" literature refers to works written from 1945 through the 60s, often as late as the 80s. The adjective poses several problems that both suggest the limitations in current assessments of 60s poetry and point to the ideological stakes involved in such assessments. World War II, of course, marked a turning point in U.S. history and a watershed in U.S. culture; the United States emerged from the war a military, economic, and political "superpower." At the same time, American literature became a legitimate object of academic study. University English departments established their first American literature programs, and a new generation of scholars set about to define and evaluate this literature. It was during these years that the New Critics helped establish what would become the critical orthodoxy for the new generation of teachers and critics.

Universities in this period were also rapidly becoming the centers for research in defense, political policy, and social thought for the new military-industrial alliance that emerged from World War II, an alliance charged by an intensified sense of competition with communism. Concomitantly, the construction of American literary studies as a discipline reflected the atmosphere of anticommunism broadly characteristic of U.S. social life in the period. The historical revelations of fascism and Soviet totalitarianism lent legitimacy to the American academy's repudiation of the Communist-inspired social protest literature and criticism of the 30s. New Criticism's promotion of formalism reflected a profound disenchantment with the doctrinaire politics of earlier twentieth-century Marxist criticism, and it was consistent with the national mood of a triumphantly prosperous and self-confident "American century." The New Critical doxa largely secured its hegemonic position in the academy on the basis of these sociopolitical contexts. As Donald E. Pease has argued, the New Critical narratives about American literary history in the 40s and 50s, such as those by F. O. Mathiessen, Henry Nash Smith, and Lionel Trilling, "explicitly related the construction of the field of American Studies to liberal anticommunist consensus."[38] In establishing the disciplinary dimensions of an American literature and literary tradition, academic critics were meeting the new superpower's needs for ideological stability.

The periodization of 60s poetry as "postwar," then, evokes the genesis of American literary studies, its historical roots in World War II experience, and the ideological assumptions fundamental to the disciplinary formation of American literary studies since World War II. The adjective presupposes that poetry written after 1960 can be contained within the historical paradigms appropriate to a previous age of economic prosperity, military dominance, and relative political conformity. Further, it resonates with a nostalgia for a time before the political upheavals of the 60s; before people of color, women, gays, and lesbians burst onto the historical stage with their unruly cries for justice, equality, and self-determination; before the military's role in public life faced widespread scrutiny; before the hegemony of white, Protestant, masculinist culture suffered its most popular and widespread challenge in U.S. history. The adjective "postwar" erases this whole counternarrative of U.S. history.

Periodizing 60s poetry as "postwar" marks World War II as the defining moment in twentieth-century American literary history. It stands as an imaginary line neatly dividing the century almost at its numerical midpoint. Yet U.S. involvement in World War II spanned only four years; the Vietnam War, on the other hand, occupied the U.S. military, much of U.S. industrial production and economy, its national and foreign politics, and the "hearts and minds" of the American people from as early as 1963 to almost 1975.[39] Indeed, we can trace U.S. military involvement in Indochina to 1955, when military "advisers" and covert operatives were stationed in Vietnam to monitor events in the country after the defeat of the French forces at Dien Bien Phu.[40] And although formal U.S. troop withdrawal from

Vietnam was completed by 1973, the last Americans at the U.S. embassy in Saigon were not evacuated until April 1975.

Unlike World War II, Congress never officially declared the U.S. intervention in Vietnam a "war."[41] There is no Library of Congress classification for the U.S. *war* against Vietnam; instead one finds it identified as the "Vietnamese Conflict 1961–1973," thus casting it as something like an argument, a struggle, or a controversy involving only the Vietnamese. The longest, costliest, and most controversial U.S. war in the twentieth century similarly goes "undeclared" in literary studies. It remains "in country," at the borderlands of accepted literary history, displaced by the adjective "postwar."

American poetry of the period from 1965 to 1975 should be periodized as Vietnam-era poetry for a number of interrelated reasons. First, it seems ahistorical to discuss any U.S. poetry produced during this period without recognizing the inescapable fact that it was written during a time of war. Literary histories have long acknowledged major wars as periodizing markers, and the insistence on viewing 60s poetry as "postwar" confirms this, while at the same time negating the significance of the war actually being waged at the time. This "undeclared war" persists as the repressed of literary history's narratives. As such it haunts our attempts to understand one of the most explosive periods in U.S. history.

Further, to read 60s poetry as "postwar" is to cling to a mythic vision of the U.S. as the heroic guardian of liberty around the world, an ideal shaped by the historical contingencies specific to 1940s and 1950s culture, and to deny that the Vietnam War and the ideological ruptures it manifested have significantly shaped the directions of contemporary U.S. literature and culture. This struggle between "postwar" and "Vietnam-era" visions of national history remains one of the central generational struggles of our time, even twenty years after the last Huey lifted off the embassy roof in Saigon. The Bush administration successfully deployed World War II imagery and tropes in its consolidation of public consensus about the war with Iraq, articulating these elements into a hegemonic formation over and against a Vietnam-era liberal viewpoint, one imbued with antimilitaristic views and a distaste for masculinist traditions. And the right wing's continued exploitation of Bill Clinton's antiwar past exemplifies how a struggle between "postwar" and "Vietnam War" generations over control of the historical record is very much at the center of contemporary politics and culture. That the Vietnam War could still elicit the fierce debates that have been waged in editorials and speeches across the country suggests that its effects are still very much with us, that we cannot will our involvement in Vietnam away by categorizing it as a "Vietnamese Conflict" or the poetry of the Vietnam era as "post-war."

The present study, while primarily focused on the oppositional body politics articulated in poetry, also insists that these articulations were shaped within the global and domestic historical contexts of the Vietnam War. In my discussions of corporeality, I will consider how the war generated compelling subject matter, metaphors, and tropes, which poets drew upon to construct their texts. In doing this, I do not mean to suggest that the plethora of cultural practices current in these years can be neatly generalized. Yet, as Fredric Jameson has written, "[T]o those who think that cultural periodization implies some massive kinship and homogeneity of identity within a given period, it may quickly be replied that it is surely only against a certain conception of what is dominant or hegemonic that the full value of the exceptional—what Raymond Williams calls the 'residual' or 'emergent'—can be assessed." In periodizing 60s poetry as "Vietnam-era," then, I seek to map out "the sharing of a common objective situation, to which a whole range of varied responses and creative innovations is then possible, but always within that situation's structural limits.[42]

Although one might reasonably argue that other "wars" best epitomize 60s culture, such as the war in the United States over racial justice or the war for women's rights, I will maintain that after 1964 the cultural politics of movements for racial and sexual liberation often drew on tropes and symbols of the Vietnam War to articulate resistance, which thus suggests that the war constituted "a common objective situation," a discursive field within which the politics unique to the years from 1965 to 1975 could be articulated.[43] What distinguishes the oppositional culture of this period is its vernacular of liberation politics, Third-Worldism, guerilla warfare, and cultural nationalism. As Jameson has noted, "[P]olitically, a First World 60s owed much to Third-Worldism in terms of politicocultural models."[44] This is not to suggest, however, that the Vietnam War was either definitive or even the main focus of oppositional activism in the late 60s and early 70s. Rather, it is to point out how the war constituted a terrain of tropes within which oppositional cultures fashioned discourses of resistance. By inflecting their rhetorics with the images, tropes, and symbols of the war, activist groups could construct themselves as a vanguard in the domestic struggle, an extension of the revolutionary struggles of Third World peoples against the United States, and position themselves alongside the Vietnamese against the imperialist state. Through such inflections, the Black Liberation, Women's Liberation, GI Resistance, and other oppositional movements, "and indeed everyone conscious of the way his or her experience of capitalism, even at the psychic level of alienation from one-self, recapitulated the situation of Third World people—had thus a 'Vietnam' of his or her own, a lived experience of imperialism."[45]

It is important, then, to understand the status of the war in oppositional cultural discourses as more inflective than constitutive. While the war obviously constituted the ground on which GI Resistance activism was founded, it operated at a more figurative level for civilian activists. Obviously, social activism on the terrains of race and gender has deep sources in American history, and its expression in the 60s was intricately configured by issues and concerns beyond the scope of the war years. The Black Arts poets, for example, often cited the Negro Renaissance of the early twentieth century as models of black self-assertion, as celebration of black vernacular culture and a distinctive black heritage. At the same time, however, these poets often cast their images, language, and subjects in ways that appropriated the discourses of liberation and revolution generated through the U.S. intervention in Vietnam. The textual evidence suggests, as I will demonstrate, that oppositional discourses shifted to a decidedly "Vietnam War" perspective after 1964 when SNCC issued its controversial statement against the war. The Black Panthers, for example, specifically linked their struggle to the struggles of the National Liberation Front, and much of their philosophy was based on readings of Ho Chi Minh, Ché Guevara, Mao Zedong, Amilcar Cabral, and other Third World liberationists. According to William L. Van Deburg, revolutionary black nationalism's

> multifaceted, anti-capitalist ideology, expressed in numerous variations throughout the period, was a melange of the theories of Marx, Lenin, and Mao; DuBois, Garvey, and Malcolm X; Nkrumah, Nyerere, Toure, and Cabral. International in scope, but Afrocentric in its promotion of black Americans . . . as the liberating vanguard, it was flexible enough to be adapted to the needs of a wide variety of black leftists. All felt that they were reading history correctly by linking their cause to Third World liberation movements.[46]

The deployment of "liberation" as the vernacular of resistance after 1964 signals the distinctive significance of Third-Worldism, which is a direct effect of U.S. involvement in Vietnam. A prevalent rhetorical strategy in U.S. oppositional discourses was to claim solidarity with Third World liberation struggle, and for U.S. radicals, in the immediate historical moment of the 60s, the Vietnam War epitomized this struggle.

I do not mean to suggest, however, that the Vietnam War was *the* dominant issue in Black Liberation and Women's Liberation, nor to consider these groups opposed to the war in the same way that the antiwar movement was. As numerous studies of movement politics in this period have shown, the antiwar movement was often viewed by Black Liberationists and feminists as white and male-dominated. But while the organized movement against the war may not have effectively forged alliances with the Black Liberation and feminists, clearly the war itself was of great concern to a broad cross-section of oppositional cultures. And even though the organized antiwar movement alienated many African Americans and feminists, significant opposition to the war was mobilized within and through the political and cultural discourses of Black Liberation[47] and Women's Liberation.[48] My goal in periodizing 60s poetry as "Vietnam era," then, is not to subsume the varied oppositional practices of this period under a dominant narrative of the war, or to privilege "war" as the definitive historical factor in the 60s. Rather, it is to acknowledge a shared situation that oppositional cultures experienced in U.S. history and responded to in different ways. It is also to acknowledge how the unique fragmentation of the "body politic" in the 60s resonates with the very material experiences of rupture generated by war at a structural level in U.S. society.

By examining how the war configured a general historical field and appears as a trope in Black Liberation and Women's Liberation literature rather than as a sole motivating factor for resistance, I hope to suggest how the war's effects can be read as more pervasive and less fixed than has been generally considered. Furthermore, on the rare occasions when literary critics focus on "political poetry" of the 60s, they invariably focus on antiwar poetry, usually written by prominent writers (such as Bly, Levertov, and Lowell) who were involved in the antiwar movement. Usually discussions of African American and feminist political poetry of the period ignore the salient effects of this literature's production during a time of war. Current accounts of 60s poetry produce a strangely alienated and deeply divided view of the period: only white, professional poets wrote poetry for the antiwar movement; African American and feminist poets wrote as if the war had never happened. By highlighting the ways that the Vietnam War was manifested in the work of the Black Liberation and Women's Liberation, I hope to correct what I believe has been a myopic and strategically limited account of 60s oppositional culture. In doing this, I also hope to unwrite a false division between domestic social struggle and global threats to U.S. hegemony that has tended to contain and destabilize the radical scope of resistance forged during this period. As I will maintain throughout this study, domestic cultural resistance during the 60s must be seen as interrelated to the uprisings of Third World liberation movements and the U.S. war in Vietnam. The U.S. military intervention both produced economic, political, and social conditions specific to the development of widespread unrest in America and was itself the effect of crises in global history, such as the post–World War II globalization of capital, the intensification of the Cold War, the decolonization of the Southern Hemisphere, and, concomitantly, the destabilization of the liberal subject that emerges as the West faces these crises and experiences vast cultural shifts from modernity to postmodernity. Such conditions help make possible the shift in U.S. leftist political opposition to a politics focused on identity, which will come to characterize the late 60s and continue to motivate resistance in the post-Vietnam era.

2

"The Transfiguration of Blackness": The Body in Black Liberation Poetry

"Poems/like fists"

When it first appeared in the January 1966 issue of *Liberator*, LeRoi Jones's poem "Black Art" cleared new ground in African American poetics and served as a stunning wake-up call to the literary establishment. Demanding a politically engaged and physical poetry to act as a weapon in the revolutionary black struggle, the poem begins:

> Poems are bullshit unless they are
> teeth or trees or lemons piled
> on a step. Or black ladies dying
> of men leaving nickel hearts
> beating them down. Fuck poems
> and they are useful, they shoot
> come at you, love what you are,
> breathe like wrestlers, or shudder
> strangely after pissing. We want live
> words of the hip world live flesh &
> coursing blood. Hearts Brains
> Souls splintering fire. We want poems
> like fists beating niggers out of Jocks.[1]

Embracing the vernacular, expressive culture of urban black life in America, Jones's poem insists that words make tangible differences in the lives of African Americans, that the black poem address the physical, material needs of black people. The poem envisioned would not only *embody* African American experience, it would also be corporeal, with organs and orgasms, its own bodily odors and fluids. David L. Smith has written that Jones's poem "expresses not just a desire for poems to become physical things but more specifically for poems literally to embody and enact forms of human activity."[2]

The poem's appearance in 1966 both marks a turning point in Jones's career and signals a new direction in African American political activism and cultural discourse. "Black Art" explicitly rejects the white Euro-American poetic norms established by New Criticism. It also rejects the elision of racial differences promoted by the integrationist aesthetics of early post–World War II African American writers. "Black Art" emphatically asserts the adjectival difference, the overdetermined sign of blackness, as a political and aesthetic positivity, a distinctive presence constitutive of African American culture. Fusing an objectivist belief in words as matter with an urgent need in African American culture for pragmatic, tangible changes in political and socioeconomic conditions, "Black Art" can be seen as indicative of Jones's decisive break from the white avant-garde of Greenwich Village and Black Mountain and his move to Harlem and the black revolutionary vanguard.

As William J. Harris has noted, the poetry of Jones's Beat period is characterized by a "propensity for fantasy." "In Memory of Radio," for example, "valorizes 'pretending' . . . [and] rejects the role of poet as an active agent in the world."[3] After his trip to Cuba in 1960, and with the Civil Rights struggle increasing in its urgency, Jones's poetry became more overtly political, more inflected by a militantly problack perspective, and more concerned with the demands of the historical moment. Jones's poems of the early 60s also seem more troubled by the poet's seeming inability to effect tangible change in the struggle for racial equality and freedom. His critically acclaimed book *The Dead Lecturer* (1964) shows Jones struggling to assert a distinctively black cultural heritage, still demonstrating an allegiance to the white avant-garde and the Black Mountain aesthetic. These poems employ the procedural techniques of projectivism often meditating on metaphysical, philosophical concepts. Here Jones would write, "Let my poems be a graph/of me."[4]

In "An Agony. As Now." the poet expresses deep confusion over the meanings of blackness and the physical consequences of being a black poet in a white world:

> I am inside someone
> who hates me. I look
> out from his eyes
> . . . .
> This is the enclosure (flesh
> where innocence is a weapon. An
> abstraction. . . . (DL, 15)

Trapped within a public self fashioned in the white-dominated world, the man inside his black body is represented here as suffering. Corporeality constitutes a limiting enclosure, a boundary, a prison; the black body bars the self from full experience. As in the works of many

African American poets and critics of the post–World War II era, blackness here is considered a hindrance, a limitation in a white-dominated world. Similarly, the opening lines of "Short Speech to My Friends" contrast markedly with the expressions of "Black Art": "A political art, let it be/tenderness" (DL, 29). And although "Rhythm & Blues (1" is dedicated to Robert Williams, who advocated armed defense against white racist violence in the South during the 1950s, Jones has still not issued a call to arms.[5] Yet there are clear portents in *The Dead Lecturer* of the rejection of avant-garde aestheticism Jones would boldly declare in "Black Art." The first lines of "Rhythm & Blues (1," for example, point to the political (and corporeal) impotence of the avant-garde: "The symbols hang limply/in the street" (DL, 44). By contrast, "Black Art" renounces symbol and metaphor and demands action, corporeal presence, a tangible black revolt. Here Jones wants "poems/like fists" to beat a new consciousness into black people; he wants "'poems that kill.'/Assassin poems, Poems that shoot/guns" (BF, 302). Whereas previously Jones envisioned the poem and the body as the graphic inscriptions of self, in "Black Art" he calls for a corporeal poetic articulating a revolutionary black body and an assertion of racially essential identity.

"Black Art" had a profound impact on the African American literary vanguard of the Vietnam era. Eugene Redmond deemed Jones's "Black Art" the "embodiment of the black aesthetic."[6] Larry Neal stated that "Black Art" epitomized what the new black poetry should achieve: "Poems are physical entities: fists, daggers, airplane poems, and poems that shoot guns. Poems are transformed from physical object [sic] into personal forces."[7] And as Smith states, the poem "became a central icon of the Black Arts Movement" and has become "a crucial document" of Black Liberation aesthetics.[8] The caustic, self-consciously shocking images of "Black Art" not only gave voice to a rage felt throughout African American society after 1965 but also indicated a new willingness in black poetry to reject the "integrationism" of post–World War II era black poetry. Jones's "Black Art" appeared in the historical context of a turning point in the ongoing black struggle for justice. In the wake of persistent white violence against Civil Rights activists in the South, the reluctance in the federal government to follow through on the political goals of Civil Rights, and the increased attention to the war in Vietnam, a new vanguard had emerged in African American activism; it promoted black nationalism, self-determination, and racial pride through a cultural discourse inflected by Third World liberation politics.

The new black poetry that was emerging in this period took hold of white America's worst fears about African American bodies to refashion them into self-assertive representations of blackness. Ahmed

Alhamisi's "The Black Narrator" (1966) both attests to the impact of Jones's "Black Art" and exemplifies the corporeality of the new black aesthetic evident in Neal's assessment:

1
White poems
are daggers. guns. cops.
                piercing hearts in weird designs. Ofays
                beating niggers to their knees. Coloured
                girls with wigs passing & cutting Afro's
                minds. Or black poems judged by whitey's
                standards. . . .

. . . .

2
Black poems are beautiful. . . .
                . . . A
poem for wooly-haired brothers. natural-haired sisters.
  Bimbos.
boots & woogies. Or nappy-headed youngsters
                Cause they want what i
                want: blood from revolutions. . . .

3
Here in america i want black thoughts, in forms of con
crete skies
tumbling down
on dingy ofays. on negro
middleclass heads (konked-haired hipsters. wig-wearing
  whores. . . .)
Crush their minds & lives thoughts. Talk to them in
  chinese

                              vietnamese
                                or
                    black language

. . . . [9]

As in "Black Art," Alhamisi's poem envisions poetry as material, physical, corporeal. Poetry can be a weapon for or against black people. And like the discursive strategies of "Black Art," "The Black Narrator" configures an ideological struggle between "white" and "black" through corporeal images. Wigs and konked hair signify the lack of "black consciousness" in "negro/middleclass heads" and position them as ideological traitors to the black struggle, whereas nappy, wooly, and natural hair signifies political correctness. Just as poetry is cast as material, the human body "matters." In this sense, the materiality of the body is written as "the effect of a dynamic of power," and it is through a discourse of race which reifies perceived corporeal difference that the materiality of the body is compelled and is also made to register *political* difference.[10] It is on the body that Alhamisi seeks to inscribe a political "black" identity.

The revolt against white culture expressed in poems such as Alhamisi's and Jones's involved a subversion of some of the most fundamental conceptual binarisms and hierarchies structuring American racial discourses. As Stephen Henderson asserted, "[T]he real revolution . . . occurring in America today is the Black Consciousness Movement, the *transfiguration of blackness,* a necessary first stage in the liberation of black people, and conceivably of all Americans."[11] Although Henderson conceived of "blackness" here in the sense of an overall cultural, political, and historical totality for African American experience, "blackness" also signifies the body, and Henderson's advocacy of a "transfiguration" is grounded in a notion of phenomenological metamorphosis. The word "transfigure" means to change in form or appearance, to transform outwardly; Henderson employs the term to mean both a change in the meaning of "blackness" culturally and in its meaning corporeally. By transfiguring the representation of African American bodies the Black Aesthetic sought to redefine "blackness" and the African American subject. Although the exact nature of "blackness" during the late 60s was often hotly debated among black writers and critics, common to its many articulations was its grounding in a re-*vision* of the African American human body. The "new Black Poetry," the "Black Aesthetic," "Black Arts," "Black Power" all foreground in the word "black" a positive, distinctive presence that signifies both culturally and physically. By foregrounding "color" as the constitutive sign of difference, these writers sought to engage the dilemma of race relations in America at its heart.

An examination of Stephen Henderson's statements about the "blackness" of African American poetry may serve to illustrate the corporeal essentialism of the Black Aesthetic. Henderson's essay "The Form of Things Unknown," the introduction to his anthology *Understanding the New Black Poetry* (1973), has been widely regarded as the definitive statement of the Black Aesthetic. Henderson sums up many of the paradigmatic statements regarding the Black Aesthetic of the late 60s and early 70s and systematizes them into a comprehensive theory of "blackness" in African American poetics. This theory of black poetry involved an implicit corporeal essentialism. Henderson argued that black poetry is:

1. Any poetry by any person or group of persons of known Black African ancestry, whether the poetry is designated Black or not.
2. Poetry which is somehow *structurally* Black, irrespective of authorship.
3. Poetry by any person or group of known Black African ancestry,

which is *also identifiably* Black, in terms of structure, theme, or other characteristics.

4. Poetry by any identifiably Black person who can be classed as a "poet" by Black people. Judgment may or may not coincide with judgments of whites.

5. Poetry by any identifiably Black person whose ideological stance vis-à-vis the history and the aspirations of his people since slavery is adjudged by them to be "correct." [12]

Henderson's model rests on the identification of "blackness" as a racial essentialism, *structurally* identifiable. Although point number 2 of his outline seems to suggest that a poem can be structurally "black" regardless of the author's race, all the other definitions emphasize the necessity of an *identifiably* African American authorship. In items 4 and 5, the poem must have been written by an "identifiably Black person." Implicit in this is the understanding that the poet must be *visibly* black, identifiable (perceived, recognized, *seen*) by distinct corporeal features as of "Black African ancestry." Throughout his introductory essay, Henderson maintains that only black people can truly understand, judge, and write black poetry. The unexamined ontological ground for this argument is the notion of what physically constitutes "Black people." Although Henderson refers to these people as a group of "Black African ancestry" who have a shared history of slavery, they also share "color"—an embodied, "structural" difference. Since ancestry and history cannot be known without recourse to other biographical contexts, "blackness" remains the embodied trait that ultimately signifies a person's being correctly judged a "Black poet." Thus, while "blackness" symbolizes a whole range of shared cultural and historical experiences, it operates as a metonym for the corporeal, *structural* difference *identifiable* in a white racist society.[13]

The insistence on the corporeality of "blackness" in the Black Aesthetic and Black Liberation cultural politics points to a key problematic in the discursive construction of race in the United States. "Black" has little objective, "epidermal" specificity (and indeed, as several African American writers have pointed out, "black" skin is rarely even black[14]); but it is on the flesh of the body that racial difference has been principally inscribed in U.S. society. The fixing of racial difference on the flesh constitutes a principal means of oppression, as Frantz Fanon has noted:

If there is an inferiority complex [in blacks] it is the outcome of a double process:
   —primarily, economic;—subsequently, the internalization—or better, the *epidermalization*—of this inferiority.[15]

For Fanon, the psychosocial problems facing black peoples derive from an economic colonialist system which supports itself by inscribing black corporeality as a negativity and casting black peoples as essentially this corporeality. Fanon writes, "To suffer from a phobia of Negroes is to be afraid of the biological. For the Negro is only biological. The Negroes are animals. They go about naked."[16] In other words, the colonialist system reduces colonized black peoples to the biological, the corporeal, the sensual. Being constructed as only their bodies, bodies marked as "black," the negative, the Other, colonized black peoples internalize the sense of inferiority this system has fixed on the epidermal surfaces of the black body. They have been disciplined to consider their "race" as a "corporeal malediction."[17] The color of flesh has been invested over history with the meanings of racial difference; but these meanings are not inherent in color. Rather than some biologically objective fact, "race," to paraphrase Judith Butler, is a "regulatory ideal whose materialization is compelled."[18]

This is not to say, however, that Fanon sees "race" as only an abstraction devoid of materiality. As he points out, and as many recent theorists of race have argued, the concept of "race" produces physical, psychic, and material effects.[19] Yet, at the same time, it is important to bear in mind that Fanon sees "blackness" as simultaneously real and imaginary, essential and constructed, and that in this dialogic perspective, the corporeality of blackness can be articulated as a site of ideological struggle. According to Diana Fuss, "For Fanon, the body image of the black subject is not constituted by biological determinations from within but rather by cultural overdeterminations from without." But as Fuss goes on to assert, Fanon's title, *Black Skin, White Masks*

> is suggestive: it foregrounds the possibility of culturally assuming racial identities ("white masks") at the same time it underscores the priority and ineradicability of the racial body ("black skin"). The gap, marked by the comma, between "Black Skin" and "White Masks" allows simultaneously for an essentialist and a constructionist reading: it unhinges "race" from skin color at the same time it reinscribes the problematic association of race with biology.[20]

Fanon's critique suggests how "blackness" could signify as both a corporeal essence and an ideological construct at the same time in Black Liberationist discourse. Insofar as "blackness" has been inscribed on African corporeality, it is this inscription of "blackness" that must be contested.

As young African American activists became impatient with the pace of the Civil Rights movement in the mid-60s, and as cities

around the United States burst into racial riots, the move away from
Martin Luther King's tactics of integration and coalition and toward
the militancy and separatism of Malcolm X was accompanied by the
rejection of "Negro" for the term "black." This shift indicates not only
a rejection of a taxonomy inscribed on African Americans by whites
and rationalized by a scientism of "race"; it also foregrounds the culturally overdetermined sign of epidermal difference as a trope of racial contestation and contradiction. By appropriating and invoking
the very sign that has historically overshadowed their existences in
the United States, Black Liberationists emphasized the significatory
antagonism in a binary opposition that has organized American race
relations (black/white). In this sense, the discourses of Black Liberation and "blackness" invariably foregrounded the body, specifically
the inscription of racial difference in the flesh.

My use of the term "Black Liberation" in this chapter is meant to
signal what I believe is one of the dominant cultural themes of this
period in African American politics, poetry, and culture: a direct link-
age articulated by radical black activists to Third World liberation
struggles. The cultural nationalism of Black Liberationist discourse in
the Vietnam era, of course, is rooted in oppositional political traditions that predate the war, and it would be ahistorical to claim that
decolonization and the Vietnam War alone dominated African American oppositional politics during the late 60s to early 70s. Clearly, the
nationalism of black oppositional politics after 1966 was predicated on
the historical tradition of black nationalisms stretching back to the
early nineteenth century and extending into mid-twentieth-century
Garveyism. The cultural nationalism of the Vietnam era, then, must
be seen as a reappearance of an important historical tradition of African American resistance. The historical specificity of Black Liberationist cultural nationalism, however, is its theoretical links to the post–
World War II anticolonialist movements in the Third World. Although
African American social activism during the Vietnam era was highly
differentiated and varied, there emerged in the nexus of the mid-60s a
distinctly new hegemonic articulation of black struggle organized
around the tropes of national liberation. This liberationist form of
struggle begins to assert itself as early as the late 50s as the effects of
African decolonization reverberated through the African American
intellectual community. It gained considerable momentum in the
presence of Malcolm X's early 60s speeches after his break from the
Black Muslims and with his formation of the Organization of Afro-
American Unity (OAAU).[21] The liberationist discourse established its
hegemony in the vanguard of radical black struggle in the wake of the
SNCC statements against the Vietnam War and in its calls for "Black
Power" during the June 1966 march in Mississippi. By 1966, this new

political vanguard shifted the focus away from the Civil Rights perspectives of Martin Luther King, Jr., largely rooted in rural, southern black church culture, and toward the race-assertive perspectives of Malcolm X and a predominantly urban-oriented, Marxian cultural struggle. The various groups, revolutionary cells, and organizations that emerged in this context—the Black Panthers, US, Spirit House, the Black Workers League—while often deeply divided, also shared important discursive features. Among these were an insistence on viewing the African American struggle as a nationalist liberation struggle, an ideological project to construct a unified social, political, and cultural vision of "blackness," and a concomitant rejection of white social, political, and cultural norms. Throughout my discussion of the various African American poems published in the Vietnam era, I will refer to those that endorse and produce this perspective as "Black Liberationist," not to efface the compelling differences between various activist groups and poets of the period, but rather to underscore critical alliances, confluences, and coalitions in their ideological and aesthetic projects.[22]

The corporeal discourses of Black Liberationist poetics signal an important historical shift in racial discourse and in oppositional cultural activism. The assertion of a revolutionary identity through a semiotics of corporeality diverges markedly from the politics and aesthetics of mid-twentieth-century black literature. To demonstrate this difference I will begin my analysis by discussing the representational strategies of post–World War II African American poetry and criticism. The shift from what Houston A. Baker, Jr., has called an "integrationist poetics" and its attempts to erase the "color line" to the Black Aesthetic and its insistence on what Frantz Fanon called "the fact of blackness" underscores the specific ways issues of political identity, corporeality, and decolonization traverse each other in U.S. oppositional culture during the Vietnam era.[23] Alhamisi's poem, for example, cited earlier in this chapter, establishes a relational chain between Black Liberation and Third World revolution: "Talk to them in chinese/vietnamese/or/black language." As I will demonstrate, throughout Black Liberationist poetic and political discourses, the refashioning of the African American body reveals the interconnectedness of historical conditions specific to the American encounter with decolonization in the 60s epitomized by the Vietnam War.

Conquering the Color Line

Although more than three million African American men registered for military service and five hundred thousand were stationed overseas during World War II, the war against fascism often only underscored for these men how little freedom they had in their own land. African American soldiers suffered the indignities of segregation in the U.S. military, for example, until the Korean War.[24] At the same time, though, their experiences in World War II empowered African Americans to challenge the fascism of the Jim Crow system. This sense of power was bolstered by new economic opportunities; African American union membership, for example, rose from 150,000 in 1935 to 1.25 million by war's end.[25] After the establishment of the United Negro College Fund in 1943, more African Americans had access to higher education than ever before. As Manning Marable has written, "On balance, greater progress in improving black educational prospects was achieved [from 1943 to 1950] than during the previous three decades."[26] Membership in the NAACP rose by 300 percent from 1934 to 1944, and the NAACP Legal Defense Fund helped repeal Jim Crow laws through appeals to the Supreme Court. African Americans were also gaining new political clout, as dozens of states elected blacks to their legislatures in the months following the war. The Truman administration, anxious to counter Soviet criticism of its race relations, seemed to be moving toward dismantling barriers to racial equality at home. The conditions seemed right for equality and integration after the war; black writers and intellectuals sought to build on the global political and economic strengths African Americans had helped secure for the United States by pressing for equal rights through appeals to the sense of common cause fostered among Americans during and after the war. The protest voices of the 30s receded into the background as voices of reform came to the fore in African American culture.

A prevailing concern in the popular black press and among many writers in this period centered on the eradication of what W.E.B. Du Bois had called "the problem of the color-line."[27] In the December 1949 issue of *Negro Digest*, an article by Walter White, then secretary of the NAACP, exemplifies both the extent of this concern and the ways in which corporeality underscored it. White's article reported on the discovery of a new chemical, monobenzyl ether of hydroquinone, that could supposedly change skin color from black to white by removing melanin, the pigment that determines darkness in skin tone. The author proclaimed, "If completely perfected and widely used, this chemical could hit the structure of society with the impact of an *atomic bomb*." He further claimed that monobenzyl "could, in fact, *conquer* the color line."[28] Later in his article, White quoted himself from a 1946 report in which he meditated on the implications of skin color: "Suppose the skin of every Negro in America was suddenly to turn white. What would happen to all the notions about Negroes, the idols on which are built race prejudice and race hatred? Would not

Negroes then be judged individually on their ability, energy, honesty, cleanliness as are whites? How else *could* they be judged?"[29] Although African American popular culture is replete with claims of "skin-whiteners," I draw attention to White's article because it marks a significant confluence of discursive elements unique to the African American cultural politics of the early post–World War II era.[30]

White's comparison of monobenzyl to the atomic bomb both implicitly celebrates U.S. victory in the war and redeploys its technology against the threat to democracy racism posed on the home front. Ostensibly, White's dream of a "colorless" society pivots on the obsessions with skin color central to U.S. racism. The color line is exposed as an imaginary mark drawn between whites and blacks, coloring Euro-American perception of African Americans. Concomitantly, though, the article also targets the "blackness" of the African American body. White's rhetoric situates the problem of racism in the visually perceived color of the African American body: an effect of seeing dark pigmentation, racism could be "cured" if only the *discoloration* of African-American skin could be "cured." "Whiteness" is thus cast as normal and "blackness" as a pathological condition.

Walter White was a powerful figure in African American literary culture and in the Civil Rights movement. He played an important role in the Harlem Renaissance, and in 1949, as secretary of the NAACP, he had a hand in aligning the organization with the emerging anticommunist liberal consensus of the postwar years. Manning Marable describes White as the major force behind NAACP's move to the right, a prominent supporter of the anticommunist McCarthy hearings, and an opponent of W.E.B. DuBois.[31] White was a light-skinned, blond-haired, and blue-eyed African American deemed "legally white," and his own physical "color" was a key problematic in his career. In his autobiography, *A Man Called White* (1948), White recalled being attacked often when he went through black neighborhoods. The problem of color prejudice within the African American community was the subject of his 1925 article "Color Lines." Yet when Alain Locke asked White to revise his article for *The New Negro* by incorporating work on this subject by the white anthropologist Melville Herskovits, White's indignant letter in response viewed color quite differently from his article of 1949: "I have read [Herskovits's] article and, frankly, I don't see there is anything in it which would improve my Survey article. As a matter of fact, every one of us who is colored knows more instinctively about color lines within the race than almost any white man can ever know."[32] Here skin pigmentation determines an essential self-knowledge and can be read as indicative of one's insights into a race. In the 1949 article, the "color" of African American skin is the line that bars knowledge; it keeps whites from seeing blacks as fellow human beings and it keeps blacks from attaining both equality and full realization as subjects. While White's letter demands that the physical color matters in the hermeneutics of race, the 1949 article argues that the insistence on *seeing* color blinds us, and further, that dark skin color itself is pathological.

White's vision of "conquering the color line" parallels an elision of blackness in African American poetics that became prominent in the late 40s. Many African American critics and poets rejected the "race-consciousness" of the Harlem Renaissance and the social realism of the 30s and sought to elide racial difference in African American poetry. This trend, which Houston Baker has called "integrationist poetics," was not, I would suggest, a cultural dominant, and a number of African American writers in the period challenged it. Yet I want to examine this discourse in the early Cold War years in order to investigate a nascent politics of the black body that reveals much about the meanings of race in the period. The elision of blackness evident in this criticism registered the emerging hegemony of New Criticism and the rise of a new black middle class, the building momentum of civil rights gains under Roosevelt, and the overall drive for national unity during the World War II era.[33] Further, it expressed the liberal consensus on race, based in the "ethnicity paradigm" promoted by the University of Chicago sociologists of the 30s and secured as hegemonic by Gunnar Myrdal's *An American Dilemma* (1944). Myrdal argued that the central "dilemma" in race relations was that African Americans had not assimilated like other immigrant ethnic groups.[34] As many critics have since pointed out, the ethnicity paradigm ignores fundamental social and historical conditions specific to the African American diaspora. As William Van Deburg has noted, views such as Myrdal's "stressed the black community's Americanness. . . . The Afro-American was, in effect, 'a white man in a black skin.' "[35] It was precisely in this assertion of the national over the racial that Cold War liberal consensus speaks itself. But, further, I want to underscore this notion of the "white man in a black skin" because I believe it reflects on the corporeality underlying the "Americanness" stressed by the ethnicity paradigm and often asserted in African American literary criticism of the early Cold War era. Many writers of the 40s insisted on the "Americanness" of black literature while concomitantly calling for an end to "race-consciousness" in African American poetry, a rejection of black vernacular forms in favor of Anglo-American poetic forms, and an erasure of race-distinctive adjectives to describe their work. Insofar as this discourse pivoted around the notion of "blackness" as the perceptible, material sign of racial difference, it implicitly involved an elision of black corporeality. Although the meaning of the "color line" trope exceeds skin color, I want to trouble its seemingly "obvious" ground in order to consider how the politics of race in this critical period at the threshold of the Civil Rights era were articulated as a concern about the perception of the "black" body in the ragged "lines" of African American poetics.

In several essays and writers' symposia, poets were enjoined to seek "nonracial themes" and write "literature"—not "Negro literature." Arthur P. Davis's introduction to his 1941 collection *Negro Caravan* epitomized this:

> The editors . . . do not believe that the expression "Negro Literature" is an accurate one. . . . "Negro Literature" has no application if it means *structural peculiarity*, or a Negro school of writing. The Negro writes in the forms evolved in English and American literature. . . . The editors consider Negro writers to be American writers, and literature by American Negroes to be a segment of American literature.[36]

Davis's rejection of any "structural" difference in "Negro Literature" ostensibly seeks to combat the effects of biologistic racism underlying much early twentieth-century criticism of black poetry, which many later black writers felt "exoticized" their literature. This desire to erase the adjectival difference is, like White's dream of conquering the color line, a desire to transfigure the perception of the "black" body in U.S. culture. It is the presence of the racially identifiable mark, whether, as in White's case, "black" skin or, as in Davis's, the "Negro" of Negro Literature that is targeted as intolerable to an "evolved" literature. Paradoxically, of course, the very title of Davis's anthology calls attention to its racial body. Yet just as White's "cure" for the "race problem" was to "whiten" African American flesh, Davis and other writers of the 40s sought to "whiten" black literature by eradicating the "structural peculiarity" of race-consciousness and its insistence on the distinctiveness of black "forms." As Baker argues, Davis's statement proposes that a *marked* African American tradition of cultural expression is "unfit" (unhealthy, incapable) literature: "The distinctive *forms* of Afro-American culture must remain *unknown*, or they must be transcended by Negro writers who adopt 'evolved' forms of English and American literatures."[37] As Baker suggests, Davis's view resonates with inherent anxieties about the African American body, which in racist culture is a body regarded as coarse, unfit, unevolved. "Corporeal properties," David Theo Goldberg has argued, serve as "the metaphorical medium for distinguishing the pure from the impure" in racist discourse.[38]

Like Davis's anthology, Beatrice Murphy's *Ebony Rhythm: An Anthology of Contemporary Negro Verse* (1948) expresses a conflicted view of the color line. A popular anthology widely available in school libraries, Murphy's book collects 226 poems from African American magazines and newspapers, featuring primarily love poems and poems about the war, the latter usually written by veterans. Ironically, even though the collection's title underscores racial difference, less than twenty-five percent of its contents specifically discuss race, race relations, or "the color line."[39] Further, despite the title's pointed reference to black music as cultural resource, virtually none of the poems anthologized explicitly draws on black musical traditions.[40] Murphy's preface resembles Arthur P. Davis's in its rejection of African American poetry's "adjectival difference":

> A critic . . . made the observation [concerning Murphy's earlier collection, *Negro Voices*] that she was disappointed because the work of the Negro poets was not dissimilar to that of any other race. We have never understood exactly what she meant, but interpreting what we believe she meant—that somehow anything a Negro does must be different simply because it was done by a Negro—we are sure some will be just as disappointed here. The Negro poets write, as poets have since they first began, about love, nature, and everyday events in the world they live in—which is an *American*, not a *Negro*, world.[41]

Murphy implicitly asserts the national over the racial and reiterates the ethnicity paradigm of the Cold War liberal and integrationist consensus. Like Walter White, several poems in *Ebony Rhythm* see the difference of "blackness" as a handicap, something to be cured. Walter G. Arnold's "Entreaty," for example, asks God to justify the speaker's "malediction": "Grant me, O God, for all the things that I/Will never know except as dreams, because/Thou made me black, the sight to see just why/It must be thus" (2). In another poem, Arnold again asks "Why must a man who loves his country well/. . . . //. . . .be in his nation's eyes/Seen always as a loyal colored man,/And never as a true American?" (3). While Iola M. Brister's "Epigram" indicts racist obsession with dark skin color, it also situates the problem, as Walter White did, in that color: "Were I not black/You would not turn/And stare at me" (13). William Cousins also sees color as a physical handicap, writing in "Black Gauntlet," "I sent my challenge out to Life/To find that he had challenged first—/And made me black" (53). In "You Are Black," Helen F. Clarke attacks racism but focuses on skin color as the problem: "When the ladder to success is broken/They all tell you . . ./Dontcha know, boy, you are black?" (41). Ed Lee's "Blend" poses a melting pot view that erases physical color even as it asserts it: "Black, brown, yellow, red, and white:/Mix them together . . . that's right./They were poured in the pot;/What have we got?/America!" (99). Such views of racial difference do not, however, characterize every poem in this collection. John Henrik Clarke, for example, advocates resistance to white racism through distinctively black cultural traditions in "Sing Me a New Song":

> Sing me a new song, young black singer,
> Sing me a song with some thunder in it,
> And a challenge that will
> Drive fear into the hearts of those people
> Who think that God has given them
> The right to call you their slave. (42)

Like Jones's "Black Art," Clarke's poem envisions a song that can serve as a weapon of resistance. In "Black Faces," Anita Scott Coleman's celebration of blackness as an epidermal sign of identity resembles the body-politics of Black Liberationist poetry: "I love black faces:/They are full of smoldering fire" (51). But such representations of black corporeality are an exception to the norm. J. Farley Ragland advocates a seemingly contradictory position on color in "Uncle Tom": "[W]e must be strong,/And take more pride in the Black Man's Song!//It matters not if we're black or tan; It doesn't take color to make the man!" (124). Even though these poems all critique white racism, their focus on skin color as the putative object of that racism belies deeply conflicted views of the black body in U.S. society. If the African American body were not black, racism would not exist. These images both deny the significance of skin color and at the same time assert it, in much the same way as early Cold War U.S. society implicitly asserted whiteness as hegemonic by viewing the remedy to the American dilemma as assimilation.

Conquering the color line in African American literary criticism of the 40s and early 50s similarly involved an elision of blackness. In 1949, J. Saunders Redding praised Renaissance writers who focused on "nonracial themes," such as William Stanley Braithwaite: "Save only a few essays written at the behest of his friend, W.E.B. DuBois, nothing that came from his pen had anything about it to *mark* it as Negro."[42] Charles I. Glicksberg, writing in 1946, applauded Countee Cullen for writing as "an American rather than as a Negro": "With the exception of a few poems, his work, rooted in the American and English poetic tradition and universal in theme, gives no indication that it was written by a Negro."[43] Similarly, Edward Bland, in a 1944 article for *Poetry*, criticized black poetry for its inability to "escape [the] preindividualistic, group point of view," which for Bland meant "race consciousness." "It is the *presence* of this limitation," Bland continued, "only partially broken through, if at all, that is to a large extent responsible for the dissatisfaction one feels about Negro verse, and it is a limitation, at least in the opinion of this writer, which detracts from whatever poetic skill may be otherwise present."[44] Often this literary critical elision of blackness went hand in hand with an assertion of patriotic American unity. In *Phylon's* Winter 1950 symposium on the Negro Writer, Redding argued that the "Roosevelt revolution" and World War II had enabled the African American writer "to see himself as in no fundamental way different and particular. . . . He began to see that the values were human, not racial."[45] In the same issue, Hugh Gloster argued that "the preponderating use of racial subject matter has *handicapped* the Negro writer," and he praised mainstream publishers' advertisements for black literary works that "make no mention of the racial identity of the writers."[46] Margaret Walker, assessing the current poetry scene of the time, wrote, "Race is rather used as a point of departure toward a global point of view than as the central theme of one *obsessed* by race. . . . The new poetry has universal appeal coupled with . . . the return to form."[47] Walker's praise of a "return to form" is also an elision of "black" form, the "structural peculiarity" that would seem to keep black poetry from a white-dominated critical canon. Just as Walter White sought to "cure" the physical features of the black body that most marked it for racist oppression, literary critics sought to erase the adjectival difference in black poetry, the "color line" that marks a black writer as different. Insofar as the most dominant "color" is the most unmarked, this call to erase the "Negro" of "Negro Literature" addresses whiteness as hegemonic and poses black literary difference as the pathological condition to be "cured."[48]

Writers otherwise noted for their "protest" literature also sought to "conquer color." In the foreword to his 1948 collection, *47th Street*, Frank Marshall Davis recounted a number of scientific studies to prove that race and color were not definitive. Davis specifically denies the "structural peculiarity" of the African American body: "With science throwing out color as a basis for classifying mankind according to race, what have we left? Surely not physical structure, for in the last half century research has shown that people with dark skin and kinky hair no more form a distinct group than do those with light colored eyes, hair or skin." Despite this, Davis contends that race has become invested with a cultural and political significance that has tangible material effects on the lives of African Americans. He concludes, "America will have Negro writers until the whole concept of race is erased."[49]

While these critical views express a Cold War liberal consensus, they also register the emerging dominance of New Criticism in American poetry. For New Critics, such as Allen Tate and Cleanth Brooks, extratextual social factors (such as race) are considered irrelevant to the understanding and appreciation of a poem; meaning coheres in the text alone. Allen Tate's introduction to Melvin B. Tolson's *Libretto for the Republic of Liberia* (1953) both expresses classic New Critical views and parallels the critical trend toward eliding race also evident in African-American criticism of the period:

> For the first time, it seems to me, a Negro poet has assimilated completely the full poetic language of his time and, by implication, the language of the *Anglo-American* poetic tradition. . . . It seems to me only common sense to assume that the main thing is the poetry, if one is a poet, whatever one's color may be. I think that Mr. Tolson has assumed this; and the assumption, I gather, has made him not less but more intensely *Negro* in his apprehension of the world than any of his contemporaries or any that I have read. But by becoming more intensely Negro he seems to me to dismiss the entire problem, so far as poetry is concerned, by putting it in its properly subordinate place.[50]

Tate's assumption that true poetry stems from an Anglo-American tradition asserts the color line even as he denies its significance. Tate argues that it is by writing in the Anglo-American tradition, and thus "subordinating" the "problem," that Tolson achieves full "assimilation." What makes Tolson a "true" poet for Tate is an elision of the "structurally peculiar" black poetic forms that embody African American experience. Through this Tolson reveals his ability to write in the evolved forms of the English language, the white body in black skin.[51]

My reading of the elision of the "black" body in African American poetics of the 40s and early 50s is not meant to overgeneralize the complex textures of literary and racial discourses in this period. Writers such as Gwendolyn Brooks, Margaret Walker, and Melvin B. Tolson placed racial difference "on the line" throughout their careers; and many of the poets and critics I've cited made important contributions to black poetics. Nor do I mean to oversimplify the problematics of skin color within the U.S.[52] I am interested rather in the ways a desire to "conquer color," to dismiss "structural peculiarities," and erase the adjectival difference of African American poetry demonstrates deeper cultural anxieties about the black body in this liminal historical moment as the country was poised before epistemic shifts in race relations. The 1943 race riots, in which hundreds of African Americans were brutalized by white workers, and the increased racialization of urban geography and politics point to the underlying white anxiety about the expanded presence of black people in post–World War II America.[53] While the urge to elide black corporeality in African American poetry of these years was founded on notions of racial justice and optimism for race relations, it was also inflected by the overarching pressures in early Cold War America for national unity, pressures that in many ways impinged on the very possibility for blackness, on the limits of the black body's tolerability in the body politic of the newly dawned "American century."

Clearly the "integrationism" of mainstream black politics that fueled the Civil Rights struggles of the 50s forged profound gains in racial justice and laid the groundwork for the emergence of radical black struggle in the Vietnam era. Despite the conservatism represented by White and the NAACP during the early postwar years, history was quickly leading African Americans into the forefront of social change. The startling victories of the southern Civil Rights actions taken by Martin Luther King's Southern Christian Leadership Council and other organizations both achieved legislative victories and thrust the racial dilemmas that had been festering in the country since Reconstruction into white America's living rooms, on their televisions. The deployment of U.S. troops to quell white riots at Little Rock in 1957 brought the racism of the South into the national arena at the same time that television was becoming more of a common appliance in American homes.[54] The nonviolent, dignified, rational tactics of the Civil Rights activists contrasted sharply with the vicious hatred of Southern whites and made for spectacular news coverage. According to Adolph Reed, Jr.,

> [I]t was through its coverage of black resistance in the south that television developed and refined its remarkable capabilities for creating public opinion by means of "objective" news reportage. . . . However, television was not alone on the cultural front of the ideological struggle. *Life*, *Look*, the *Saturday Evening Post*, major non-southern newspapers, and other national publications featured an abundance of photo-essays that emphasized the degradation and brutalization of black life under Jim Crow.[55]

These campaigns opened up the terrain for contestation over the meanings of race and racial identity and set the stage for the militant cultural politics of Black Liberation, partly through the circulation of images depicting African American bodies brutalized by southern racism.[56] Television's attention to the racial struggles in the South increased black presence in popular culture and paralleled the increasing attention to struggles for national liberation around the world. At the same time that Little Rock and Montgomery became news to millions of Americans, Kwame Nkrumah's Convention People's Party won independence for Ghana and Egypt's Gamal Nasser was defying England. In the midst of desegregation campaigns in the United States and the apparent victories in Third World decolonization, many African Americans began to place their struggles in a global context. As Marable notes, "The contradiction of a 'free' Africa and their 'unfree' descendants in the U.S. was an immediate and important parallel which was reiterated by many civil rights advocates."[57]

Along with the political interventions of the Civil Rights movement, African American literature and culture were making profound impacts on dominant U.S. culture. Works by Ralph Ellison, James Baldwin, Gwendolyn Brooks, and Lorraine Hansberry achieved unprecedented recognition and helped give white audiences more exposure to African American experiences. LeRoi Jones had also emerged by the late 50s as an important figure in the New York Beat scene and had begun publishing his influential journal, *Yugen*. In popular culture, jazz and the folk blues had captured the imagination of the post–World War II avant-garde, and Elvis Presley's reinterpretation of southern black culture both scandalized white American parents and energized the increasingly restless "baby boom" population. Despite the appearance of white conformity during the 50s, then, African American literature and culture were significantly shaping American popular culture.[58] The fact that the rock music explosion of the 60s, which continues to define the period in the popular imagination, was predicated on African American music points to the importance of black culture in the 50s. Insurgent black subcultures, particularly in the urban North with youth gangs, the drug culture, and the growing influence of the Black Muslims, prepared the way for the dramatic explosions of black militancy in the Vietnam era. With the rise of racial tensions in the United States and a concomitant rise in Third World struggle, increased black presence in U.S. cultural discourse, and a growing impatience among younger black intellectuals with the pace of Civil Rights reforms, an important shift was taking place in the discourses of race that would eventually find expression in Black Liberation and would definitively reconfigure race relations in the United States.

The work and legacy of Malcolm X were instrumental in this shift. The literature on Malcolm X's importance in late twentieth-century African American politics, culture, and society is enormous and has been growing rapidly with his recent revaluation in hip-hop culture. Since the present chapter could not possibly provide an adequate analysis of Malcolm's role in Vietnam-era African American activism, I would like to focus more specifically on his articulation of a Third-Worldist position concerning African American oppression and its links to his assertion of black corporeality. As Robert Allen stated in 1969, one of Malcolm X's most important contributions to African American politics was the notion that

> the struggle of blacks in this country was bound up with the outcome of revolutionary struggles in the Third World. This message was especially timely because it was at the end of 1964 and beginning of 1965 that the United States started its massive buildup in Vietnam, and Malcolm was one of the first black leaders to stand in opposition. He did so not because he was a pacifist or morally out-

raged. He opposed the war out of a sense of solidarity with the Vietnamese liberation fighters.[59]

In many of his speeches, Malcolm X made explicit connections between U.S. military interventions and economic exploitation in the
Third World and racism in the United States. In his April 8, 1964,
speech, "The Black Revolution," sponsored by the Militant Labor Forum, for example, Malcolm X articulated Third-Worldist positions
that would come to dominate Black Liberationist politics after 1965:

> What happens to a black man in America and Africa happens to the
> black man in Asia and to the man down in Latin America. What
> happens to one of us today happens to all of us. . . . 1964 will see the
> Negro revolt evolve and merge into the world-wide black revolution
> that has been taking place on this earth since 1945. The so-called
> revolt will become a real black revolution.[60]

At this point in his career, Malcolm had split with the Nation of Islam
and had begun to promote a pan-global revolutionary philosophy.
This speech delineates a view of African American struggle sharply
contrasted with the hegemonic liberal consensus positions of the
leading spokespersons in the Civil Rights movement at the time. It
expresses a growing empathy felt among leftist vanguard black intellectuals toward the movements of decolonization in the Third World.[61]

Malcolm's speeches repeatedly criticized both whites and the African American middle-class leaders of the Civil Rights movement for
making blacks ashamed of their bodies. This politics of corporeality
went hand in hand with Malcolm's insistence on the links between
decolonization in the Third World and African American struggle.
Malcolm began his February 14, 1965, speech, given just hours after
his home had been bombed, by asserting that the United States,
France, and the United Kingdom were chiefly anxious about "the African revolution." He continued by again claiming direct correlations
between Third World and African American struggles. Emphasizing
African revolutions, Malcolm asked his audience, "Now what effect
does [the struggle over Africa] have on us?" Malcolm argued that because colonialist whites had portrayed Africans negatively for hundreds
of years, African Americans began to hate Africa, and thus began to
hate themselves. He then connects the effects of this colonialist system
of representation on African American identity to corporeality:

> You know yourself that we have been a people who hated our Afri-
> can characteristics. We hated our heads, we hated the shape of our
> nose, we wanted one of those long dog-like noses, you know; we
> hated the color of our skin, hated the blood of Africa that was in our
> veins. And in hating our features and our skin and our blood, why,
> we had to end up hating ourselves. And we hated ourselves. Our

color became to us a chain—we felt that it was holding us back; our color became to us like a prison which we felt was keeping us confined. . . . We felt that all of these restrictions were based solely upon our color, and the psychological reaction to that would have to be that as long as we felt imprisoned or chained or trapped by black skin, black features and black blood, that skin and those features and that blood holding us back automatically had to become hateful to us.[62]

Liberation from white colonialist domination, then, is inextricably linked with liberation from a corporeality shaped by that domination. The black revolution invariably demands a transfiguration of blackness as a physically essential, anatomical, embodied identity. The pride in black corporeality and black culture that Malcolm promoted had an enormous impact on the shape of African American identity in the Vietnam era. In 1966, the actress Denise Nicholas would say, "I never knew I was black until I read Malcolm."[63] Malcolm X's view of black corporeality contrasts markedly with Walter White's dream of conquering the color line, Arthur P. Davis's goal of eliding the "structural peculiarity" of blackness, and the post–World War II mainstream African American cultural politics of integrationism. His insistence on black corporeality as a site of ideological struggle, a ground for the assertion of racial empowerment, and the source of revolutionary awareness would become articulated as the epistemological ground for Black Power, Black Liberation, the Black Aesthetic, and other modes of cultural revolutionary discourse in the Vietnam era.

Rewriting Blackness in the Vietnam Era

The "denigration" of African American corporeality in white U.S. cultural history has been enabled by the investment of certain physiological signs, such as dark skin, with the meanings of race. "Blackness" is not *of* the body, but rather fixed on the body by a systematic history of white cultural perceptions. Yet, obviously, corporeal and epidermal differences can be visually verified, *seen*, among humans. These tangible differences have been compelled to signify "race" in the United States. Although "race" may be historically and socially constructed, this does not alleviate the fact that its inscription on the body quite powerfully structures the material existences of people of color in the United States. It is crucial to recognize how, as Omi and Winant define it, race operates as a "social formation" that is not an ahistorical essence but is nevertheless a tangible determinant of social relations.[64] As a "transcendental signified" in American social relations, moreover, race is always unstable, in "dialectical flux."

Writing on the emergence of identity politics in the 60s, Kobena Mercer argues, "It was precisely because of the recognition of the meaninglessness of race that the signifier itself became the site for the making and remaking of meanings."[65] In other words, it is important to recognize how the *discursivity* of race, its instability as a signifying system, constitutes it as a terrain of political struggle. The transfiguration of blackness mounted by Black Power, Black Liberation, and the various manifestations of black cultural nationalism were possible precisely because of the openness of "blackness" as the sign of an embodied racial difference in U.S. culture. Although the totality of "blackness" clearly involves a complex variety of cultural, political, or historical repertoires for African American experience, "blackness" is always at the same time metonymic of the corporeal difference overdetermined as racial difference in U.S. history.

The corporeality that underwrites black cultural politics in the Vietnam era asserted itself in the emerging militancy of SNCC activists as they linked their cause to the national liberation struggles in the Third World. In 1964 John Lewis noted the change:

> Something is happening to people in the Southern Negro community. They're identifying with people *because of color*. . . . They're conscious of things that happen in Cuba, in Latin America, and in Africa. Even in SNCC, we talk about integration, about the beloved community, but there have been great changes going on. There's been a radical change in our people since 1960; *the way they dress, the music they listen to, their natural hairdos—all of them want to go to Africa.* . . . I think people are searching for a sense of identity, and they're finding it.[66]

By the mid-60s, young black intellectuals began asserting "blackness" as both cultural and embodied difference.

This politics of black corporeality was viewed as central to the revolutionary potential of Black Liberation. In 1968 Hoyt Fuller wrote:

> Across this country, young black men and women have been infected with a fever of affirmation. They are saying, "We are black and beautiful," and the ghetto is reacting with a liberating shock of realization which transcends mere chauvinism. . . . After centuries of being told, in a million different ways, that they were not beautiful, and that whiteness of skin, straightness of hair, and aquilineness of features constituted the only measures of beauty, black people have revolted.[67]

With the emergence of Black Liberation and black cultural nationalism, the black body that had been "denigrated" (from the Latin *de-* + *nigare*, to blacken) by white culture would now be celebrated, its distinctiveness asserted as a positive presence of "blackness" as a cultural totality.

Poetry played an instrumental role in the political and cultural environment of the Black Liberation. In his study of African American literary history, C.W.E. Bigsby wrote, "If the dominant form in the 1950s had been the novel, in the 1960s, it was the public arts, drama, and poetry in performance."[68] The production of African American poetry mushroomed during the Vietnam era; not even at the height of the Negro Renaissance of the 20s were so many writers publishing so much poetry. Small presses and literary journals sprang up across the country, not only in New York City or on the West Coast, but in midwestern urban centers such as Chicago, St. Louis, and the Twin Cities, as well as in the South. Increased African American enrollments in colleges and universities contributed to a proliferation of writing workshops and campus political groups, which in turn fueled the expansion of black underground and small press production in this period. The many politically oriented black underground newspapers that had sprung up around the country in the wake of the call for Black Power regularly featured poetry. *The Black Panther*, for example, included a regular feature called "Revolutionary Poetry," which usually comprised ten or more poems. Writers associated with the avant-garde literary groups of the late 50s and early 60s, such as Umbra and Dasein, would reemerge as important leaders of the cultural front for the militant black poetics of the mid-60s to early 70s, and they would find new energy and develop new audiences in the fervor of the Black Aesthetic. LeRoi Jones's short-lived Black Arts Repertory Theatre/School (BARTS) in Harlem became an archetype of the new black literary groups organized in African American communities across the country during the Vietnam era.[69] BARTS promoted and developed a new vanguard of politically engaged African American poets, fiction writers, and dramatists, and it also served as a model for literary groups around the country, such as the Detroit Black Arts, BLKARTSOUTH Poets centered in New Orleans, and the Black Arts Center in Houston.[70] In addition, African American writers organized conferences and symposia that would help consolidate a writing community separate from the white-dominated literary world. The number of conferences aimed at black writers became so extensive that *Negro Digest* began running a special column called "On the Conference Beat."[71] Conferences in Berkeley (1964), New York (1965, 1968), Newark (1966), Detroit (1966, 1967), Fisk University (1966, 1967, 1968), and Dakar, Senegal (1966) helped U.S. black writers forge a sense of solidarity amongst themselves and with black writers across the world. These conferences and the many writing groups and small publishing venues that emerged in the Vietnam era gave African American writers an important forum for the circulation, exchange, and production of views concerning the new Black Aesthetic.[72]

The Black Aesthetic has been widely discussed in African American literary criticism, and I will not attempt to summarize these statements here.[73] My primary concern will be to show how the Black Aesthetic articulated a cultural politics of corporeality that elaborated on the Third-Worldist politics of Black Liberation inflected by the historical experience of the U.S. involvement in the Vietnam War. To initiate this discussion, however, some tentative description of the Black Aesthetic seems necessary. The Black Aesthetic differs markedly from the aesthetics dominant in early post–World War II African American literature. Whereas critics in the period from the 40s to the late 50s argued that African American poets should be "poets" first and foremost, and only circumstantially "African American," thus downplaying and even eliding racial difference in order to obtain an "integrated" critical regard equal to that of white poets, African American critics of the Vietnam era vigorously argued that black poetry was first and foremost "black." Racial difference is foundational to the various arguments and theories of the Black Aesthetic. The assertion of "black" as the constitutive difference in African American literature stems from the turn toward Black Power and its coalescence as Black Liberationist politics. Many of the writers associated with the Black Aesthetic, such as Leroi Jones/Amiri Baraka, Larry Neal, Don L. Lee, H. Rap Brown, and Carolyn Rodgers, also played important roles in the new black political vanguard that emerged after 1966. In many ways, the Black Aesthetic was viewed as the revolutionary cultural front of Black Liberation.[74]

The Black Aesthetic's major goals included emphasizing the distinctiveness of African American culture. The symbols, myths, and tropes of the historical black experience were cultivated as a revolutionary discourse of black self-assertion. The hegemonic Euro-American literary and cultural traditions were rejected or utilized to critique and caricature white culture. According to Henry Louis Gates, Jr., the Black Aesthetic was forged as "a reaction against the New Criticism's variety of formalism. The readings [Black Aesthetic] critics advanced were broadly cultural and richly contextualized; they aimed to be 'holistic' and based formal literature firmly on black urban vernacular, expressive culture."[75] In the wake of the urban riots of the early 60s and the emergent black nationalism of Malcolm X, the city—most often metonymically represented as the ghetto—was conceived as the space of revolutionary black culture. Central in this celebration of black life was the importance of jazz and rhythm and blues as musical analogues to black poetry. As Van Deburg notes, "The use of poly-rhythms, short and explosive lines, delayed rhymes, and other tech-niques borrowed from verbal rituals of the street such as the rap, the toast, scatting, and signification assured audiences that black writer/performers no longer cared about 'talking white.' Instead they would utilize a distinct lexicon, syntax, and phonology."[76] Although rural black gospel music played a significant role in establishing rhythmic patterns in the poetry, the improvisatory riffing and multilayered me-ters of jazz and rhythm and blues constitute the distinctive analogues of Vietnam-era black poetics.

The Black Aesthetic was also articulated as a political project in line with the overtly Third-Worldist perspectives of Black Liberation. The emergence of race-assertive discourses in African American op-positional politics and the move from a politics of integration to one of separatism and nationalism occur at the same time that the United States faced a number of challenges to its political hegemony in the Third World. The liberation struggles in Algeria, Ghana, the Congo, Egypt, Indonesia, and Vietnam, to name a few, made a significant impact on the African American community, particularly when the nonviolent struggles of the Civil Rights era seemed to reach an im-passe against entrenched racism in America. Throughout the litera-ture of the Black Liberation, specific parallels are drawn between these struggles, especially in Vietnam, and those of African Ameri-cans for self-determination. The Black Panther Party, theoretically informed by Mao Zedong and Ho Chi Minh, made solidarity with the National Liberation Front a specific platform in its agenda. In his popular and influential book, *Soul on Ice* (1968), Eldridge Cleaver insisted on a direct relationship between the war in Viet-nam and racism in the United States and advocated an interna-tionalist perspective to Black Liberation: "The black man's interest lies in seeing a free and independent Vietnam, a strong Vietnam which is not the puppet of international white supremacy."[77] Cleaver's view, and the Third-Worldist perspectives of the Black Panthers, reiterated Malcolm X's insistence late in his life on the global significance of the African American struggle: "It is incorrect to classify the revolt of the Negro as simply a racial conflict of black against white, or as a purely American problem. Rather, we are today seeing a global rebellion of the oppressed against the op-pressor, the exploited against the exploiter."[78]

Contrary to arguments made by authors of many historical and cultural studies of African American activism of the 60s, the Vietnam War constituted both an important reference point in the formation of the Third-Worldist perspectives of Black Liberation and a critical con-cern in African American literature and culture of the period. *Freedom-*

ways regularly featured articles, editorials, and literature (mostly poetry) condemning the war as racist and imperialist. Its editorial practices repeatedly linked the struggles of African Americans to the war. In the Spring 1967 issue, inside front cover photos of U.S.-engineered destruction and brutalities in Vietnam were compared with photos of police brutality against African Americans on the back inside cover. The first photo's caption read: "IN VIETNAM . . . detention, death, destruction . . . made in U.S.A."; for the back cover, the caption read: ". . . in the U.S. south."[79] An editorial entitled "Rescuing the NAACP" argued, "Today the victims of American military intervention overseas are the colored people of Vietnam, Laos, Cambodia and the Dominican Republic."[80] The cover story of a 1968 issue of *Black Vanguard* mourned the combat death of an African American soldier and argued that, by forcing this man to fight in an unjust war, the U.S. military was guilty of murder. The article went on to state, "We of the BLACK VANGUARD feel that there must be a complete termination of all black participation in the aggression that is being perpetrated by white America against the world." The back page of the same issue reproduced a photo of four white GIs showing off severed Vietnamese heads. Below this grisly photo is an article by a USAF lieutenant pleading with readers to resist the draft.[81]

Black nationalist discourse in the period often asserted analogies to the Vietnam War. In 1968, the Republic of New Africa (RNA), a group that demanded that the United States turn over five southern states to serve as a black homeland and attempted to negotiate with the State Department as a separate nation, cited the Vietnamese struggle against the United States as a model for a black war of liberation within the United States. As Van Deburg summarizes their views, "If the Vietnamese could force an American retreat from Southeast Asia 'without ever being able to land a single bomb on a single American city,' certainly the RNA and its allies had the potential to win far greater concessions."[82] In 1970, the Congress of African Peoples "went on record as being unalterably opposed to the war and urged black troops to cease firing on the Vietnamese." Eldridge Cleaver suggested that black troops could sabotage the military from within and advocated fragging any officer who tried to interfere.[83]

The parallels drawn by Black Liberation between the African American and the Vietnamese struggles stemmed in part from an analysis of the war's increasing impact on the lives of African Americans, particularly the urban working class. Although from the early 60s to about 1966 many African Americans supported duty in the newly integrated military as a move up and out of ghetto unemployment, by 1968 attitudes had shifted markedly. A disproportionate percentage of troops assigned to combat duty were African American;

programs such as Project 100,000 specifically targeted low-income, urban black males for the draft, and the numbers of minority soldiers killed in Vietnam outweighs their relative presence in the field.[84] A 1966 poll by *Newsweek* showed that 35 percent of African Americans polled opposed the war; in 1968, however, opposition rose to 56 percent. By a two-to-one majority, African Americans polled believed that their young were being made to bear an unequal burden in the war.[85] African American activists often argued that military expenditures for the war would exhaust funds for social programs and inner-city development. As Gwendolyn Patton wrote in a 1966 article in *Liberator:*

> Black people saw that the Vietnam war was the reason why the war on poverty had diminished. Black people in Washington D.C. saw . . . low-rent housing made into an airbase . . . saw Black militants and activists forced into the army because of inequities in the draft . . . . saw Black students forced into the army to become Black mercenaries because this country does not allow them enough economic stability to continue their college education.[86]

Similarly, the League of Revolutionary Black Workers often spoke out against the war, calling for its end so that defense expenditures could be reallocated "to meet the pressing needs of the black and poor populations of America."[87] Black Liberationists viewed the Vietnamese as people of color who, like themselves, were victims of a racist, imperialist First World power. Malcolm X articulated this view in his 1965 speech in Rochester, New York, when he stated:

> Right now in Asia you have the American army dropping bombs on dark-skinned people. . . . It's racism. Racism practiced by America. Racism which involves a war against the dark-skinned people in Asia, another form of racism involving a war against the dark-skinned people in the Congo, the same as it involves a war against the dark-skinned people in Mississippi, Alabama, Georgia and Rochester, New York.[88]

In his poem "Junglegrave," S. E. Anderson expressed how many black people felt about the war: "Vietnam: land of yellow and black genocide."[89]

The Black Aesthetic and Black Liberationist poetry in this period often expressed the historical and cultural effects of African American concern with the Vietnam War. The racism and imperialism that black activists discerned in U.S. military interventions in Southeast Asia were viewed as extensions of the white mentality that had historically oppressed black Americans and "denigrated" black vernacular culture. In a statement on poetics, Etheridge Knight argued, "The Caucasian has separated the aesthetic dimension from all others, in order that undesirable conclusions might be avoided. . . . [T]he red of this aesthetic rose got its color from the blood of black slaves, exterminated Indians, napalmed Vietnamese children, etc."[90] Knight links the violence of the war with the Cartesian rationalism of white culture. Significantly, Knight's statement portrays this rationalism as a separation of intellect from corporeality and an indication of white culture's inability to see how its civilization has been secured through the subjugation of the bodies of nonwhite peoples. Ron Welburn's poem, "First Essay on the Art of the U.S.," similarly indicts white aesthetics: its "chaos is in the scattering of Man/in fright, in Watts/ Harlem, in Africa or/Vietnam" (BF, 264). Clyde Taylor makes a similar point in the introduction to his anthology, *Vietnam and Black America:* "By following the distant points of Vietnam and Black America down far enough, you reach a funky depth where the roots of racism, imperialism, and war become a tangled web."[91] By articulating such connections, African American activists both asserted theoretical links between militaristic violence and racism and constructed African Americans as the revolutionary vanguard in the United States. Black Liberationists realized that the Vietnamese, without the technology and overwhelming firepower of the U.S. military, were thwarting U.S. imperialism. The Viet Cong and the NLF came to be viewed as exemplary models of guerilla resistance against whites.

The political ideologies of the Black Aesthetic were significantly inflected by the black intellectual vanguard's reading and adaptation of Third-Worldist cultural revolutionary concepts. According to Gates, the Black Aesthetic envisioned art as a revolutionary tool:

> Art was a fundamental part of "the people"; art for art's sake was seen to be a concept alien to a pan-African sensibility, a sensibility that was whole, organic, and, of course, quite ahistorical. What was identified as European or Western essentialism—masked under the rubric of "universality"—was attacked by asserting an oppositional black or "neo-African" essentialism. In place of formalist notions about art, [Black Aesthetic] critics promoted a poetics rooted in a social realism, indeed, in a sort of mimeticism; the relation between black art and black life was a direct one.[92]

The Black Aesthetic held that the critical ideology of "art for art's sake" was "Caucasian idolatry of the arts." Maulana Karenga, the leader of the US movement and highly regarded by LeRoi Jones in 1965, pointed out that African Americans "do not need pictures of oranges in a bowl or trees standing innocently in the midst of a wasteland. If we must paint oranges and trees, let our guerrillas be eating those oranges for strength and using those trees for cover."[93] As LeRoi

Jones embraced nationalism in the mid-60s and became Amiri Baraka, he would argue that all cultural and social activities were inherently political. "In Baraka's world, black art forced change, enabling blacks to *recreate themselves.*"⁹⁴

This notion of "recreating" self and "transfiguring" blackness was articulated both through an assertion of distinctive aspects of black vernacular, expressive culture and through a discourse of corporeality. This "transfiguration" of African American corporeality as a key project of black cultural nationalism reiterates a tradition in Third World liberationist cultural practices of asserting identity and inverting the terms of oppression. Amilcar Cabral, a leader of the Guinea (Bissau) liberation movement, asserted, for example, that the vanguard in a nationalist liberation struggle seeks to affirm and define an identity distinct from the colonial power. This identity, "individual or collective, is at the same time the affirmation and denial of a certain number of characteristics which define the individuals or groups, through *historical* (biological and sociological) factors at a moment of their development." Furthermore, "To make a total definition of identity, the inclusion of the biological element is indispensable."⁹⁵ As Manning Marable has noted, "Books by African socialists and leaders such as Tanzania's Julius Nyerere, Ghana's Kwame Nkrumah, and Guiné-Bissau theorist Amilcar Cabral became an integral part of the African American revolutionary nationalists' lexicon."⁹⁶ One of Ho Chi Minh's famous statements, that "to make revolution one must first and foremost remould oneself," closely parallels black cultural revolutionary thought. His campaign for revolutionary morality sought to forge an indissoluble link between the Party and personal life and became characteristic of the Vietnamese Communist Party.⁹⁷ Ho's concept of revolutionary morality can be seen in many of the rules for personal behavior espoused by the Black Panthers.⁹⁸ As is evident in the numerous references in Black Liberationist poetry to the liberation struggles of the Vietnamese, the Vietnam War had a profound impact on black culture in this period.

Throughout the Black Liberationist poetry published during the Vietnam era, the body is foregrounded as the terrain for the signification of a racially assertive and empowered subjectivity. Many poems celebrate African American culture and self-identification by focusing on physical features idealized as characteristics of black corporeality. Sandy Robinson's "I HAD TO BE TOLD" represents the speaker's consciousness-raising as a process of reexamining her body. Written in capital letters, the text loudly declares the corporeal presence of blackness:

I HAD TO BE TOLD THAT BLACK WAS BEAUTIFUL
I HAD TO BE TOLD MY BLACK SKIN WAS SEXY AND
    EXCITING
I HAD TO BE TOLD THAT MY BIG LIPS AND WIDE FLAT
    NOSE WERE NOT UGLY MISTAKES OF NATURE, BUT
    BEAUTIFUL TRAITS OF A BEAUTIFUL PEOPLE.
I HAD TO BE TOLD NOT TO WORRY ABOUT THE NAPS
    AND KINKS OF MY HAIR AND WEAR IT
    NATURALLY.[99]

Robinson spells out in capital letters both a body "epidermalized" by white culture as an "ugly mistake" and a body reconstructed by Black Liberationist discourse. She celebrates the new assertiveness of blackness signaled by the cry for "Black Power" as a new perception of her own female body. Often, Black Liberationist poems present such corporeal revisions as the key to racial self-awareness. Carl Clark's "No More" traces the distinctive corporeality of blackness as evidence against a false consciousness promoted by white culture he can no longer accept: "My hair curls sharply./My nose is flat./I am black./I celebrate."[100] S. E. Anderson similarly celebrates the distinctive physical beauty of black people in "Soul-Smiles":

> I be moved by ebony's
> snow capped teeth
> ready to speak in the name
> of blackness
> ready to grimace in
> the struggle for freedomblack. . . . (BF, 357)

The recognition of blackness as a positive presence is also bound up with a vision of the black body as transgressive sign in white-dominated America. In a 1967 issue of *The Black Panther*, Emory's poem "On Revolutionary Art" portrays the act of representing the distinctive corporeality of African Americans as revolutionary:

> Painting beautiful things
> Light skin, brown skin
> black skin, too.
> Painting beautiful
> things curly hair,
> straight hair,
> nappy hair, too.

Next to this poem is an illustration by the poet of a black man with an ammo belt slung around his torso, automatic rifle in one hand, knife in the other, lunging forward over a pig.[101] Similarly, another poem in *The Black Panther*, this one by Ericka, views black corporeality as essentially revolutionary:

> strong black flesh squeezed through channels of hate hope
> ugly red wrinkled snout of racist perversion
> soft brown round smoothness of birth
> our warriors, our enemy, our hope[102]

Black Liberationist poetry emphasized images of distinctive physical features associated with African Americans that seemed to transgress the hegemony of white corporeality.

Such images were cast as synecdochal of revolutionary consciousness. This is especially the case in images of hair: the natural, which emphasized a kinkiness viewed as essential and natural to African American hair, was often portrayed as a sign of liberation. Raymond Washington's "Freedom Hair," for example, celebrates the natural:

> unrestricted/unrestrained/uncompromising
> untamed/not straightened/natural/protesting
> kinky/nappy/Revolutionary hair/Black folks
> hair[103]

Sharon Scott's "Oh——Yeah!" similarly locates liberatory potential in hair:

> my nappy hair grows/lives in. and
> lights my fire allthroughout my
> being.[104]

But Scott also cautions in another poem, "For Both of Us at Fisk":

> is your nappy hair
> skin coloring
> and your diggin
> chitterlins but.
> it is your
> being.
> in your pores
> is your blood
> and your
> breeding![105]

Yet while these lines reject a superficial stylization of blackness and assert that true blackness is a state of being, they end in images of corporeality to demonstrate that blackness is more deeply embodied than hairstyle.

In the Black Aesthetic, it is by transfiguring blackness to signify power that African Americans can free themselves from oppression. Raymond R. Patterson's "Black Power" emphasizes this by representing the speaker's affirmation of his body:

> I stepped from black to black,
> It was so simply done—
> Like walking out of shadow
> And going forth in sun—
> And I will not look back.
>
> But if you ask me how
> That day was, what I saw,
> These memories linger now:
> An easing at the core,
> A clearer sense of what
> I am, a keener taste
> for life; the urge to touch
> My shining hands and face—
> And marvel at how much
> They please me in each case. (NBV, 316)

The recognition of blackness represented in such poems corresponds to the political ideologies of Black Power. According to Van Deburg, "[T]he core assumptions and directives" of "black consciousness" or "the new blackness" in the period involved an ideology of psychosocial "black self-actualization."

> This black self-actualization was accompanied by a corresponding questioning and rejection of many normative values forwarded by the majoritarian society. . . . Traditional color associations would be reversed: black skin color and physical features were to be considered good, not bad characteristics. Black lifestyles and distinctive cultural forms such as religious and musical expression would be affirmed, acclaimed, and elevated in status. In this respect, the new blackness encouraged Afro-Americans to seize control of their own self-image and to validate that image via a wide array of cultural productions.[106]

Poets often deployed images of black corporeality and white corporeality in binary hierarchical oppositions to transfigure black self-image. As Al Young's "The Prestidigitator [1]" describes the role of black poets: "The poet is a prestidigitator, he makes/your old skins disappear & re-clothes you/in sturdy raiment of thought, feeling, soul" (NBV, 370). Blackness may encompass the whole panoply of African American cultural and historical experiences, but it is also grounded in a cultural construction of the body.

This construction was also deployed to consolidate a group cohesiveness and sense of nationhood. S. E. Anderson's "The Sound of AfroAmerican History Chapt. 1" emphasizes the corporeal as the distinctive ground from which a national, historical African American cultural experience stems:

the history of blacklife is put down in the notions
of mouths and black hands with fingering lips
and puckered ravenfingers bluesing the air of
today and eeking [sic] out the workgrunts getting down
to earth the nittygritty. . . . (BF, 359)

In a similar sense, Lance Jeffers's "There is a nation" renders black nationalism corporeal:

There is a nation in my brawny scrotal sac,
a nation in my spine,
a nation in my graveled throat,
a nation in the succored egg that climbs my womby well
(NBV, 267)

In constructing nationhood through corporeality, Black Liberationist poems from the Vietnam era often celebrate the black body as a manifestation of a pre-diasporic utopia. Imamu Amiri Baraka (LeRoi Jones), for example, writes in his 1967 poem "Ka 'Ba":

We are beautiful people
with african imaginations
full of masks and dances and swelling chants
with african eyes, and noses, and arms,
though we sprawl in grey chains in a place
full of winters, when what we want is sun. (NBV, 208)

Herschel Johnson's " 'We Are Not Mantan' " rejects the inherently violent stereotypes that whites have historically inscribed on the black body in favor of the idealized images of African warriors:

WE ARE NOT MANTAN
   or BUCK/wheat
false comic images
singers&dancers
. . . .
we are
HANNIBAL
coming through the alps
and SHAKA
defending his homeland. . . . (WSAL, 79)[107]

Edward S. Spriggs celebrates the black body as inherently expressive of African culture in his "Every Harlem Face is AFROMANISM Surviving":

. . . this
Source of power keeping on
Keeping our past present

> & indelible in ourselves
> In our blood in our genes
> In our sons on our faces
> In our minds in our lives. . . . (BF, 341)

The "nation" (that is, Africa) is "indelible" in the black body, and it is through the body that "AFROMANISM" is signified.

Black Liberationist poetry also likened the transfiguration of black corporeality to riots and violent insurrection against white domination. Joseph Bevans Bush's "Nittygritty," dedicated to Leroi Jones, exemplified this:

> We all gonna stop sliding stuff, tighten
> Up, stop locking Black asses and start
> Locking Black arms, hearts and souls.
> We gonna come from behind those
> Wigs and start to stop using those
> Standards of beauty which can never
> Be a frame for our reference; wash
> That excess grease out of our hair,
> Come out of that bleach bag and get
> Into something meaningful to us as
> Nonwhite people—Black people.
> We all gonna grab the minds of our
> Children, make them vomit up the
> Super white patriotism fed them
> In the public schools as history
> And inform them that: "We are beautiful
> People with African imaginations"
> . . . .
> All of this is to say: throat-
> Cutting time is drawing nigh and
> We all gonna be ready. (WSAL, 4–5)

Bush draws together a representation of black communality through images of the body. Black people must band together physically to overcome white oppression. This oppression is manifested in the ways they have been taught by white culture to construct their bodies through cosmetics designed to make black people seem white. Bush even portrays the history taught to black children by whites as something ingested, taken into their bodies, something that can be physically expelled. In the concluding lines he echoes Jones's sentiments in "Black Art," that only violence against the bodies of racial others will bring about the revolution.

Violence is often represented as physically liberatory and cathartic in Black Liberationist poetry. Rolland Snellings's "The Song of Fire," for example, graphically portrays a revolution against white oppression for all people of color in the world:

BLOOD will wash your pain away!
  (Fire!)
Bright red flames! Burnt, charred death,
    grinning skulls,
    rolling eyes, and mad-mad
    cries to mute Madonnas!
  (Fire!)
will scorch the "Lonely Crowd" with Death's embrace
    like Mushroom Suns . . . in mutant Hiroshima!
  (Fire!)
will vindicate the blues; sanctify the earth;
    resurrect the mangled Jesus from . . . the Nordic
    lynch-tree!
  (Fire!)
will cauterize the Racist Plague! (BF, 326)

Dedicated "for Africa, Asia, Latin & Afro-America—the Wretched of the Earth," Snellings's poem articulates the internationalism characteristic of Black Liberationist cultural politics. The images draw upon the tropes of lynching in order to invert them against whites; these images emphasize how liberation for people of color will come through a mutilation of the white body that will lead to the reconstruction (resurrection) of the black body. A. X. Nicholas also evokes the imagery of lynching to represent the violence of urban riots as cleansing and redemptory for the black body in "This Baptism with Fire . . . ":

The invisible blood burning
in our black faces—we huddle
bitterly at bay in this hovel—
cops clutching their stiff
rifles—eager to kill.
This baptism with fire, people,
is our redemption—our kindled candle.
Our dreams have long ago drowned
in the guts of the sea. We leap
blindly at dragons—our bloody bones
bolting through the skin's edge. (WSAL, 115)

Here violence is considered necessary for the liberation of black people; their bodies must bear this violence in order to bring forth the new body within. Amiri Baraka's "Sacred Chant for the Return of Black Spirit and Power" celebrates the violence of riots as a rearticulation of the oppression of black people by whites:

Work smoke-blood streams out thick bushes.
We lay high and meditating on white evil.
We are destroying it. They die in the streets.

Look they clutch their throats. Aggggg. Stab him.
. . . .
To turn their evil backwards
is to
live. (NBV, 209)

Baraka represents mutilation as the liberatory violence that will un-
leash a new black life; his poem envisions blackness as transgressive,
even poisonous to whites. In "Riot Rimes," Raymond Patterson portrays rioting as the result of an embodied condition, the racial oppression that must be overcome:

> I felt this itching all over
> My skin
> So I smashed that plate-glass window in,
> And all that fancy furniture
> And easy credit plans
> Were right there in my hands—
> All the things that I've been needing.
> And I didn't even know my hands were bleeding.[108]

Patterson's poem envisions revolutionary action as being predicated
on the conditions of the body. Once the speaker of the poem acts by
destroying (white) property, he seems to have physically crossed the
barrier of material wealth that is also a barrier of epidermal difference.
The final image suggests that in his looting the speaker acquires a
new consciousness that is not dictated by his body, a liberation from
the limitations of the body as subject in white culture. Al Young's "A
Dance for Militant Dilettantes" satirizes a purely intellectual militancy
and argues that authentic revolutionary action stems from a new
awareness of black corporeality:

> soul is not enough
> you need real color
> shining out of real skin
> nappy snaggly afro hair
> baby grow up & dig on *that!*
>
> You got to learn to put in about
> stone black fists
> coming up against white jaws
> & red blood splashing. . . . (NBV, 367–368)

And in Norman Jordan's "Black Warrior," revolution proceeds from
the recognition of "African-ness" in the body:

> At night while
> whitey sleeps
> the heat of a

> thousand African fires
> burns across my chest (BF, 389)

A number of Black Liberationist poems represent black corporeality as a weapon. Lebert Bethune's 1966 poem "To Strike for Night," for example, represents black identity as the embodiment of a weapon against white Western culture:

> The man with the blood in his sight
> with the knife in his voice
> and nothing to lose but that life
> which in living like them
> comes to death—is me
>
> . . . .
>
> The man who will win is me
> the man who cant die anymore
> the man who forged behind patience and smiles
> a long black gun of justice
> that man is me[109]

The black man is defined according to the corporeal trauma he has suffered or his family has suffered. More importantly, the poem represents the very means of signifying for black people grounded in the physical mark of their oppression. The images of "the blood in his sight" and "the knife in his voice" signify doubly and bear the double-consciousness that W.E.B. Du Bois so accurately noted black Americans live with: the black man's eye may be bloodied but he also has his eye/gun-sights set on blood, murder, revolt, and the raging passion of vengeance; the black man's throat may have been cut, but now his words will cut down his oppressor. The means of corporeal oppression have been rearticulated as potent attributes of the black body, a body in revolt, a militant body rising up against white America. Bethune's vision of the black male body rising up against white America exploits the fear of black masculinity, particularly in its last image of the black man waiting to knife someone in the night, an image that exploits the white stereotype of the black man as urban mugger. Raymond Patterson's "What We Know" envisions blackness as having the destructive force of nuclear weapons:

> There is enough
> Grief-
> Energy in
> The blackness
> Of the whitest Negro
> To incinerate
> America. (NBV, 315–316)

Michael Nicholas similarly imagines his body as incendiary in "Today: The Idea Market": "I'm napalm in Watts./I shall be gas from other hydrogens" (NBP, 94). Black Liberationist poetry seeks to invest "blackness" both as a cultural and epidermal sign with a corrosive power, a power to destabilize the legacy of white hegemony.

Nicholas's reference to napalm indicates how this politics of black corporeality was also articulated within the historical experience of the Vietnam War. While many Black Liberationist poems from the period represent black corporeality as a weapon in a war of liberation, the Vietnam War constitutes an important frame of reference for such representations. Further, the war is often cited as evidence of U.S. racism. In Bob Bennett's "It's time for action," the war in Vietnam is represented as a genocidal campaign against all people of color:

> The devils are closer to pullin' an out & out
> genocide now
> Than they have been since we got off the boat
> . . . .
> Yeah man, Right now
>   In Viet Nam and
>   In your home town
>
> Viet Nam is almost funny, man
>   Really funny.
>   (I cry about it often)
>
> Here he's got a double genocide goin'
>   You and the VietNamese
> The funny part is that he's got you killin'
>   each other (BF, 420–421)

In a similar vein, Clarence Major's "Vietnam #4" offers a grim joke about this connection. Hanging out on a street corner of an unnamed city, the poem's speaker is asked:

> how come so many
> of us
> niggers
>
> are dying over there
> in that white
> man's war

The man asking this question finally suggests that black people are dying in Vietnam for the same reason the Vietnamese are: "you know, he said/two birds with one stone" (NBV, 299). Bobb Hamilton asserts solidarity with the Vietnamese in his "Brother Harlem Bedford Watts Tells Mr. Charlie Where Its At":

Help you fight in
Viet Nam?
Man, them's my folks
you fucking with over there,
Viet Cong
            or
Hong Kong
They is colored. . . . (BF, 450–451)

Gerald W. Barrax's "The Old Gory" sees the Vietnam War as only the most recent manifestation of the historical war against people of color and compares the war to the U.S. war against Native Americans and the U.S. enslavement of Africans:

Now it's yellow reds.
The color of the land never changes
neither do the tongues
whether splitting truth
(with or without treaties)
or chemical fire licking
tenderly lovingly the round snub-nosed faces
of the evil menace. (NBV, 212)

In all of these examples, the link asserted between the African American and the Vietnamese struggles rests on a corporeal essentialism, the "epidermal difference" that connects all people of color as subject to oppression by white U.S. imperialism.

For an African American to participate in this war against people of color was viewed as either an ideological betrayal or an example of the ways black people are exploited by white racism. Black Liberationist poets often argued that the costs of fighting "the white man's war" and of not joining the Vietnamese in the struggle against white hegemony would all too often result in the loss of young black lives. Carolyn Rodgers's "A Non Poem about Vietnam" pointedly criticizes any black participation in the war:

no black man (or negro) should fight the
hunkie's war, cause everytime we kill a Vietnamese, we
are widening the crack in our own asses for the hunkie
to shove his foot into. (WSAL, 152)

Renaldo Fernandez's "legacy of a brother" mourns the loss of an African American to the war:

. . . markings on a shitter wall
WILLIE WAS HERE IN 59
but willie died in 63

> fighting vc
> and his body was never found (NBV, 380)

The emphasis on the body's loss underscores how the U.S. military's exploitation of African American labor disrupts the black nationalist body politic. Prentiss Taylor laments a similar loss of a young African American in "Tony":

> look up brothers, look at the sun.
> THE STRUGGLE IS IN this COUNTRY.
> . . . .
> look at tony
>
> laid out in a closed casket
> cause he didn't look human no more
> after the undertaker sewed
> his head
> back
> together.
> > you went to war, tony, and it ain't even
> > our war.[110]

The mutilation of the black soldier's body by the war parallels the disintegration of the black body politic that results from the war's continued exploitation of black men.

Etheridge Knight's "2 Poems for Black Relocation Centers" similarly focuses on the ways the U.S. military decimates the black community by convincing young African American men to fight against other people of color. The poem tells the story of Flukum, who joined the army because he "wanted inner and outer order." The white military convinced him that killing Vietnamese was right:

> . . . And sin? If Flukum ever thought about sin
> or Hell for squashing the yellow men, the good Chaplain
> (Holy by God and by Congress) pointed out with
> Devilish skill that to kill the colored men was not
> altogether a sin.

When he returns from his tour of duty, however, Flukum is shot and killed in his own community: "He died surprised, he had thought/the enemy far away on the other side of the sea."[111]

Perhaps the most extended treatment of the link between the war's destruction of the black soldier's body and its decimation of the black body politic is Michael Harper's "Debridement" (1972). This poetic sequence traces the post-traumatic stress and eventual death of Sgt. Stac John Henry Louis, a black soldier from Detroit decorated with the Medal of Honor as the sole survivor of a tank explosion in

Dak To. Throughout the sequence, the triage technique of debridement, cutting away unhealthy flesh to prevent infection, is compared to the gradual mental and physical disintegration of Louis, which in turn symbolizes the war's devastating effects on the black community. Louis's name evokes both Stackolee and John Henry; but the war renders Louis impotent, an "electronic nigger," the white state's Uncle Tom—he is neither the heroic trickster, like John Henry who died trying to prove the human body superior to the machine, nor the "natchal man." Instead, as his mother tells us in "Mama's Report," Louis does little more than watch slides he brought back with him of dead Vietnamese. By focusing on how the war experience has corrupted and debilitated Louis, Harper represents the war as destructive of black culture's masculine ideals. As the opening text tells us, "BLACK MEN ARE OAKS CUT DOWN" by the war; Louis's story is: "A CLINICAL HISTORY://BODY POETRY TORN ASUNDER."[112] Harper's poetic sequence seeks to enact a debridement for the African American community wounded by the war.

Although the war was viewed as a destructive exploitation of black men by white imperialism, the Vietnamese struggle also served as a model to Black Liberationists of the possibilities for resisting this imperialism. The Last Poets, whose street and concert performances involved rap poetry recited over a persistent ground beat provided by congas in an early prototype of hip-hop and rap music, celebrated the defiance of Ho Chi Minh in Suliaman El Hadi's "Ho Chi Minh." In this poem, when Ho Chi Minh rejects the United States offers to Americanize his country, Uncle Sam responds:

> I'll send my helicopters out
> to hunt the peasant down
> I'll send my jets and tanks
> to burn his villages to the ground
> **The old man looked up at this fool**
> **and did not even bat an eye**
> **He said** *Before we would submit*
> *you see, we all would rather die*

The poem views Ho Chi Minh's guerilla struggle as exemplary for black revolution and struggle.[113] A. B. Spellman's "tomorrow the heroes" represents Black Liberationists and the Viet Cong as fighting the same war:

> tomorrow the heroes
> will be named willie. their
> hair will be the bushes that grow
> everywhere the beast walks. america

is white. america is not. white
is not the slow kerneling of seed
in earth like the willies, the grass
the roots that grapple the beast

in the swamps. the williecong are earth
walking. ile-ife succor the williecong.
there is no other hope. (VBA, 301)

Spellman draws upon the Yoruba myth of ilé-ifé, "the house from which all earthly dwellings originated"[114] and the black vernacular tradition (Willie) to articulate an alliance between oppressed peoples who, through their solidarity, can rise up against American racism. Here people of color are represented as formidable foes of white America. Similarly Ted Joans's "FOR THE VIET CONGO" conflates an Afrocentric Black Liberationist struggle with the struggle for national liberation of the Viet Cong:

THEY CAME WITH SYPHILIS ON THE
END OF THEIR BLONDE TONGUES AND
OPEN SORES OF GONORRHEA SPEWING
PUS FROM THEIR SKY BLUE EYES. . .
. . . .
THE THIRD WORLD EVERY NON-WHITE MAN/
   WOMAN/BOY & GIRL
THE MAJORITY OF HUMAN BEINGS ON THIS OUR
   EARTH/WE STAND
   READY TO DO
WHAT HAS TO BE DONE/WE SHALL NOT STOP OUR
   REVOLUTION/UNTIL WE HAVE WON
WE OF THE THIRD WORLD/KNOW WHO THEY ARE/
   WHO WORKS WITH
   THEM/AND WHAT SHALL BE DONE. . . . (VBA, 303–304)

Just as Black Liberationist poetry sought to celebrate and assert the black body, it also represented the white body as diseased, decadent, debased. In Joans's poem, the decadence of whiteness is opposed to the righteousness of Third World peoples (which here means all people of color).

In order to reconstruct the body, black poets also sought to reject the body constructed by white culture. As Peter X articulated this position:

Black is the basic of all colors; All colors come from black. White is the absence of color—no color. If the white persons who are blond and light-skinned, brunette and dark-skinned, or red-haired and freckled can call themselves white, why can't we, who are black, brown, yellow, and red call ourselves black?[115]

The rejection of white culture involved a promotion of traditions, expressions, and values distinctive to African American history and rooted in African culture. Askia Muhammad Touré's "Extension (for Imam El Hajj Heshaam Jabeer and Leroi Jones)" argues: "We must live again—in our minds./You know, shed the white plaster of our 'negroness.'"[116] K. William Kgositsile's "Towards a Walk in the Sun," for example, contrasts whiteness as a degraded corporeality to the empowered corporeality of blackness. Kgositsile, an African emigré, meditates on the possibility of black memory as a revolutionary awakening. His poem begins by questioning, "Who are we?" and argues that without reflection on the history of black oppressions, African Americans are consigned to a half-life servitude to white culture. This "Negro" mentality is metaphorically linked to a physical degeneracy of African American corporeality:

> You who swallowed your balls for a piece
> Of gold beautiful from afar but far from
> Beautiful because it is colored with
> The pus from your brother's callouses
> . . . .
> You who bleached the womb of your daughter's
> Mind to bear pale-brained freaks
> You who bleached your son's genitals to
> Slobber in the slime of missionary-eyed faggotry. . . .
>
> (BF, 228)

The poem addresses those black people who ignore their blackness and seek to assimilate with the white world. Gold signifies both the material riches to be gained through this assimilation and the light color of white corporeality (both in skin and hair). The false beauty of whiteness is colored with the (white) pus on the bodies of black laborers. Kgositsile portrays such assimilation as sexually degenerate. The poem ends by prophesying that "THIS WIND YOU HEAR IS THE BIRTH OF MEMORY. . . . THE ONLY POEM YOU WILL HEAR WILL BE THE SPEARPOINT PIVOTED IN THE PUNCTURED MARROW OF THE VILLAIN." African Americans who dress, talk, look, and act like whites are reviled in Black Liberationist poetry as degenerates and traitors to the race. James Danner's ironically titled "My Brother" attacks a black moderate politician:

> . . . Look at yourself,
> With your little moustache and greased hair
> And looking more like a Spaniard every day,
> You fear the nigger
> In you. . . . (BF, 271)

The black moderate exhibits his accommodation and subservience to white culture through his corporeality: his body has been fashioned to repress the blackness he fears in himself.

The cultural politics of the body espoused by Black Liberationist poetry has been often criticized for chauvinistic tendencies. "Black Art," for example, calls for poems to physically defend black people, but it also calls for them to be "daggers . . . in the slimy bellies/of the owner-jews" and for poems "cracking/steel knuckles in a jewlady's mouth" (BF, 302–303). The noxious antisemitism and misogyny of these images overshadow the poem's concluding weak images of a black people who

> understand
> that they are the lovers and the sons
> of lovers and warriors and sons
> of warriors Are poems & poets &
> all the loveliness here in the world. (BF, 303)

Such vague platitudes and clichés pale in comparison to the violence of the earlier images. Jones's poem expresses a common sentiment in Black Liberation that certain ethnic groups (not only Jewish but also Italian and Irish Americans are targeted in the poem) who do not bear the physical mark of "blackness" often find a material success in the United States that has been unattainable for blacks, and often their successes are achieved through the economic exploitation of blacks.[117] That Jones's poem so violently attacks ethnic groups who are often themselves the target of economic oppression in the United States and elsewhere serves to underscore how central and determining the epidermal difference, blackness as an embodied sign of racial identity, was in the Black Arts. In 1968, the same year that Jones's poem appeared in the anthology *Black Fire*, Nikki Giovanni would write,

> Nigger
> Can you kill
> . . . .
> Do you know how to draw blood
> Can you poison
> Can you stab-a-jew
> Can you kill huh?[118]

Henry Dumas's "cuttin down to size," printed in *Black Fire*, similarly positions Jewish Americans as the scapegoats for the exploitation of blacks. Written in the voice of a young black hood, the poem represents the vicious murder of a Jewish shopkeeper as an act of triumph for the black man over a system of economic oppression (BF, 349–350). These poems exemplify the grotesque extent to which Black Liberation could romanticize any transgressive act by black people as another blow for the revolution. The hatred in such poetry cannot be neatly explained away; I point it out to demonstrate how, despite the very real conditions of ethnic bias and the sociohistorical facts of anti-semitism in U.S. culture, for Black Liberationists the palpable and visual sign of "blackness" was the essential determining difference.[119]

Black Liberationist body-politics often conflated black empowerment with patriarchal values. White women would be reviled, while black women were often celebrated, yet in both senses the female was objectified. A typical means of rejecting white culture in black male poetry was by representing white women as prostitutes who emasculate black men. Larry Neal's "The Baroness and the Black Musician," for example, represents a wealthy white woman who frequents Harlem jazz clubs as vampiric:

> Tangled in sea weed minutes;
> her eyes suck your blood.
> the baroness glides into the Harlem houses,
> leaves her touch on the lips
> of the young blacks,
> spits out your manhood with Chase
> Manhattan check books—is a lover of *Negro* art.
> (BF, 309)[120]

Ed Bullins represents sexual relations between white women and black men as another form of slavery in "When Slavery Seems Sweet":

> When slavery seems sweet
> its scent is Chanel
> and rustles Sachs silk
> upon an ivory slide
> that presses
> your Black balls
> like Burgundy grape. . . . (NBP, 32)

In order to demonstrate the poet's allegiance to "blackness" and to compensate for white culture's stereotypes of black women, male poets often objectified the black woman as muse, idealized black beauty, or mother of the new black nation. Neal, for example, portrays black women as the embodiment of Afrocentric consciousness in "For Our Women":

> Black women, timeless, are sun breaths
> are crying mothers
> are snatched rhythms
> are blues rivers and food uncooked
> lonely villages beside quiet streams,
> are exploding suns green yellow moons. . . . (BF, 310)

The pronoun in Neal's title to this poem underscores the possessiveness many black male poets of this period expressed toward black women. "You Are the Black Woman," a poem that appeared in a 1969 issue of *Liberator*, represents the black female as the embodiment of a feminine aspect of an Afrocentric nation:

> You are the Black Woman.
> Within the marvelous Temple, which is your warm body, reposes
>   the Black Nation.
> You are both Sustainer Of The Ember and Bearer Of The Flame.
> You are the Nation's strength and you are the Nation's glory.
> I am but Protector of and Servant unto the Temple.
> Our combined mission is that of protecting and bearing the Flame.
> You are my strength, the Nation is my glory, you are the Nation.
> I need you, my Black Woman.
> You need me, your Black man.
> The new Black Nation waiting within your body
> Is dependent on us both.[121]

Throughout these poems although men celebrate black women, the male is always represented as dominant and dominating. In the images quoted here, the woman "sustains," contains, and embodies the black nation's strength, yet does not wield that strength. The black nation is the man's "glory" and the woman is the nation. Although the black nation is dependent on both male and female, it "waits" inside the female body; the male body's union with the female will enact it.

A number of black female poets supported the patriarchal practices of the Black Aesthetic. Linda Goss reiterates the patriarchal discourse evident in Theodore's poem in her "Revolution Man Black":

> Revolution Man Black
> Before you go
> and win the battle
> plant in me a seed
> your son
> your daughter to produce a grandson.
>
> Revolution Man Black
> while you are gone
> winning the battle
> I will feed your son
> your ways of politics and love
> our child will know Black Truth. . . . (WSAL, 61)

In one sense, such positions can be read as a response to the prevailing stereotypes of the failure of the black family.[122] In another, however, they point to the crucial significance of the body as the site of ideological struggle for Black Liberation. By envisioning the nation and liberation in terms of reproduction, such rhetoric emphasizes the embodiedness of "blackness."

Of course, the misogyny and antisemitism in poems such as "Black Art" were not universally endorsed by all African American writers associated with the Black Liberation. Ishmael Reed, for example, has insisted on a multicultural perspective in his poetry, and he broke with Black Arts poets when they accused his Jewish girl-friend of being a "Zionist agent."[123] Mari Evans, Sonia Sanchez, and Carolyn Rodgers often challenged the misogynist stances asserted by male Black Liberationists. Paula Giddings, in "Rebirth," questions the masculinist doctrine of Black Power and the inability of black poets to see black women as anything more than an abstraction:

> I am called sister and now you want to protect and write poems
>   about me.
> But what I don't understand about my new beauty is. . .
> Why is it not reflected in your eyes? (WSAL, 49)

Michele Wallace provoked a national controversy among African American critics when she denounced sexism among black men and argued that men in the Black Power movement "were primarily interested in gaining access to the bodies of white women."[124] It is important to note, however, the latent reactionary extremes this discourse could lapse into in some cases, as they point to the limitations of the cultural politics of Black Liberation as an effective means of resistance against social oppression. According to bell hooks, "While the 60s black power movement was a reaction against racism, it was also a movement that allowed black men to overtly announce their support of patriarchy." Although racial oppression often figuratively and literally emasculated black men, hooks questions the viability of compensating for this through an assertion of masculinist sexuality. She argues that the sexism of Black Power indicates the extent to which black men have adopted forms of social injustice that have enabled white men to maintain power in the United States. The sexism of Black Power operated as a bond between black and white males, and, consequently, a terrain of struggle with white males could be defined by Black Liberationists over the control of women.[125]

Many have argued that Black Power and the discourse of self-determination ultimately served to generate a new black middle class and failed to achieve its revolutionary goals.[126] The physical essentialism of the black aesthetic may be strategically limited and a dangerous idealization of blackness, as recent critics such as Adolph

Reed, Jr., Henry Louis Gates, Jr., and Kwame Anthony Appiah have argued, but it also illustrates how during the Vietnam era oppressed Americans envisioned the body as the site of ideological struggle. Although the negative, violent, misogynist, and antisemitic tendencies of much Black Liberationist poetry have kept it on the margins of the mainstream African American canon, works by Jones, Giovanni, Neal, and Lee were widely popular and highly influential, and illustrate how black poets envisioned the human body as a terrain upon which racial meanings could be contested and the relations of public and private negotiated.[127] The images of black people empowered and ready to assert themselves in U.S. society "by any means necessary" had a considerable impact on the shape of race relations. As Michael Omi and Howard Winant state, "The black movement *redefined the meaning of racial identity,* and consequently of race *itself,* in American society."[128]

As Omi and Winant describe it, the "great transformation" in post–World War II racial discourse came about over both the contestation of the meanings of race in the Civil Rights movement and the emergence of insurgent theories of race based on class and nation paradigms. It is the nation-based paradigms, however, that Omi and Winant identify as central to African American political thought in the Vietnam era:

> The nation-based paradigm, to a far greater extent than the ethnicity- or class-based approaches, is a theoretical convergence, a resultant of disparate currents. . . . Despite the wide range of specific approaches, nation-based theory is fundamentally rooted in the dynamics of *colonialism.* . . . In the nation-based paradigm, racial dynamics are understood as products of colonialism and, therefore, as outcomes of relationships which are global and epochal in character.[129]

Where Civil Rights activism had advocated an end to "race-thinking" in American society and focused on equal rights within the prevailing U.S. political systems, Black Liberation activism repudiated the existing systems and sought to change the fundamental structure of U.S. society. Through the "rearticulation of black collective subjectivity," Black Liberation called for a new racial awareness based in a redefinition of the African American body and cultural experience.[130] In so doing, Black Liberation initiated the dissolution of the split between personal and political that would come to characterize oppositional culture in the United States during the Vietnam era. The rearticulation of the black body and the assertion of the "epidermal difference" distinguish Black Liberationist poetics from the integrationist poetics of the early postwar years. While the Vietnam-era movement evoked early twentieth-century black nationalism and radicalism, in the 60s and early 70s the black struggle intersected in a number of ways with the struggles of Third World peoples, especially with the Vietnamese. The cultural politics of Black Liberation articulated a complex convergence of historical, political, and social moments that enabled it to effect a profound challenge to the paradigms of racial discourse in the United States.

3

"The Territory Colonized": Siting the Body in Women's Liberation Poetry

"The Final Revolution"

Black Liberation had an enormous impact on the politics of Vietnam-era social movements, particularly Women's Liberation. The Black Liberation movement opened up discursive spaces for the dramatic emergence of "new classes," new historical subjects identified through the corporeality of their race, gender, and/or sexuality rather than through their economic status. The relationships between African American and Vietnam-era feminist activisms are both practical and theoretical. Many of the women who would later organize Women's Liberation were active in the Civil Rights campaigns from the mid-50s to the 60s.[1] They learned tactics of civil disobedience, direct action, and street theater, and they learned that they could signify resistance through their bodies. According to James Forman, by 1961 SNCC activists "had begun to walk, talk and dress like the poor black farmers and sharecroppers of rural Georgia and Mississippi."[2] The emerging feminists active in the Civil Rights movement during the early 60s learned from their SNCC compatriots that cultural practices of the body (clothes, grooming, manner, speech, gesture) could also be deployed in their cause. Feminists who dressed like Vietnamese women, for example, or wore Mao jackets, reiterated the SNCC tactic of walking, talking, and dressing like the oppressed.

Women in Civil Rights began to apply the principles of equality espoused by the movement to their own situation, beginning with their "second-class" status within the movement itself. The ground for what would be called "the Second Wave" had been long in preparation, but by 1961 President Kennedy's founding of the Commission on the Status of Women brought a new political legitimacy to the analysis of women's roles in U.S. society. In 1963, both the commission's report, which decried the "pervasive limitations" on women's roles, and Betty Friedan's *The Feminine Mystique* appeared, generating extensive attention to the place of women in U.S. society.[3] Friedan's book exploded the ideology of domestic containment perpetuated during the 50s and brought a political analysis to bear on the private experiences of women in American society. Friedan's enormously popular book radically changed many women's perceptions about themselves and their relations to men.

In the Civil Rights movement, white female activists typically played supportive roles, often replicating the very stereotypes Friedan's book attacked in mainstream culture. Many women activists, both white and black, attempted to broach the issue of sexism within the ranks, but black male activists were generally unsympathetic and often openly hostile to these attempts. Many black activists, both men and women, considered feminist demands for gender equality racist and a diversion from the struggle for racial justice. Stokely Carmichael's oft-cited response to the position paper on the status of women in the movement presented by Casey Hayden and Mary King at the 1964 Waveland SNCC conference epitomized this conflict: "What is the position of women in SNCC? . . . The position of women in SNCC is prone!" Carmichael's remark exemplified for many women in the movement the sexually exploitative and hostile attitudes male activists fostered toward them.[4] Furthermore, Carmichael's conflation of women with their bodiliness, stating their "position" as nothing more than their (sexual) bodies, underscores the corporeality of gender tensions in Civil Rights that would culminate with the emergence of mid-60s feminism.

Along with the reactionary postures of African American men to feminism, African American women in the movement often resented white women for their privileged position in a racist culture. The interlocking dynamics of race and gender, which masculinized "blackness," thus marginalizing black women as nonfemale, hampered the ability of white and black women in the movement to forge effective alliances based in feminism.[5] Again, the race-gender system articulated in these conflicts pivoted on corporeal difference: the body was viewed as political. Often northern white female students would be placed in prominent positions on a demonstration line precisely because their *physical* presence was considered a strategic blow to white racists' assumptions about the movement. In such cases, it was because they were visibly white and women that they were placed on the front lines; their place in the political structure of the movement mattered little. In contrast, while whites felt they played a "second-class" role in the movement, black women often held significant positions of authority in its structure. Many African American women active in the movement were instrumental in developing strategy, and they became the first to raise questions of gender equality within the ranks of 60s American resistance movements. By 1964, black women in SNCC and SCLC were demanding more prominent roles and questioning their "second-class" status within the ranks. The example set by these women would prove instrumental to the feminists who would later form the Women's Liberation movement. Alice Echols cites this as fundamental to the rise of 60s feminism: "[W]hite female activists began to question culturally received notions of femininity as they met powerful, young black women in SNCC and older women in the black community who were every bit as effective as male organizers and community leaders."[6]

With Black Liberation's move toward separatism, whites empowered by their experiences in Civil Rights activism became more deeply involved in the antiwar movement and the New Left. Yet white women often encountered as much resistance to their calls for gender equity in the male-dominated antiwar movement and the New Left as they had in both the black movement and mainstream culture. Like many Black Liberationists, Students for a Democratic Society (SDS) tended to look upon feminism as a bourgeois diversion from the important issues of the war, race, and class. According to Echols, "Women who were demanding that their oppression be acknowledged ran up against a left concerned only with supporting the struggles of blacks, the working class, or the Vietnamese."[7] Men in the New Left may have supported women in theory, but in practice many male leaders of the movement rejected the "prefigurative politics" and the linking of personal and political that the feminist focus on sexual relations and gender threatened to effect.[8] As Sara Evans has written:

> For all its emphasis on personal relationships, on openness, honesty, and participatory democracy, the northern student left was highly male-dominated. Where SNCC had provided an open environment within which women utilized the skills they already had to grow in strength and self-confidence, the northern movement reinforced the traditional roles by building on a competitive intellectual style.

Evans goes on to point out that in the northern movements, "public positions were virtually monopolized by the men," and that "until 1966 no major national office was held by a woman."[9] Their emerging struggles marginalized by the male-dominated politics of Black Liberation and the New Left, feminists seized the ideological ground upon which they had been rejected and forged a Women's Liberation movement that pushed 60s oppositional activism into a new arena of conflict: the realm of gender. Just as Black Liberation manifested a cultural politics of the racial body, Women's Liberation would articulate a cultural politics of the gendered body. According to Susan

Bordo, "Feminists first began to develop a critique of the 'politics of the body'. . . in terms of the material body as a site of political struggle."[10] The gendered body became the terrain of ideological struggle in Vietnam-era feminist discourse, and representations of the body figure prominently in the political rhetoric and cultural practices of feminists during this period.

The rise of Women's Liberation from the black movement parallels other moments of feminist activism in U.S. history (most obviously in the post-Abolitionist period), but the use of a nation-based paradigm to analyze the oppression of women distinguishes Vietnam-era feminism from the feminism of earlier periods.[11] The popular feminist slogans of the period, such as "off our backs," "seizing our bodies," and "hands off our bodies," underscore how the body was viewed as colonized territory. As the prominent spokeswoman for Women's Liberation Robin Morgan would proclaim in her poem "Monster": "No colonized people so isolated one from the other/for so long as women."[12] On a theoretical level, women's involvement in the black movement gave rise to conceptual links between the politics of gender and the liberation politics of decolonization in the Third World. The emergence of Black Power ideology by 1966 and the general trend in the African American left toward racial separatism forced whites to reexamine their position in oppositional struggle. In the early 60s, white activists, who tended to come from privileged backgrounds and were often college students, had been primarily concerned with the struggles of "others" (African Americans, the Vietnamese, the working class). In Gramscian terms, white radicals operated as "traditional" rather than "organic" intellectuals; they were not of the oppressed social class but came to that struggle from the preexisting institutions.[13] Many white activists were products of the very economic, political, and social institutions that Black Liberation set itself against. In fact, black activists often looked upon whites as colonizers of the black struggle. With increased pressure from Black Power for black ownership of the struggle, white activists were enjoined to "organize around your own oppression." In Women's Liberation, this would be partly achieved through the deployment of an analogy to colonialism.

As we have seen, Black Liberationist cultural discourses often envisioned black people as a distinct nation. The political subject of history, in this theory, became defined by color; the "black" color of the flesh signified one's subjectivity in the "black nation," and, hence, the struggle, and to be "nonblack" automatically defined one as outside the nation. The cultural discourse of blackness fused the American black nationalist tradition with Third World liberationist concepts of articulating oneself as a subject of the oppressed nation. This discourse would prove essential to the formation of the cultural politics of Women's Liberation.[14] Just as black activists viewed the "epidermal difference" as the ultimate contradiction in the struggle for black liberation, feminists envisioned (biological) gender difference as the ultimate contradiction in Women's Liberation, and indeed, any revolutionary struggle. Marilyn Webb, for example, declared in 1968, "Women's liberation is the final revolution." Women's Liberation sought to rearticulate the female body as the new political subject of history. According to Echols, "Radical feminists argued that women constituted a sex-class, that relations between women and men needed to be recast in political terms, and that gender rather than class was the primary contradiction." Gender, in this analysis, however, was understood by most feminists during the Vietnam era as a biological essence. Just as Black Liberationists essentialized race as corporeal, many feminists essentialized gender so that Women's Liberation was construed as a movement organized against the oppression that all women were subjected to principally on the basis of their sexual anatomy. An anatomo-politics emerged in Women's Liberation that mobilized the terms for revolutionary struggle around the biologically female body.[15]

The position paper presented by Jane Addams (of SDS), Elizabeth Sutherland (a former SNCC member), Susan Cloke, and Jean Peak at the June 1967 SDS National Convention marks one of the earliest articulations of this feminist politics of the body. The authors argued, "As we analyze the position of women in capitalist society and especially in the United States we find that women are in a colonial relationship to men and we recognize ourselves as part of the Third World." As Echols points out, the paper goes on to argue for "communal child-care centers, accessible abortion, the dissemination of birth-control information, and the sharing of housework to free women from the confines of domesticity."[16] The SDS paper links issues of health, particularly reproductive health, and women's struggles for control of their bodies to Third World liberation struggles. The rhetoric also implies that, like geographical territory, the female body constitutes a political terrain under the colonial domination of men, who, by extension, are linked to the state (especially the United States in its relations with the Third World). The problems inherent in the SDS paper, later published as "Liberation of Women" in a 1967 issue of *New Left Notes*, have been noted by Evans:

> The evident inadequacies of this analysis made it a short-lived one. In the context of the new left at that time, however, it served several purposes. Any activist knew that third world peoples—the Viet-

namese, the blacks in Africa and in the United States, Chicanos, American Indians—were oppressed. Their struggles constituted guideposts for the movement and front page news to the entire nation.[17]

The paper, nevertheless, represents an important discursive shift in feminist thought of the late twentieth century. While a discourse of control over the body has circulated in women's rights activism since at least Margaret Sanger, the "Liberation of Women" paper envisions (biological) women as a *nation* oppressed through internal colonialism, and the issue of control becomes articulated to resemble a discourse of territorial rights.[18] The rhetorical strategies of the "Liberation of Women" paper seek to rearticulate (white) women in the movement specifically and all women generally as a social group unified by common anatomical traits. The effect of this would be to place feminists, such as Addams, Sutherland, Cloke, and Peak, as the "organic intellectuals" and the vanguards of the emergent social class seeking self-determination in a struggle for "national liberation."

The internal colonialism model expressed in the SDS "Liberation of Women" paper appears in a number of feminist analyses during the Vietnam era, such as "The Fourth World Manifesto." Originally drafted by a group of feminists from Detroit in response to a 1971 conference of American and Vietnamese women against the Vietnam War, the manifesto was later revised by Barbara Burris and appeared in *Radical Feminism*. The paper attacks the conference for claiming to be a "women's liberation" conference even though it focused almost exclusively on antiwar issues. Burris argues that the conference subordinated the liberation of women to a male-defined anti-imperialist cause. Further, the manifesto rejected the conference's claim to be anti-imperialist on the grounds that, as women are the principal victims of colonization, and since the conference offered no analysis of this, it could not be truly anti-imperialist. The manifesto represents women as colonized and defines the relationship of colonized and colonizer according to biological gender differences:

> We find it self-evident that women are a colonized group who have never—anywhere—been allowed self-determination. Therefore, all women who fight against their own oppression (colonized status) as females under male domination are anti-imperialist by definition. . . . It should go without saying that those of us connected with the "Fourth World Manifesto" are deeply opposed to the war in Indochina. . . . The anti-imperialist women, like the rest of the anti-war and anti-imperialist Left movement, never question war and national imperialism as male-supremacist institutions. They ignore the roots of domination, aggression, imperialism, and war in male-supremacist society.

Burris goes on to declare that "women are a colonized group in relation to men all over the world, in all classes and races, including the Third World." The manifesto's analysis of the Vietnam War is grounded on biologically essential gender differences:

> The demand for an end to sex roles and male imperialist domination is a real attack on the masculine citadel of war. After all, women don't declare or fight in offensive wars. War is a male institution—as are all other institutions in the society—and war is simply an extension of the colonial policy of the subjection of the female culture and "weaker" male cultures, i.e., "weaker" national cultures.

While on the one hand Burris argues that biologically defined "women" do not declare wars of aggression, she also claims that colonization feminizes the colonized; thus, all colonized people occupy the "female" position in a system of oppression conceived of as analogous to the structure of relations between biologically defined males and females. This rhetoric imputes the characteristics of biological gender to colonized nations. Rather than emptying gender of any corporeal essentialism, however, this move reasserts biological gender as foundational to the dynamics of oppression. In the first instance, therefore, "women" constitute the principal object of oppression and, in the context of the Vietnam-era Third-Worldism in which the manifesto is expressed, by extension, women must also be seen as colonized. By this logic, therefore, women can be viewed as constituting a nation, a group identified by biological gender systematically subjected to superexploitation, domination, and institutionally based external control. Burris goes on to argue as much when she claims that "women were the first group to be subjected as a caste all over the world, thousands of years ago—long before blacks were subjected to whites in America or anywhere else." The nation-status of women is further defined in a section of the manifesto called " 'National' Culture is the Dominant Male Culture." This section critiques the dominant U.S. concept of the "nation" as inherently masculine and argues for a feminine "national" culture.[19]

Burris's analysis illustrates the theoretical importance of the national liberation paradigm in shaping feminist discourse. In order for feminists during the Vietnam era to constitute themselves as the vanguard of revolutionary struggle, the legitimate subjects of history, it was necessary to invoke the dominant tropes of Third World struggle. By rearticulating "woman" as oppressed within a nation-based paradigm, feminists developed a unique remapping of subjectivity and corporeality. Comparing feminist struggle to the Third World anticolonial struggles Frantz Fanon describes, Burris emphasizes the body:

Fanon and the whole black liberation struggle have recently extended the dictionary definition of imperialism or colonialism to
mean a group which is prevented from self-determination by another group—whether it has a national territory or not. The psychological and cultural mutilation is particularly intense and the
colonialism more brutal when the group that colonizes and the
group colonized have different defining physical characteristics that
set them clearly apart. . . . Women, set apart by physical differences
between them and men, were the first colonized group. *And the territory colonized was and remains our women's bodies.*[20]

According to Echols, the Fourth World Manifesto was "an embryonic
but highly influential expression of cultural feminism. It should be
read as a transitional work, one that straddled the line between
radical and cultural feminism." Where radical feminists tended to
advocate a social constructionist view of gender, cultural feminists
tended to essentialize gender and sought to celebrate "the female
principle." Echols describes the latter as the feminism most dominant
in the post-Vietnam 70s.[21] Cultural feminism, then, might be read as a
"cultural nationalism" similar to the black cultural nationalism that
emerged out of Black Power.

It should be stressed, however, that the Third World analogy was
never uniformly endorsed by all feminists in Women's Liberation.
The 1968 paper by Beverly Jones and Judith Brown, known as the
"Florida Paper," criticized the analogy for its reductionism. Referring
to Marilyn Webb's comparison of feminist struggle with the struggles
of the Vietnamese National Liberation Front, Brown writes, "Now
Marilyn Webb is cool. She can strain the analogy between the US left
and the NLF just enough to make it look reasonable for the American
women, who can't be in the black thing, and want to do something, *to
think of themselves as Vietnamese.*" As Brown points out, American feminists wanted to rearticulate themselves as the colonized.[22] Echols
notes that this paper presented an early case for total gender separatism. It also argued that resistance to the war should be subordinate
to the liberation of women. Moreover, Brown was one of the first
radical feminists to explore the political utility of lesbianism, advocat-
ing that women could gain "political strength" from such sexual practices. Despite its radical feminist line, however, the representation of
gender in the "Florida Paper" is informed by essentialism. According
to Echols, "both Jones and Brown, in contrast to other radical feminists, raised the possibility that gender differences might be biologically rooted."[23] Similarly, Shulamith Firestone's *The Dialectic of Sex*, a
key statement in radical feminist theory, argued that the inequalities
inherent in the hegemonic sex-class systems stem from the inherent
differences in biological reproductive systems. While Firestone's anal-

ysis has been criticized by feminists for its biological reductionism, it nevertheless exemplifies how notions of corporeal essentialism were key to the articulation of Vietnam-era feminist discourses.

From the movement's earliest political statements to its theorizations of the early 70s, feminism constructed corporeality as the principal locus of its political and social struggles. The strategic significance of the feminist politics of corporeality is that it enabled Women's Liberation to articulate itself as the vanguard in sociopolitical struggle. As Michael Omi and Howard Winant have written, arguments against oppression based in a theory of internal colonialism "attempted the synthesis of different aspects of racial oppression: economic, political and cultural, through the invocation of a colonial model." According to Omi and Winant such approaches share the following elements:

1. a colonial *geography* emphasizing the territoriality or spatial arrangement of population groups along racial lines;
2. a dynamic of *cultural domination and resistance*, in which racial categories are utilized to distinguish between antagonistic colonizing and colonized groups, and conversely, to emphasize the essential cultural unity and autonomy of each;
3. a system of *superexploitation*, understood as a process by which extra-economic coercion is applied to the racially identified colonized group, with the aim of increasing the economic resources appropriated by the colonizers;
4. institutionalization of *externally based control*, such that the racially identified colonized group is organized in essential political and administrative aspects by the colonizers or their agents.[24]

If we substitute "gender" for "racial" in this description it becomes evident that Women's Liberation derived much of its analysis of women's oppression from a nation-based paradigm.

Robin Morgan's "Taking Back Our Bodies," in fact, enacts just such a substitution. In the article's first sentence, Morgan declares, "As a radical feminist, I make an analogy between women and colonized peoples." Citing Fanon, Morgan summarizes the nation-based model of colonial oppression as directly analogous to women's oppression.

The oppressed are robbed of their culture, history, pride, and roots—all most concretely expressed in the conquest of their *land* itself. They are forced . . . to adopt the oppressor's standards, values, and identification. In due course, they become alienated from their own values, their own land—which is of course being mined by the oppressor for its natural resources. They are "permitted" (forced) to work the land, but since they do not benefit from or have power over what it produces, they come to feel oppressed by *it*. Thus, the alienation from their own territory serves to mystify that territory, and the enforced identification with their colonizing masters provokes eventual contempt for both themselves and their land. It follows, of course, that the first goal of a colonized people is to *reclaim their own land.*[25]

Emphasizing the "land" and "territory" usurped in colonialism, Morgan's argument sets the stage for articulating female corporeality as analogous to colonized territory.

Women are a colonized people, with our history, values, and cross-cultural culture having been taken from us—a gynocidal attempt manifest most blatantly in the patriarchy's seizure of our most basic and precious "land": *our own bodies.*[26]

Morgan's substitution of biologically gendered female bodies for colonized land posits a problematic conflation. The materiality of female corporeality has often been erased in masculinist discourses through metaphoric renderings of women's bodies as land. Yet by rearticulating this substitution, feminists during the Vietnam era also situated their struggle within the paradigms of the Third-Worldist, anti-imperialist, Black Liberationist, and antiwar struggles hegemonic in oppositional culture.

The use of gender categories to designate colonizer and colonized also works to establish the unity of women. The analysis of women's oppression as a superexploitation based on gender enables a critique of the exploitation of women's labor as "extra-economic coercion" of a gender-identified group. And the critique of women's "internalized oppression" through the cultural institutions of sex roles also suggests how the nation-based paradigm of race constituted an important model for the cultural politics of Women's Liberation. Class, race, and national differences were often subsumed in this political discourse under the general term of "gender."[27] This strategy ultimately proved inadequate, but at the time it offered a distinctive intervention that would reverberate throughout U.S. culture.[28] Just as Black Liberation's invocation of a nation-based model sought to synthesize various aspects of racial oppression, feminists' use of the tropes of colonialism to characterize their struggle attempted to synthesize aspects of gender oppression. In the Vietnam era, feminist deployment of a nation-based conception of oppression and resistance would prove decisive in shifting American oppositional culture toward "personal politics" and questions of identity.

In the same way that groups like the Black Panthers could see the black struggle as equivalent to the armed anti-imperialist guerilla movements in the Third World, other social groups articulated their struggles in a nation-based paradigm consistent with movements of decolonization. Kobena Mercer has argued that

the political positions of the Black Panthers had an empowering effect in extending the chain of radical democratic equivalences to
more and more social groups precisely through their dramatic visibility in the public sphere. At the level of political discourse, it was
this system of equivalences that generated women's liberation and
gay liberation out of analogies with the goals, and methods, of black
liberation, which were themselves based on an analogy with third
world struggles for national liberation.[29]

The Black Panthers were widely recognized as the vanguard of revolutionary struggle by both the New Left and many Women's Liberation groups. The Panthers, furthermore, specifically aligned the
struggle for black liberation with the NLF struggle in Vietnam and
often advocated subversive antiwar activism as a means of demonstrating internationalist solidarity with the NLF war against the
United States.[30] Mercer goes on to argue:

> The ten-point platform of the Black Panther Party . . . formed a dis-
> cursive frame work through which the women's movement and gay
> movement displaced the demand for reform and "equality" in favor
> of the wider goal of revolution and "liberation." The ten-point char-
> ter of demands of the Women's Liberation Movement (1968) and the
> Gay Liberation Front (1969) were based on a metaphorical transfer of
> the terms for the liberation of one group into the terms for the libera-
> tion of others and it was on the basis of such imagined equivalences
> that the connotative yield of slogans such as Black Power and Black
> Pride was appropriated to empower movements around gender and
> sexuality. Black pride acted as metonymic leverage for the expres-
> sion of "gay pride" just as notions of "brotherhood" and "commu-
> nity" in black political discourse influenced the assertions of "global
> sisterhood" or "sisterhood is strength."[31]

In this way, the "new social movements" of the Vietnam era demonstrate "the indeterminacy and ambivalence that inhabits the construction of every social identity."[32]

A principal arena for the construction of feminist identity in the
Vietnam era was in poetry. According to Jan Clausen, "[A]ny serious
investigation of the development of contemporary feminism must
take into account the catalytic role of poets and poetry . . . . there is
some sense in which it can be said that poets have made possible the
movement."[33] Indeed, a number of the major spokespersons for
Women's Liberation, such as Adrienne Rich, Robin Morgan, Marge
Piercy, and Susan Griffin, were also poets. Furthermore, as Clausen
points out, "[p]oetry has become a favorite means of self-expression,
consciousness-raising, and communication among large numbers of
women not publicly known as poets."[34] Poetry readings were an important part of Women's Liberation meetings, and the poems read

often focused on the body as a site of political struggle. Reflecting on her own experience in the movement, Clausen writes, "Poetry represented the clearest opportunity for the direct statement of women's experience; it was the literary counterpart of the [consciousness-raising] groups' attempt to break down the distinction between the personal and the political." The feminist poetry often read and published during the Vietnam era relied heavily on a social-realist style that emphasized bodily, material experiences deemed common to all women. "In the beginning," Clausen writes, "we had an enormous appetite for *the evidence,* for anything that could provide testimony concerning the conditions of women's lives."[35]

Alicia Suskin Ostriker observed in her important study of women's poetry, *Stealing the Language,* "During the last two decades, American women poets have been writing about their bodies with decreasing embarrassment and increasing enthusiasm. . . .whether or not they deal directly with the self, or with sexuality as such, contemporary women poets employ anatomical imagery both more frequently and far more intimately than male poets."[36] Ostriker's assertion is supported by a survey of poems collected in the major feminist anthologies of the early 70s. For example, in the Florence Howe and Ellen Bass anthology *No More Masks!* anatomical imagery occurs more frequently in poetry published after 1960.[37] Poetic images celebrating female anatomy were key to the political ideologies articulated in feminist poetry of the Vietnam era. The attention to corporeality in women's poetry of the Vietnam era seeks to transfigure the masculinist construction of the female as "the body" and, by virtue of this, a negativity. Simone de Beauvoir argued that women had been constituted as the body, "weighed down by everything peculiar to it," while men positioned themselves as "the inevitable, like a pure idea, like the One, the All, the Absolute Spirit."[38] By focusing on, celebrating, and politicizing the intimate details of female corporeality, feminist poetry of the Vietnam era sought to invert the terms by which the female historically has been denied access to subjectivity. As Susan Bordo has suggested, the Women's Liberation articulation of personal politics and a critique of the body as site of political struggle stems from the pervasive construction of women's intimate experiences in bodiliness: "[F]or women, associated with the body and largely confined to a life centered *on* the body. . . , culture's grip on the body is a constant, intimate fact of everyday life."[39]

In the section that follows I will discuss some ways that feminist poetry of the Vietnam era articulated a politics of corporeality that situates the female body as the principal subject of historical struggle. Images, tropes, and symbols of female anatomy, biology, and corporeality often associate the female body with colonized territory. Specifically, such figurations draw analogies between the female body and Vietnam. Ruth Rosen has written that "during the peak of the Vietnam War, the women's liberation movement frequently combined a radical critique of America's involvement in the third world along with their analysis of women's subordinate position in society."[40] For feminist poets writing during a time of war, the subjects of war and war-making, themselves historically figured as gendered and gender-making rituals, constituted key terrain for imaginative interrogations of gender and gendering.[41] Throughout Vietnam-era feminism, the war constitutes a palpable, compelling source of images of oppression that feminist poets drew on to express this analogy. Discourses of corporeality in this poetry also exemplify an important confluence of oppositional concerns in the leftist vernacular of the Vietnam era. Literal and figurative images of the body's insides map the analogies articulated between "women" as nation and Vietnam. Women's strength, subversiveness, and political renewal were viewed as organically internal. Reproductive organs are figured as sites of struggle: celebrating and becoming "in tune" with the uterus, the womb, the vagina signaled heightened political and revolutionary awareness; these organs are also represented as targets of masculinist oppression. Oppression is cast as a penetration, invasion, and colonizing of corporeal interiority. The Third World analogy thus came to encompass the politics of reproductive rights and the Women's Health movement. Male-dominated medical practices were cast as tools for the colonization of women's bodies. In these ways, a number of feminist poems focusing on motherhood, pregnancy, abortion, and sex linked concerns about the war with women's reproductive rights and health.

"My politics is in my body"

The politicization of the body's interior in feminist poetry of the Vietnam era registers the traces of neoromantic beliefs in an inner truth that the creative individual must contact and express, as well as the Marcusean ideas, prevalent among leftists, of a true sensual self repressed by society.[42] Women's Liberationist poetry also more specifically articulates this political discourse in terms of female physiology. Images, tropes, and symbols of women's subversive political resistance are often associated with pregnancy. Female corporeality in these poems tends almost exclusively to focus on reproductive and gynecological physiology. Insofar as it has been this biology specifically that masculine society has written as women's corporeal "otherness," images of pregnancy, genitalia, and menstruation in feminist poetry serve both as the most obvious choice for articulating women as a distinct class and as a strategic terrain of struggle over the meanings of female corporeality and subjectivity in society. The politicization of female corporeal interiority furthered the discourse of personal politics into the most intimate spaces of female subjectivity and, concomitantly, intensified the feminist analysis of masculinism in the corporeal zones that male society had most sought to possess, penetrate, monitor, and manage in the patriarchal system. During the Vietnam era, this "siting" of resistance within female anatomy articulated critical equivalencies with the war.

Adrienne Rich's 1968 poem "Tear Gas," for example, emphasizes the corporeal interiority of the political. Written in response to the tear-gassing of a GI Resistance rally against stockade conditions at Fort Dix, Rich draws associations between the corporeal sufferings of demonstrators and her own life. She considers what the human body must endure to be tear-gassed and compares this to her feelings of frustration and rage at the oppressions she encounters as a woman. Recognizing that language alone will not enact change, she writes:

> The will to change begins in the body not in the mind
> My politics is in my body, accruing and expanding with every act
>   of resistance and each of my failures
> Locked in the closet at 4 years old I beat the wall with my body
> that act is in me still[43]

Rich imagines political resistance as deeply embodied and, like a pregnancy, "accruing and expanding." Her image suggests that feminist politics emerges not simply from raised political consciousness but from embodied sensations, physiological changes, and that resistance must arise out of physiological experiences unique to biological females. Susan Sherman's "Lilith of the Wildwood, of the Fair Places" opens by asking, "And how does one begin again//(Each time, each poem, each line, word, syllable/Each motion of the arms, the legs/A new beginning." A celebration of the Biblical Lilith, Sherman's poem asserts, "I do not have to read her legend in the ancient books/. . . /She is here inside me/. . ./My body my breath my life."[44] The feminine subversiveness of Lilith is seen both as a power that must be constructed through a reconstruction of the female body and as a power internal to female corporeality. Sandra McPherson reiterates this concept more emphatically when she describes her pregnant body in the 1970 poem "Pregnancy" as "highly explosive."[45] McPherson represents a female body that has taken in the destructive force of military (masculine) weaponry to re-create it as feminine power. The female body becomes the means of "exploding" masculinist hegemony; its otherness disarticulates the patriarchal language. The political resistance of the female body, as in Rich's poem, resides within.

Alta's "Living in a Country at War/1968 Version" similarly internalizes the painful guilt she feels about the war in images that call to mind pregnancy:

> inside hurts
> standing up means
> unbend
> shoulders hunch
> belly hurts[46]

A change in political consciousness for the speaker, sparked by guilt over the Vietnam War, is figured as a physiologically experienced pain located inside the body.

For feminists during the 60s, many of whom had been deeply involved in the antiwar and draft resistance movements, the liberation movement in Vietnam served as a compelling model of resistance. Echols argues that radical feminists "initially took their inspiration from the revolutionary women of Vietnam, Cuba, and China." The example of the NLF was often cited by feminists to promote a revolutionary vision of Women's Liberation. Marilyn Webb, for example, praised "the Vietnamese woman [who] has literally won her equality with a weapon in her hand and through the strength of her arms."[47] The image of Vietnamese women fighting for liberation offered U.S. feminists a militant vision of the female body. Kathie Sarachild of New York Radical Women (NYRW) and Redstockings has written that a photograph of a Vietnamese militia woman *"capturing* a [U.S.] serviceman" was widely reproduced in the Women's Liberationist press and demonstrated to U.S. feminists that women could succeed in physical combat against men and patriarchy.[48] Specific analogies were made between the Vietnamese struggle against U.S. imperialism and the Women's Liberation struggle throughout the women's underground press of the 60s.[49]

The consciousness-raising (CR) sessions that became vital to the formation of feminist groups and their analyses of personal issues exemplify the importance for Women's Liberation of these conceptual links to Third World liberation theories and practices. According to Echols, Kathie Sarachild coined the term "consciousness-raising" and explained that she was using a technique she and other women activists had learned in the Civil Rights movement. Echols writes, "The proponents of consciousness-raising took their inspiration from the civil rights movement where the slogan was 'tell it like it is,' the Chinese revolution when peasants were urged 'to speak pains to recall pains,' and from the revolutionary struggle in Guatemala where guerrillas used similar techniques."[50] CR sessions stem from and emulate Third-Worldist liberationist practices, such as "speaking bitterness" in the Chinese revolution. The technique also resembles Ho Chi Minh's principle of regular "self-criticism" sessions among cadres to emphasize how the revolution needed its activists to "remold" themselves, to consolidate a sense of tight-knit community, and to emphasize personal interactions within the revolution. Ho's hope was that such sessions would alleviate the debilitating problems of bureaucracy and corruption in the revolution.[51] In Women's Liberation, remaking oneself, refashioning identity, transfiguring the body, and articulating self as revolutionary all pivot on the dissolution of barriers between the personal and the political. One important Women's Liberation group called The Feminists, for example, "made the process of re-creating oneself the central feminist task." As Echols notes, the Feminists' "conflation of the political and the personal made lifestyle synonymous with political struggle."[52]

While the theory of CR sessions was significantly modeled on the practice of self-criticism in Third World revolutionary cadre training, the analogy between Women's Liberation and Third World liberation movements was often explicitly staged in street theater and direct actions. At an April 1968 antiwar demonstration, for example, members of the group New York Radical Women (NYRW) "dressed like Vietnamese women, handed out leaflets about women's liberation to women only, and ran through the crowd ululating like the Algerian women in Gillo Pontecorvo's 1966 film 'The Battle of Algiers.'" In this theatrical spectacle, NYRW activists "cross-dress" as Third World people and stage an elision of nation, race, and class that renders the female body as the ultimate target of oppression.[53] Such conflations sought to locate the dynamics of oppression in biological gender essentialism. Marilyn Lowen Fletcher's 1969 poem "A Chant for my Sisters," which re-creates a feminist protest chant, links Women's Liberation and Third World struggles in images of a universal female body:

> it's all right to be woman
> dishwasher, big belly, sore back
> swollen ankles
> . . . .
> a chant for my sisters
> strong in battle
> la bandita killing generals with zapata
> maria in mexico and mississippi
> haydee with the rest at moncada
> a chant for my sisters

dead before i could meet them
victorious
in havana
and dien bien phu[54]

This poem/chant represents the female body as both laboring in the kitchen and pregnant; oppression is inscribed both on and in the bodies of women everywhere. The poet essentializes these physiological conditions as universal for women throughout the world; and thus, the female body, regardless of race, class, sexuality, or nationality, experiences oppression in similar ways. The historical specificities of the liberation struggles she invokes (the Cuban Revolution, the French-Indochina War) are collapsed under the category of gender inevitably presented as biological essence.[55] Significantly, the most specific images describe physiological conditions that women experience during pregnancy: "big belly, sore back/swollen ankles." Solidarity with Third World liberation emerges out of the "fact" of women's shared reproductive biology.

Bearing children could be viewed as a moral dilemma in the context of the war. A number of feminist poems from the period represent women refusing to bear children as a protest against the atrocities of war. The 1970 poem "A Womb on Strike," by "Brandy French" (a pseudonym), begins by recounting the speaker's sensual pleasure in making love to her partner:

We pass a cigarette back and forth
like a communion wafer
and while they are invading Cambodia
you are invading me
deeper, deeper
sixty miles
a hundred miles
across continents
I am a vast battlefield of love
one of your bayonet casualties
wounded with sons

Masculine sexuality is associated with the U.S. military and its invasion of Cambodia, and heterosexual intercourse is represented as a phallic penetration that "wounds" the female body.

Suddenly!
(I stand up quickly)
you have the look of a president about you
(pregnancy trickles down

into the nostrils of the earth)
. . . .

> I (forgive me)
> cannot carry (forgive me)
> death
> . . .
> your warriors inside my body

It is by refusing to keep the sperm inside her body that the speaker enacts her protest against the atrocities of war. By not bearing any more potential warriors, she will also not bear potential death. This act closes the poem, thereby placing emphasis on the speaker's resistance to the authority of the male in sexual relations. The poem begins "I lay my head on your lap"—the speaker's body is represented lying before the male. In the poem's final lines, however, the speaker is standing upright, refusing to act as a passive receptacle for masculine procreation. Furthermore, by refusing to "carry. . ./death/. . . inside [her] body," the speaker lays claim to the body's interior, which masculine penetration seeks to invade, wound, and colonize.[56]

A similar analogy between the Third World and the female body as territory colonized is drawn in Jean Tepperman's popular 1969 poem "Going Through Changes." Tracing the emergence of her radical feminist consciousness, Tepperman's poem moves from personal relationships to her political activism into fantasies of the ultimate subversiveness of female power. In section 2 of the poem, she describes her rejection of the male-dominated New Left as an experience of identifying with the plight of women in the Third World:

> I used to get very big.
> I used to be in rooms full of strangers
> and questions made me into
> China and Russia and Cuba
> ten thousand teenage draft resisters
> the history of the Communist Party
> a lone terrorist in Oakland
> the entire black population
> and Marx and Engels.
> I got so big
> there with miles
> from my mouth to your ear.
> Today,
> in my small natural body,
> I sit and learn—
> my woman's body
> like yours
> target on any street,
> taken from me
> at the age of twelve
> like Venezuelan oil. . . . (SIP, 570)

The image of the female body that opens this passage suggests a pregnant body symbolic of the poet's own body filled with (masculine) political doctrine. Again, as in Rich's "Tear Gas," the political is envisioned as inside the human body. Her body enlarges so that the distances between her and any other woman become almost insurmountable. The female (body) filled by male ideology enlarges so that it broadens the space between women, keeping women separate from each other. This intellectual and symbolic impregnation enlarges her body to geographic proportions, turning her into an abstraction, disconnected from the material "truths" of her actual body. While masculinist radical politics makes her see herself as the embodiment of Russia, China, and Cuba, her identification with the Third World in the last lines quoted here signals her recognition of the material body she inhabits. This recognition, however, is still dependent on a kind of intellectual inflation: the female body has been metaphorized as geographic space. Representing patriarchy as depriving her access to the resources of her body, "tak[ing]" her bodily riches from her "like Venezuelan oil," refigures a common archetype of woman as earth. Her recognition of the female body as Third World arises out of her sense that no matter what movement she belongs to, all women, because they are biologically female, are "targeted" by masculinist forms of oppression. Such forms are not only economic but also militaristic; a later line in the poem reminds us that those who take the Venezuelan oil also sell women commodities and buy "armies . . . with the profits."

U.S. military aggression in Vietnam is often associated with rape and other forms of sexual violence and oppression in feminist documents from this period. This is evident in a WITCH (Women Inspired to Commit Herstory) poem/chant from 1969.[57] It was read at a demonstration to protest the incarceration of several women from the Black Panthers at Niantic State Prison farm:

> WITCH knows our suppressed history:
> that women who rebel are not only
> jailed, napalmed, & beaten,
> but also
> raped, branded & burned at the stake.
>
> We women are:
> in jail at Niantic
> in the mud of Vietnam . . . . (SIP, 620)

The corporeal punishment of women rebels is seen as sexual violence and misogyny. "Women" as represented in the poem appear classless and raceless, even though the prisoners of Niantic were Black Panthers. What ultimately links the oppressed is biological gender; the victims of oppression are female, and, by implication, oppressors are male. The poem establishes a relational chain between the police brutality experienced by the women at Niantic, the war in Vietnam, and sexual violence. In this system of signifying, the female body is always the target (as in Tepperman's poem) of a masculinist political domination; by extension, it is the female body that will be the site for any revolutionary struggle.

Adrienne Rich utilizes a similar logic in her 1973 article, "Vietnam and Sexual Violence":

> The bombings [of Vietnam by the United States] . . . if they have anything to teach us, must be understood in the light of something closer to home, both more private and painful, more general and endemic, than institutions, class, racial oppression, the hubris of the Pentagon, or the ruthlessness of a right-wing administration; the bombings are so wholly sadistic, gratuitous and demonic that they can finally be seen, if we care to see them, for what they are: *acts of concrete sexual violence,* an expression of the congruence of violence and sex in the masculine psyche.[58]

According to Rich, sexual violence is "both more private and painful, more general and endemic" than the war, the machinery of the state and its military, or even class or race; the violation of the female body by an aggressive male epitomizes the ultimate form of oppression that underlies all other forms of oppression. Rich collapses the complexities of the political, economic, historical, and racial violence represented by the U.S. bombings of Vietnam and substitutes a male body violating a female body as archetypal of military aggression. According to this logic, the United States as a First World military state becomes the male, Vietnam becomes the female; violators are male, the violated are female. Rich reinscribes the very hierarchical logic that feminists argue has historically served to legitimate oppressive gender relations.[59] Yet, although "male" and "female" may act as symbols of oppressor and oppressed, the language used to convey this dichotomy relies on the assumed "naturalness" of biological, corporeal differences between men and women. Rich's analysis reiterates the gender discourses prevalent in Women's Liberation by siting the dynamics of oppression within the terrain of biologically gendered bodies, Male/Female. When Rich states that the bombings of Vietnam are "concrete acts of sexual violence," she configures the antagonistic oppositions as biologically gendered—they are "concrete" precisely because they are embodied, corporeal, physical.

A number of feminist poems from the period utilize images and metaphors of the Vietnam War and military combat. Marge Piercy's 1973 "Night letter," written to a feminist comrade, compares the effects of their long struggles to the effects of napalm or tear gas: "Now they've burnt out your nerves, my lungs" (NMM, 249). In "Freaks," Robin Morgan describes a hallucinogenic experience using the imagery of war:

> blue pineapple ridges
>> burst from anti-personnel fruits
> of your brain
>> strapped shuddering in electric-shock compassion
> leak nectars slowly
>> through water torture clogging captured Vietcong
>>> lungs[60]

The speaker of Diane Wakoski's "In Gratitude to Beethoven" likens herself to a Viet Cong guerilla in describing her wariness of sexual attachments:

> I am like the guerilla fighter
> who must sleep with one eye open for attack, a knife
> or poison, a bamboo dart could come at any time.
> No one has loved me without trying to destroy me,
> there is no part of me that is not armoured.[61]

The guerilla and the female body are both in danger of being penetrated; the enemy in both cases is figured as masculine. Yet interestingly the speaker represents her body as "armoured," impenetrable and militarized, thus subverting a dominant gender paradigm that represents the male body as armored. In Margaret Atwood's "It is Dangerous to Read Newspapers," the speaker's encounter with the reports of the war's atrocities reported leads her to question her own complicity:

> I am the cause, I am a stockpile of chemical
> toys, my body
> is a deadly gadget,
> I reach out in love, my hands are guns,
> my good intentions are completely lethal. (*Psyche*, 219)

The speaker takes in the images of destruction she sees in the news; this is "dangerous" precisely because daily exposure to the war imbues the female body with a knowledge of its own power. Although the speaker expresses a sense of complicity, she also recognizes how knowledge of the war can make the seemingly placid citizen deadly. Atwood's poem, like McPherson's and Wakoski's, portrays the female body as lethal, disruptive of the patriarchal order that can produce the atrocities of war. And as in Rich's "Tear Gas," the political resistance of women is envisioned as inside the body. Imaginative associations with war in feminist poetry register the political equivalences delineated by Women's Liberation between the oppression of women and colonialist oppression. The numerous images, symbols, and tropes of the Vietnam War in women's poetry express a general sense among feminists that their battles for justice were equivalent to the war for national liberation in Vietnam.

The politicization of interiority in feminist discourse during the Vietnam era and the concomitant increased attention to graphic images of bodies may also be seen as a response to an intensification of explicit representation in culture. As many cultural critics have argued, media and visualization technologies developed rapidly in the post–World War II years and expanded as never before the ability to proliferate photographic and cinematic images and render visible the previously unseen.[62] The expansion of visual media in the United States during the 60s dramatically increased technology's ability to capture images of the human body in graphic detail. According to Walter Kendricks, the move toward greater explicitness, evident in the history of pornography, has been characteristic of cultural development since the mid-nineteenth century:

> [D]uring the course of the pornographic era—from approximately the 1840s to the 1960s—representations of all kinds proliferated at a wildly accelerating pace in both quantity and medium. . . .The trend in all cases was toward ever wider dissemination of ever more representations, saturating the culture with words and pictures. Simultaneously, the range of content steadily broadened, in an apparently unstoppable drive towards the total availability of total detail. . . . Every mode of representations has become explicit in the same years, in every nonsexual realm; it has become possible to photograph the earth from outer space, a fetus in the womb, and Vietnamese children in the process of dying.[63]

As Kendricks suggests, modes of visual representation have developed along similar vectors in journalism, science, medicine, and pornography. As the ability to penetrate, invade, and reveal the body, to render it totally visible in its naked details, increases in the 60s "society of the spectacle," feminists articulate a politics of the body as territory that politicizes the private, interior spaces such visual technologies seek to expose.[64] Interestingly, Kendricks links the explicit visualization of the earth to that of a fetus and to that of a dying Vietnamese child. Activists in Women's Liberation, I would contend, likely perceived the same associations. The technology that seeks to reveal the earth is the same one that seeks to reveal the interior of the female body and *capture* both a fetus in utero and a child's death in Vietnam. This language of "capturing" so commonly used in the discourses of visual technologies underscores how conceptual links could be developed in the feminist analysis of the male gaze, female oppression, and colonization. For many feminists, the central factor in all the various technologies of visual representation was that they sought to increase masculinist culture's ability to fix the female body within a male gaze. And as many have argued, the privileging of the visual as the proof of authentic knowledge epitomizes masculinist discourse.[65]

Fredric Jameson locates the beginnings of a "politics of otherness" central to the U.S. cultural politics of the 60s in the Sartrean concept of the Look. According to Jameson, Sartre rewrites the Hegelian master/slave narrative so that it is in the Look that the "I" relates to its Others. The Look is the concrete mode in Sartrean philosophy of object/subject relations. The one who is looked at is alienated as the Other in her/his "being-for-other-people."

> [A]t the dawn of the 60s, the Sartrean paradigm of the Look and the struggle for recognition between individual subjects will also be appropriated dramatically . . . in Frantz Fanon's enormously influential vision . . . of the struggle between Colonizer and Colonized, where the objectifying reversal of the Look is apocalyptically rewritten as the act of redemptive violence of Slave against Master.

In the dialectical struggle between Colonizer/Colonized, Self/Other that typifies 60s liberationist cultural politics, Jameson identifies a Hegelian third term in "the tremendous expansion of the media apparatus and the culture of consumerism."[66] Within these contexts, feminists, who were not only familiar with Sartre but also with Simone de Beauvoir and Frantz Fanon, identified the male gaze as the principal mechanism of their oppressed status within masculinist culture. The female body is "colonized" by the male gaze, a gaze that has literally become increasingly present in women's lives. The reversal of the Look, then, manifests itself not only in the theatrical styles of dissidence during the 60s but also in a rearticulation of the body through poetic imagery. By "seizing the body" and rewriting its image, feminist poets sought to disrupt the paradigms of Colonizer/Colonized. Feminist poetry of the Vietnam era sought to articulate resistance precisely on the "terrain" where panoptic forms of power/knowledge that have determined gender relations in the West had so intensified in the late twentieth-century age of maximum visuality.[67] Although women's poetry of the 60s approached the representation of bodies in numerous ways, in the discussion that follows I will investigate a specific and unique aspect of feminist body-politics of the Vietnam era that continues to inform the discourses of one of the dominant agenda in feminism, dramatizing the significance of the feminist politicization of corporeal interiority.

Configuring the female body as the privileged site of oppression, and often conflating their struggles with those of Third World peoples, Women's Liberation also targeted the male gaze as a principal mechanism of masculinist power. Feminist critiques of and demonstrations against media stereotyping and pornography cite the ways in which visual technologies expose the surfaces of the female body and objectify it for the male gaze. Susan Bordo has argued:

> With the advent of movies and television, the rules for femininity have come to be culturally transmitted more and more through the deployment of standardized visual images. As a result, femininity itself has come to be largely a matter of constructing . . . the appropriate surface presentation of the self. We no longer are told what "a lady" is or of what femininity consists. Rather, we learn the rules directly through bodily discourse; through images which tell us what clothes, body shape, facial expression, movements, and behavior is required.[68]

One effect of the expansion of visuality has been to intensify the normalization of the female body and expand self-disciplinary practices of the body among women. Yet while feminism has critiqued the domination of the surfaces of the female body, its politicization of corporeal interiority responds to the expanded capabilities of visual technologies to penetrate and "colonize" the body's insides.

A major development of Women's Liberation in this regard was the emergence of the woman's health movement, which mounted a popular and extensive critique of the medical profession. The tendency in feminist poems to locate politics as immanent in anatomy suggests that many women viewed the increased ability of visual technologies to "capture" the interior of the female body as a crucial issue in the struggle for liberation. Such representations often deploy the semiotics and terminology of medical practices, images, and metaphors derived from women's experiences with a male-dominated medical profession. These images seem specific to a period when medical technologies expand the ability to penetrate and reveal the body's insides, and concomitantly more women have access to these technologies through the expansion of social services. Although the increased technological capacities of the medical profession ensured a higher standard of living for those women who could afford it, at the same time the profession's obsession with these technologies seemed to many feminists to have marginalized women and their experiences as patients, to dehumanize and objectify them. Women's Liberation mobilized specific modes of resistance around what Michel Foucault would call "bio-powers."[69] According to the 1973 feminist pamphlet *Complaints and Disorders: The Sexual Politics of Sickness*, "The medical system is strategic for women's liberation. . . . When we demand control over our own bodies, we are making that demand above all to the medical system."[70] Many women in the 60s—predominantly white, economically privileged, and college-educated women, those who had ready access to advanced medical practices and who were active in the women's movement—began to question these practices, and some began to even consider them malignant rather than benign. Male-dominated obstetrical and gynecological technologies and practices in particular seemed to epitomize the violence of the male gaze—a clinical, rationalistic, penetrating gaze that sought to expose and colonize the interior of the female body. In the atmosphere of the cultural politics of the New Left, a politics that distrusted science and technology and romanticized the "natural" body, these critiques of medical science focused resistance more precisely on the biologically gendered body.

"Our Bodies, Ourselves"

According to Ostriker many post-1945 women's poems can be classified as "doctor poems . . . which represent women as objects being probed by experts whose profession is to care for and heal, and who personally fear and despise, women's bodies."[71] Images of women's bodies in women's poetry of the 60s often utilize the terminology of medical practices. To some extent this phenomenon can be traced to the social prominence of expanded technological innovations in medicine. The enormous popularity of the poetry of Sylvia Plath and Anne Sexton also established a contemporary literary tradition for women's interrogation of medical practices. Although Plath committed suicide in 1963, her poetry, mainly in posthumous collections, looms large over Women's Liberation poetry. Ostriker writes that Plath's *"Ariel* [1965] . . . gave many readers their first taste of unapologetic anger in a woman's poems."[72] Liz Yorke claims that "Sylvia Plath is an important precursor for contemporary women poets."[73] According to Clausen, public readings of feminist poetry in Women's Liberation often included readings of Plath and Sexton, "those enormously influential poets of female anger and victimization."[74]

Many of Plath's images, much of her confessional style, and her attention to the relationships between public and private worlds figure prominently in feminist poetry of the 60s. Plath often represented masculine aggression and violence through representations that blurred the distinctions between father and doctor. Her poem "Lady Lazarus," for example, represents the father as both Nazi fascist and sadistic doctor. The female body represented in this poem emerges as a collection of body parts, scars, blood, bones, sores scrutinized by "Herr Doktor," who is also "Herr Enemy," "Herr God," and "Herr Lucifer":

For the eyeing of my scars, there is a charge
For the hearing of my heart—
It really goes.

And there is a charge, a very large charge
For a word or a touch
Or a bit of blood

Or a piece of my hair or my clothes.
So, so, Herr Doktor.
So, Herr Enemy.

I am your opus,
I am your valuable,
The pure gold baby

That melts to a shriek.
I turn and burn.
Do not think I underestimate your great concern.

Ash, ash—
You poke and stir.
Flesh, bone, there is nothing there—[75]

Represented as a probing, invasive, controlling figure, this doctor/ father seeks to uncover the secrets of her body, extract truths from it, and, at the same time, manage the subject, make her his "opus." In "Tulips," the poet's hospitalization after a suicide attempt is represented as an erasure of identity: "I am nobody; I have nothing to do with explosions./I have given my name and my day-clothes up to the nurses/And my history to the anesthetist and my body to surgeons." Attended by nurses and doctors, her body is merely an object: "My body is a pebble to them, they tend it as water/Tends to the pebbles it must run over, smoothing them gently."[76] Drawing upon her own experiences in hospitals and the psychotraumas she suffered in her relationships with men, Plath gave voice to a range of private anxieties that later women poets would articulate as public and political problems. Many feminist critics during the Vietnam era saw Plath as an archetypal victim of a masculinist medical profession. Anita Rapone, for example, declared, "Sylvia Plath's poetry is political not because it is ideological but because it presents our experience." Rapone also argues that the poet's oppression is represented in images of male doctors controlling her. The speaker in "Tulips" is "merely an object in the bureaucratic mechanics of the hospital."[77] As Jacqueline Rose has asserted, "Plath associates sexual and medical violence, links the personal and the institutional, the private and the public in a way that has become one of the hallmarks of the feminist analysis of power."[78]

Anne Sexton's earliest published poetry similarly critiques doctor surveillance as a form of masculinist domination. *To Bedlam and Part Way Back* (1960), for example, offers dramatic and disturbing portrayals of her experiences during hospitalization in a psychiatric ward. Its opening poem, "You, Doctor Martin," describes the doctor's panoptic surveillance of the patients: "Your third eye/moves among us and lights the separate boxes/where we sleep or cry."[79] Throughout her work, Sexton represented herself as a body under medical scrutiny, examined and probed, opened and revealed by doctors. The invasive gaze of her doctors is invariably associated with phallic violation and/or masculinist domination. "Unknown Girl in the Maternity Ward," "The Operation," "The Division of Parts," "Cripples and Other Stories," and many other Sexton poems represent the female body as enclosed and configured within the space of the hospital and dominated by a masculine order epitomized by the (male) doctor. "In Celebration of My Uterus" (1969) evokes images of hysterectomy to attack the masculinist view of female anatomy as pathological:

> They wanted to cut you out
> but they will not.
> They said you were immeasurably empty
> but you are not.
> They said you were sick unto dying
> but they were wrong. (SPAS, 125)

The posthumous collection *Words for Dr. Y.* (1978), written from 1960 to 1970, records a chilling narrative of a woman painfully negotiating her subjectivity against the dominating gaze of the doctor. In a poem dated "June 14, 1964" from this collection, Sexton writes:

> What has it come to, Dr. Y.
> my needing you?
> . . . .
> We make a bridge toward my future
> and I cry to you: I will be steel!
> I will build a steel bridge over my need!
> I will build a bomb shelter over my heart! (SPAS, 57)

The codependent relationship of (male) doctor and (female) patient ultimately defines the female body as a lack. Through the doctor's intervention, Sexton is saved from suicide and madness only insofar as she is a suicide and mad, that is, a patient. Sexton writes:

> With your own hands you dig me out.
> You give me hoses so I can breathe.
> You make me a skull to hold the worms
> of my brain . . . . (SPAS, 258)

The doctor constructs the female body through which the speaker must exist and recognize herself as subject. Any attempt to discern her subjectivity outside her relationship to Dr. Y. is inevitably hopeless—she is defined by her madness, by her status as Dr. Y.'s patient, by her "illness."

Although Sexton's poetry had a powerful impact on Women's Liberationist poetry, she never identified herself as a feminist, and seldom expressed any explicitly political views during the Vietnam era. Yet traces of war invade Sexton's poetry, often in ways that link masculinist domination and the male gaze with militarism. The last image in the lines quoted from *Words for Dr. Y*, for example, evokes a sense that the poet needs to protect herself from the doctor's gaze as if from a military attack. In "The Firebombers" (1972), Sexton evokes antiwar and countercultural politics, associating the slaughter of the Vietnamese with American consumerism:

> We are America.
> We are the coffin fillers.
> We are the grocers of death.
> We pack them in crates like cauliflowers.

The imagery of consumerism that typifies American imperialism here revolves around groceries, vegetables, stereotypically associated with women's shopping. Later Sexton depicts a bomb opening "like a shoebox." The poem's central image of mutilation, however, focuses on a woman:

> The woman is bathing her heart.
> It has been torn out of her
> and because it is burnt
> and as a last act
> she is rinsing it off in the river.
> This is the death market.[80]

Women, who shop at the grocery where death has been marketed, are also targets of military imperialism. Sexton articulates the violence of war as a violence against women.

The link between masculinity, war, and the domination of the female body is perhaps most disturbingly evident in the nightmarish images of Sexton's posthumously published "I'm dreaming the My Lai soldier again":

> I'm dreaming the My Lai soldier night after night.
> He rings the doorbell like the Fuller Brush man
> and wants to shake hands with me
> and I do because it would be rude to say no
> and I look at my hand and it is green
> with intestines.

Once again, the male aggressor is linked to the commercial exploitation of women. The speaker shakes hands with the salesman despite her misgivings because masculinist society teaches women to never say no, to be polite. This socialization, however, also links the speaker to the violence of the war. Because she feels compelled to fulfill the prescribed feminine role, the speaker is also violated and contaminated by the war's carnage. After this initiation into the violence of the massacre, the woman speaker of the poem is lifted up by the soldier "again and again," an image suggestive of sexual intercourse, but more likely rape. The soldier then "lowers [her] down with the other dead women and babies/saying, *It's my job. It's my job.*" This echoes the famous excuses heard at Nuremberg and from the U.S. soldiers charged with the My Lai atrocities, that they were only following orders. Furthermore, it associates Sexton's own feelings of sexual violation with the atrocities of the Vietnam War, and more interestingly, it positions the speaker with the Vietnamese. The poem's speaker becomes another victim of the male soldier and is literally placed alongside the slaughtered of My Lai. Later the speaker tells us she is given "a bullet to swallow/like a sleeping tablet." The bullet may be metaphorical of the tranquilizers regularly prescribed to treat women's emotional and physical conditions stereotyped by male doctors as hysteria; it is a panacea to experiences incomprehensible and threatening to masculinist society. Swallowing a bullet is also connotative of fellatio, which resonates with the implicit rape imagery of the preceding lines. The lines between phallic penetration, sexual dominance, and female oppression converge so that they become inextricably linked to the military atrocities of My Lai. By the end of the poem, the speaker is fully entrenched in the masculine violence so brutally epitomized by the My Lai massacre:

> I am lying in this belly of dead babies
> each one belching up the yellow gasses of death
> and their mothers tumble, eyeballs, knees, upon me,
> each for the last time, each authentically dead.
> The soldier stands on a stepladder above us
> pointing his red penis right at me and saying,
> *Don't take this personally.* (SPAS, 261; emphasis Sexton's)

The speaker, the dead women, and the children are all engulfed in the grotesque obverse of a womb. Like other women poets during the Vietnam War, Sexton associates the war with rape, masculinist power, medical practices that confine women, and the control of pregnancy.

Poems by Plath and Sexton focus extensively on their experiences in mental institutions and psychotherapy; Sexton actually began writing poetry as part of her therapy. From the 50s to the early 60s a remarkable reliance on scientists, doctors, sociologists, and therapists emerged in American culture. According to Elaine Tyler May, "Long-term individual therapy . . . reached unprecedented popularity in the mid-1950s."[81] A number of feminists during the Vietnam era, however, attacked psychiatry for seeking to normalize women, misreading traits and conditions "natural" to women as "pathological."[82] Psychotherapy, marriage and family counseling, and other forms of therapeutic practice were widely promoted and became popular in the 50s as means of controlling behavior within the family and establishing what May calls the "domestic containment" of women, a cultural ideology that emerged in response to women's increased political and economic power during World War II. May concludes that "domestic containment and its therapeutic corollary undermined the potential for political activism and reinforced the chilling effects of anticommunism and the cold war consensus."[83] Since the majority of psychiatrists, like most medical professionals other than nurses in this period, were male, psychotherapy could be seen to epitomize the patriarchal control of female subjectivity. As many have noted, the Confessional style of poetry that Plath, Sexton, Robert Lowell, and others of the late 50s and early 60s made popular emerged in response to the pervasiveness of psychotherapy.[84] The poetry of Plath and Sexton often represents psychotherapy as a means of dominating the female subject. At the same time, by speaking out on taboo and repressed topics, such as women's bodies, bodily functions, and familial dysfunctions, Plath and Sexton opened up new modes of expression that would become central to contemporary women's poetry, particularly the representation of female anatomy.

Many women poets of the late 60s and early 70s configure such representations around an implicit critique of what they imagined was the probing, rationalistic, violating gaze of doctors. In her 1964 poem "Chant for Half the World," Carol Bergé envisions the female body through a series of surrealistic images that often implicitly cite medical practices as a violating means of opening the body to this gaze:

> The women breast to breast across empty
> across lava-strewn bitter plains
> facing lidless eyes of the majestic surgeons
> who demand they empty their wombs
> of the quintuplet dolls shaped like "husband"
> . . . .
> The women as kosmotics
> wombs tipped crazily toward the source of light
> . . . .

> Tragedies of women their toothlessness
> having had the wombs wormed like sick kits
> having little to do but notice how hills
> recall flesh as it might have been
>
> . . . .
>
> The accurate synaptic traceries prohibited
> turned instead into lightning on film
> overexposed and comically brilliant[85]

These images evoke experiences of abortion, gynecological exams, hysterectomies, and fetal monitoring, associating obstetrical and gynecological practices with cold, invasive, and dominating means of controlling the female body.

Marya Mannes's 1966 antiwar poem "Assignment" links the technologies of the war with the visual penetration of bodies made possible by medical technologies. Written in a male voice, as a transcript of a radio transmission from a military control center to an atronaut or jet pilot, the poem associates the violence of the war with a masculinist desire to visualize and penetrate the human body:

> Luna Nine,
> transmit the cortex of Ky and let us see
> the brain of Ho. Show us the wombs
> of village mothers, seeded to replace
> the small lives spindled, folded stapled mutilated
> by this war.
>   We have
> pictures enough of shattered bodies, theirs and ours we
>   need
> a *special vision:* the computer eye, freed
> from the warping and wavering of moral sight, that fogs
> the lens. Quick, Luna Nine—
> land—transmit—
> reveal.[86]

The speaker demands something more than the photographs of mutilated bodies so common in Vietnam War imagery. He orders "Luna Nine" to allow him to see inside the bodies, to see their hidden secrets. To do this, "Luna Nine" must penetrate the skull of Ho Chi Minh, the wombs of mothers. The technology, "the computer eye" imagined here evokes images of the medical technology that had become widely available by the early 60s for monitoring the fetus in the womb. The "special vision" must be a "science" free of morality. Mannes associates the violence of the war with the technological, coldly rationalistic imperatives prevalent in an age of science. Yet the images of Ho's brain and the mothers' wombs suggest that this "special vision" can only be achieved through violence. The goal of such

technology is to "transmit—/reveal." The poem suggests that a masculinist insistence on visual proof is a desire to "capture" the truth of
the body; by transmitting the visual image, "Luna Nine" gives the
speaker access to the bodies of the Vietnamese. By "revealing" the
body's closed secrets, the military gains control. Mannes's poem invokes the Sartrean paradigm of the Look as an apparatus for colonizing the Other. Military and medical technologies appear linked;
similarly the targets of this technology are linked. Ho Chi Minh and
Nguyen Cao Ky, colonially oppressed leaders of, respectively, the
Democratic Republic of Vietnam and the Republic of Vietnam, are
objects of an oppression associated with the masculinist oppression
of women.[87]

Exposing the body's insides to an institutional gaze also figures as
an important trope in Etel Adnan's 1966 antiwar poem, "The Enemy's
Testament."[88] The poem is written in three parts in the voice of an
anonymous and genderless Vietcong cadre, "With no other identity
than the/letters of V.C./which sound like venereal disease" (WV 3).
Cataloging the ways her/his body has been violated by the United
States, the poem casts the persona's body as the synecdoche of Vietnam, representing its destruction through her/his wounds:

> I have been softened up,
> my backbone as soft as my belly,
>
> I have been gassed,
> my eyes as blind as a worm's,
>
> I have been brainwashed,
> told of freedom until light
>   passed out of my brain,
>
> I have been shot,
> more bullet holes in my flesh
>   than holes in a target. (WV, 3)

First softened by a decadent colonialist reign, the Vietnamese body is
later represented as gassed by napalm and defoliant. Indoctrinated by
U.S. propaganda or ruthlessly interrogated by U.S. intelligence, who
often attempted to "re-educate" captured Vietcong cadres, the Vietnamese subject is finally shot, penetrated, broken open.

Ending on an image of the Vietnamese body as opened and penetrated, the first section leads to the speaker's rearticulation of the mutilation as a means of resistance. Throughout the poem, the images
associate the violence of the war with a kind of medico-technological
will to penetrate the body, expose its insides, and dissect its parts.
The second section represents the United States viewing the Vietnamese body as pathological, diseaselike ("like venereal disease"):

"They got me out of my lair/for I was infesting my own land." By the third section, however, the speaker turns the mutilation of her/his body around so that it now serves as the "testament" to U.S. atrocities, and thus contradicts United States claims of serving the interests of Vietnam:

> I send my brain to your center of research
> so they could see what made me fight,
>
> I send my eyes to your President
> so they can look him in the face,
>
> they only knew the darkness of tunnels . . .
>
> I send my teeth to your generals,
> they bit more rifle than bread,
>
> for hunger was my companion . . . . (WV, 3–4)

The dismembered body parts become both testimony and grotesque legacy, evidence and bequest of U.S. atrocities in Vietnam, a subversive gift given by the disempowered "enemy" to the powerful. In bequeathing these body parts, the speaker reverses the Sartrean paradigm of the Look, sending her/his eyes to the President to "look him in the face," and thus subvert the roles of Colonizer and Colonized. As in Mannes's poem, these images implicitly critique the dominating power of visuality that characterizes not just the overly rationalistic state in general, but specifically medico-technology, precisely because the latter focuses on "capturing" the body's insides.

By identifying the violence of the war with invasive technologies of visualization, these poems evoked a widely held view in feminism. The proliferation and expansion of scientific and medical visual technologies in the post–World War II era predominantly cast the female body as its primary object, its "target." The "gaze" constructed in the sciences, a gaze increasingly intent on surveying, monitoring, and managing women's reproduction and health, was metaphorized in feminist theory as a form of militaristic, masculinist oppression. Feminist studies of medical practice published in the Vietnam era argued that the male-dominated profession functioned as a means of controlling the female body. Vicki Pollard's 1969 article "Producing Society's Babies" declared:

Doctors are always enemies of women. They are an ultra-conservative group resisting any kind of social change. They consistently adopt an infuriating and patronizing attitude toward women. This is especially true of most obstetricians who elect to play the role of father and god to their patients, forcing women into the role of helpless, stupid, ridiculous little girls. The way we are treated by doctors is symptomatic of the conditioning we get in all aspects of our lives. Obstetricians are almost always men; we are therefore forced to give up all control of what happens to us and our bodies to a man who makes all the decisions for us.[89]

Mary Daly reiterates this view: "[T]he mutilations and mutations masterminded by the modern man-midwives represent an advanced stage in the patriarchal program of gynocide." Daly further sees this "program" as a masculinist response to the rise of radical feminism.[90] Adrienne Rich termed the male domination of obstetrics "the theft of childbirth" and argued that regaining control of birth was crucial to the liberation of women. She concludes:

> Patriarchal childbirth. . .is exploited labor in a form *even more devastating than that of the enslaved industrial worker* who has, at least, no psychic and physical bond with the sweated product, or with the bosses who control her. Not only have conception, pregnancy, and birth been expropriated from women, but also the deep paraphysical sensations and impulses with which they are saturated.[91]

Rich's claims that the exploitation of women's birth labors by male doctors is "more devastating" than the exploitation of industrial workers subsumes the social category of class under that of gender. Her argument makes an analogy that elides the unique material conditions faced by the industrial worker and, furthermore, essentializes the experience of birth. Her analysis admits no distinctions in race, class, or nation in representing birth. The ultimate crime of "patriarchal birth" is its ability to rob women of the corporeal experience that Rich believes identifies them as women.

These approaches to medical practice and reproductive rights stem from a political discourse of the female body evident in the Vietnam era that articulated associations between the war and notions of motherhood as both a cultural role and an embodied experience. Typically, those images and tropes of female corporeality in Women's Liberationist poetry that drew these connections argue that men wage war, women bear children; that women, children, and the colonized are innocent victims of men's wars; and that aggression and colonialism are male. In the Mannes poem quoted previously, for example, the male Vietnamese are linked to the Vietnamese mothers through their common violation by the penetrating technological gaze of the U.S. military. Patricia Giggans's "Two Poems" draws connections between the oppression of women and the Vietnamese through imagery suggestive of mothering and pregnancy. In the first poem, Giggans considers her relationship to the victims of the war:

> What do you know of me
> child of the delta?

> Charred and scarred
> your missing limbs
> dangling from
> leafless trees.

The speaker's thoughts seem to have been occasioned by TV news images, as she characterizes herself as "a member/of the family/waiting for the white/light to spread." She is compelled to consider both her complicity with the war and her links to its victims through media images. Later she concludes:

> What do you know of me
> delta child?
> I am hiroshima
> looking into the eye
> of a napalmed baby.

The ambiguity of the third line in this passage suggests the speaker is both "hiroshima" as synecdoche of U.S. militaristic atrocity and "Hiroshima" as victim. This double-consciousness, the dilemma of being a citizen of the aggressor nation and also its ultimate victim, is made explicit in the second poem:

> vietnam is a crypt
> and i'm in it.
> . . . .
> shockless vietnam
> numb like a sleeping buddha
> i'm like you now.[92]

The final lines suggest the speaker has answered the question that opened the poems. She identifies with the napalmed "delta child" as a victim of masculinist, militaristic power. Further, the speaker is now *inside* the violated womb/tomb space of Vietnam.

The speaker of Helen Sorrells's 1966 poem "To a Child Born in Time of Small War" looks to the child she has borne as a sign of her independence and strength as she reflects on how the father was killed in the war. Speaking to the child, the mother recalls how she discovered her unintentional pregnancy shortly before her soldier-husband was sent to Vietnam:

> In May we were still alone. That month your life
> stirred in my dark, as if my body's core
> grew quick with wings. I turned away, more wife
> than mother still, unwilling to explore
> the fact of you. There was an orient shore,
> a tide of hurt, that held my heart and mind.
> It was as if you lived behind a door

> I was afraid to open, lest you bind
> my breaking. Lost in loss, I was not yours to find.

Presumably, the husband in this poem was sent to the war when it still seemed to many Americans that it would be a "small war," since prior to 1966 President Johnson had promised the country, "We seek no wider war." Yet, as the pregnant speaker grows, the war lingers:

> I swelled with summer. You were hard and strong,
> making me know you were there. When the mail
> brought me no letter, and the time was long
> between the war's slow gains, and love seemed frail,
> I fought you.

The woman finds herself trapped in an unwanted pregnancy, constantly reminded of the husband the "small war" has taken from her. When she finally gives birth, however, she not only finds love for the child but sees her child as evidence of a new sense of self-affirmation:

> Discipline of the seasons brought me round.
> Earth comes to term and so, in time, did we.
> You are a living thing of sight and sound.
> Nothing of you is his, you are all of me. . . .[93]

A poem by Dotty LeMieux published in a 1970 issue of *Women* questions the nature of motherhood and women's lack of reproductive freedom through reflection on the Vietnam War:

> The war is still on somewhere
> The faces of the dead
> Today lined the street
> Reminding me
> I too was wanted dead
> For the crime of life I carried inside me
> Will my daughter someday make babies
> She doesn't want
> Will my son's picture
> Proclaim his death
> Unnoticed in a forgotten war
> Closer than the war
> Are men who have decided
> I shall bear for them
> A child of hate[94]

Watching an antiwar protest where photographs of soldiers killed in Vietnam were displayed, the speaker connects their deaths at the hands of a patriarchal state to her sense of oppression as a woman. Just as men decided the fates of the dead soldiers, she sees men deciding her own fate, limiting her reproductive choices. Opposite this poem in *Women* appears an article by Carol Driscoll entitled "The

Abortion Problem" that begins, "[W]omen can never hope to be liberated in any sense if they are denied the right to control their bodies, especially their reproductive organs."[95]

In the preceding examples, as in a number of poems and texts that grounded their critique of the war in political discourses of the body and reproductive rights, women's biological capacity to bear children serves as evidence of their inherent pacifism. The "motherist" argument against war has a long history in U.S. pacifism. The Women's Peace Party of the early twentieth century, for example, "argued that women's special morality—derived from their life-giving and preserving role as mothers—provided them with a unique capacity to join women all over the globe in seeking disarmament."[96] According to Ruth Rosen, "Until the Vietnam war, in fact, American women (with the exception of those attached to Socialist or Communist parties) had traditionally based their opposition to war—and nuclear weapons—on their biological difference as mothers."[97] One of the first women-only demonstrations occurred in November 1961, when fifty thousand housewives, organized by Women Strike for Peace (WSP), left their homes and jobs to protest nuclear testing.[98] When called before the House Un-American Activities Committee in 1962, "these women spoke as mothers, claiming that saving American children from nuclear extinction was the essence of 'Americanism.'. . . These women carried the banner of motherhood into politics."[99] WSP later became a powerful force in the movement against the Vietnam War, basing its arguments against the war in female reproductive biology.[100]

To be sure, the legitimacy of the institution of motherhood as a grounds for antiwarist activism came under heavy attack from radical feminists. Shulamith Firestone, for example, argued, "The heart of woman's oppression is her childbearing and childrearing roles."[101] Heather Booth, Sue Munaker, and Evelyn Goldfield of the Chicago Women's Liberation Union issued a statement against the "motherist" assumptions of the Jeanette Rankin Brigade antiwar demonstration in 1968, arguing that "[u]ntil women go beyond justifying themselves in terms of their wombs and breasts and housekeeping abilities, they will never be able to exert any political power."[102] NYRW staged a counterdemonstration to the Brigade's that involved a funeral procession and burial of "Traditional Womanhood." NYRW member Peggy Dobbins's "Liturgy for the Burial of Traditional Womanhood" expressly rejects the "motherist" line as liberal and complicitous with patriarchy:

> Women unabashed of feelings
> Loving peace

And lively bodies
More than efficiency
And exigencies
Of war.
We also
We have sinned
Acquiescing to an order
That indulges peaceful pleas
And writes them off as female logic
Saying peace is womanly.[103]

Despite the radical rejection of the "motherist" line, however, the re-cuperation of a "matriarchal culture" would dominate much of the cultural feminism of the 70s. Dolores Bargowski's 1969 letter to the *Voice of the Women's Liberation Movement* offers an early articulation of this matriarchist position, describing

> those women today, having reached a certain consciousness about women in relation to this oppressive patriarchal society, who choose to reject its definitions and look elsewhere to affirm the values this society has repressed. This other place is the matriarchal culture which preceded the patriarchal when woman was recognized for her inherent creative potentials.[104]

One way feminists during the Vietnam era could reconstitute "woman" as a legitimate, distinct subject in a nation-based theory of struggle was to focus on specific biological functions that have de-fined "woman" as subject in patriarchal culture. The "motherist" and "matriarchist" appeal in antiwar and feminist discourses foregrounds female anatomy as the determining instance of subjectivity.[105]

These aspects of feminist body-politics during the Vietnam War stem from the struggle for reproductive rights that women had been waging since the turn of the century; at the same time, they converge with the expansion of birth control options and the new sexual free-doms of the post–World War II era. The development of new contra-ceptive technologies such as the IUD and the Pill after 1950 gave women more freedom in their sexual relations and provided support for the "Sexual Liberation" of the 60s and 70s. During the Vietnam era, however, feminists critiqued the medical establishment's domi-nation of reproductive technologies and the proliferation of birth con-trol discourses in public policies as aspects of a masculinist-imperialist dynamic. In part, this critique developed in response to programs for increased governmental control of population growth, often couched in imperialistic rhetoric. According to Linda Gordon, the dominant perspective among birth control organizations after 1950 was "popu-lation control." Theoretically linked to Malthusianism, population control represented a U.S. project to control the expanding birth rate in the Third World.[106] Population control advocates considered over-population the cause of underdevelopment in Third World econ-omies. By the 50s and 60s, funded by major U.S. corporations and industries (such as Standard Oil and Du Pont) and implemented by the U.S. government or the United Nations, population control be-came a means of conducting foreign policy.[107]

Several feminists during the Vietnam era pointed out the links between population control and imperialism. For example, Jean Sharpe's 1972 article "The Birth Controllers" details the various in-dustrial and corporate sponsors of birth control programs. According to Sharpe, "All have worked tirelessly and contributed heavily to publicizing the population menace, birth-controlling Third World peoples abroad, and influencing the U.S. government to step up its involvement in birth control both at home and abroad."[108] During the later 60s, after urban riots had exploded across the country, popula-tion control discourse shifted focus from the Third World to the inner city.[109] A 1969 mass advertising campaign sponsored by the Commit-tee to Check the Population Explosion exemplifies the underlying eu-genicist thinking of population control discourse:

> How many people do you want in your country? Already the cities are packed with youngsters. Thousands of idle victims of discontent and drug addiction. You go out after dark at your peril. . . .Birth control is the answer. . . .The evermounting tidal wave of humanity challenges us to control it, or be submerged along with all of our civilized values.[110]

In the face of such programs, opposition to birth control among women in many Black Liberation groups, most notably the Black Pan-thers, emerged to counter what was viewed as a racist, genocidal pro-gram aimed precisely at the inner-city blacks who had been threatening white hegemony.[111] That population control discourse had been deployed to target people of color both in the Third World and in America's inner cities underscores the conceptual links be-tween Black Liberation and Third World revolution. The stories that appeared in the late 60s of African American and Chicana women being sterilized either without their knowledge or through coercion seemed to corroborate these links.

The antagonisms between women and the medical profession were often articulated in terms of revolutionary politics. A number of narratives that appeared in the feminist press represented women's medical self-examinations as a liberatory practice akin to revolution-ary strategy. Ellen Frankfort's 1972 article "Vaginal Politics" exem-plifies this discourse. Her narrative describes how women of the Los

Angeles Feminist Women's Health Clinic displayed their genitals to teach lower-income women about their bodies. The clinic workers went on to describe the various instruments doctors use to inspect the vagina, and eventually they taught the women there how to diagnose themselves. Frankfort writes, "I hesitated to use the word 'revolutionary,' but no other word seems accurate to describe the effects [of this meeting]. It was a little like having a blind person see for the first time—for what woman is not blind to her own insides?" Political revolution stems from an awareness of the body's insides, according to Frankfort. The notion of inner truth that has been central to the philosophy of individuality in modernity now becomes a notion of anatomical truth. Rather than a knowledge of the soul or consciousness, it is knowledge of genitals, organs, the inner workings of the body that makes one free. This knowledge of anatomy was considered crucial for a women's revolution; women need to gain control of medical examinations and abortion in order to liberate themselves. Frankfort concludes by claiming, "Any group genuinely interested in self-help clinics ought to look at the People's Republic of China."[112]

As the lead article of the "Health" section of *The New Woman's Survival Sourcebook* (1975), Robin Morgan's "Taking Back Our Bodies" makes explicit the links between a critique of masculinist medical practices and women's colonization.

> Our bodies have literally been taken from us, mined for their natural resources (sex and children), and deliberately mystified. . . . Androcentric medical science, like other professional industries in the service of the patriarchal colonizer, has researched better and more efficient means of *mining* our natural resources, with (literally) bloody little concern for the true health, comfort, nurturance, or even survival (long-term) of those resources. . . .
>
> We must begin, as women, to reclaim our land, and the most concrete place to begin is with our own flesh.

Morgan continues by arguing that women need to educate themselves better about their bodies and their health in order not to be dependent on the male-dominated medical establishment. Through education and practice, women will achieve a revolutionary self-realization. She concludes, "That is why, as radical feminists, we believe that the Women's Revolution is potentially the most profound hope for change in history. And this is why the speculum may well be mightier than the sword."[113] Morgan's article figures the female body as the foundational site or territory of ideological struggle, and the male-dominated medical profession as a prime instrument in the "battle" for control of this territory by men.

Although the feminist critique of the medical profession often fell into reductive claims, it is important to recognize how this critique

stemmed from Vietnam-era feminism's articulation of analogies between U.S. women's historical experiences with a male-dominated
and patriarchal profession and the oppositional vernacular of libera-
tionism, revolution, and Third-Worldist critiques of imperialism. Until the post-Vietnam era, doctors in obstetrics and gynecology were
overwhelmingly male; as late as 1977, men made up 94 percent of
certified gynecologists.[114] The history of modern obstetrics is rooted in
the expulsion of female midwives from the birth room during the
nineteenth century as male obstetricians, through legislative and professional control of licensing, training, and hospitalization, sought to
consolidate their hegemony over the field.[115] Central to this process
was the profession's ability to cast birth as pathological. According to
William Arney, "Obstetricians used their ability to treat childbirth as
pathological to create their profession . . . but the continued existence
of obstetricians depended on their ability to capture childbirth, all of
it, treat it, and hold it firmly as part of their project."[116] After World
War II, the development and increased use of new technologies in
obstetrics to help decrease the mortality and morbidity rates of birth
had the concomitant effect of increasing doctors' control of birth,
technologizing it, and distilling birth from the woman, essentially
marginalizing the female body. According to Arney, "As the profession achieved its specialty status within the broader profession, the
medical gaze narrowed until the obstetrical 'case' was effectively dis-
tilled from the person. . . . Obstetrics made women faceless, vehicles
of obstetrical material."[117]

The emergence of new visual technologies in obstetrics, for example, allowed physicians to monitor the fetus more precisely than
ever before.[118] Yet these technologies were often linked in practical
and conceptual ways both by the feminist movement and by the general public to militarism. Ultrasound imaging, for example, now a
commonly used technology for monitoring fetal development, was
developed from a concept based on sonar systems used in World War
I to track U-boats. According to Ann Oakley:

> [T]he original idea, pioneered by Ian Donald and his colleagues in
> Scotland, was to use as diagnostic aids on mysterious tumors in the
> abdomens of women, the ultrasonic metal-flaw detectors used in
> industry. Their theory was that malignant tumors would look differ-
> ent from benign ones. Later it occurred to them that the commonest
> abdominal tumor in women is pregnancy, and additionally that
> there is not a lot of difference between a foetus *in utero* and a subma-
> rine at sea.[119]

Donald's view of pregnancy is consistent with the general representation of pregnancy in obstetrical practice of the early twentieth century

as pathological; here the fetus is likened to a tumor, a metal-flaw, or even a submarine. The cultural associations between sonar imaging of pregnancy and military surveillance also appear in the 1965 *Life* photo-essay "A Sonar 'Look' at an Unborn Baby." The photos' caption proclaims, "The astonishing medical machine resting on this pregnant woman's abdomen . . . is 'looking' at her unborn child precisely the same way a Navy surface ship homes in on enemy submarines."[120] Pregnancy is metaphorically transformed not simply into pathology but into a military battle, with the fetus "home[d] in on" like an "enemy." Although the *Life* text ostensibly celebrates the conversion of military technology to life-giving peacetime use, it concomitantly represents the female body as a site under masculinist/militaristic gaze. In both the *Life* photo-essay and in Donald's description of pregnancy, the woman's body must be penetrated to capture the true object of surveillance, the fetus obscured by the female body. The female body is *only* a body that must be seen through, whose presence is a hindrance that medical science must overcome. The "look" here, like the "special vision" in Mannes's poem, penetrates the female body to objectify and appropriate its inner secrets.[121]

The trope of the female body as pathological that has characterized these medical discourses became a specific site of contest in the women's health movement. Activists in Women's Liberation probably had experiences with doctors and medical technologies that epitomized for them the violence of patriarchal rule. Particularly as the number of women entering hospitals had increased and as the number of hospital outreach programs grew, making doctors readily available to more women than ever before, women's bodies during the 60s and 70s were routinely placed at the hands of male professionals. Medical practices were undoubtedly shaping the experiences and perceptions many women had of their bodies in the mid to late twentieth century. Citing National Center for Health Statistics reports, Paula Treichler notes, "In 1900 fewer than 5 percent of births took place in hospitals; by 1940 it was 50 percent, and by 1980 it was more than 95 percent."[122] Outside their relationships with male sexual partners, women's relationships with doctors constituted their principal experience of intimate physical contact with men. As Colette Price put it in her 1971 article "The First Self-Help Clinic," "For all practical purposes, men have probably had more intimate contact with, and certainly far greater accessibility to the vagina than women ever had."[123]

In many ways, Vietnam-era women's health activism could be said to culminate in the publication in 1971 of *Our Bodies, Ourselves*, a self-help medical guidebook written for women by The Boston Women's Health Book Collective. This book marked a significant intervention in the medical profession's control over women's health and epitomized the feminist struggle for control of the female body. The book's enormous popularity demonstrates the widespread appeal the women's health movement had in Vietnam-era America. By 1973 over 250,000 copies had been sold, and twelve hundred women's health collectives had been established around the country. Linda Gordon points out that *Our Bodies, Ourselves* and the women's health movement "strongly influenced regular medicine, especially gynecology and obstetrics."[124] The idea for the book arose out of a meeting about "women and their bodies" at a 1969 Boston Women's Liberation conference. According to the preface of *Our Bodies, Ourselves*, "We had all experienced similar feelings of frustration and anger toward specific doctors and the medical maze in general, and initially we wanted to do something about those doctors who were condescending, paternalistic, judgmental and non-informative." Identifying themselves as primarily white and middle-class, the Boston Women's collective explained, "In some ways, learning about our womanhood from the inside out has allowed us to cross over the socially created barriers of race, color, income and class, and to feel a sense of identity with all women in the experience of being female."[125] *Our Bodies, Ourselves* explicitly links the politics of women's bodies and their internal modes of existence with the dissolution of race and class differences. Inside the body, the book seems to suggest, all women are the same. To underscore the importance of body-politics in the affirmation of an empowered identity, the second part of the book's preface offers a poem, "Our Faces Belong to Our Bodies," from the It's All Right to Be a Woman Theatre of New York. The poem insists that self-empowerment resides in politically aware practices of the body:

> Our anger is changing our faces, our bodies.
> Our anger is changing our lives.
>
> Our power is changing our faces, our bodies.
> Our power is changing our lives.
>
> Our struggle is changing our faces, our bodies.
> Our struggle is changing our lives.[126]

As in other documents and poems from Vietnam-era feminism, the personal is not just the political, the political is the corporeal, and becoming politically aware as a feminist entails corporeal transformations.

Siting political resistance within female physiology, Women's Liberationist poetry often refigured the feminist struggle for reproductive rights in ways that could overlap with opposition to the war. The rhetoric of reproductive rights articulated during the Vietnam era linked these rights to decolonization. Ellen Willis has written, "Radical feminists' first major public effort was a militant campaign for abortion law repeal; more than any other issue, abortion embodied and symbolized our fundamental demand—not merely formal equality for women but genuine self-determination." Willis points out that the issue of reproductive rights remains one of the most crucial struggles for feminists:

> In the aftermath of the Supreme Court's *Webster* decision narrowing the scope of women's constitutional right to abortion and inviting a state-by-state struggle over abortion laws, commentators have repeatedly declared that "abortion is our new Vietnam." But in fact it is less the act of abortion that so deeply divides us than what that act represents: it is women's freedom that's our new Vietnam.[127]

Written in the 80s, Willis's statement demonstrates the persistence in feminist thought of the Women's Liberationist analogies drawn between the struggles for women's rights to bodily self-determination and the Vietnamese rights to national self-determination. The female body is considered colonized in the same sense that Vietnam is colonized.

Although the approaches to female corporeality in Women's Liberation often differed, a key aspect they shared was the demand for liberation, self-identity, and female control over women's health. These demands were articulated in the paradigms of anticolonialism characteristic of both Black Liberation and Third World liberation movements. The problems that essentialism poses to feminist theory have been widely debated, yet it remains important to recognize how the biological essentialism of Women's Liberation traverses other political and cultural discourses of the Vietnam era. The essentialism of Women's Liberation marks a historically complex and unique remapping of female subjectivity and a recognition of the pervasiveness of power in the life of the private body.

Indeed, feminism in the Vietnam era and after has developed the most systematic critical and theoretical approaches to corporeality. While the impetus for the specific inflections of Women's Liberationist corporeal politics I have been discussing arose out of Black Liberationist and Third World liberation practices, feminism has elaborated on these practices and extended them further than any broadly defined sociopolitical movement before or since. A vast and diverse corpus of feminist theory and criticism on discourses and politics of the body is currently available.[128] Indeed, the contemporary interest in corporeality is undoubtedly rooted in feminism and in Vietnam-era Women's Liberation's politicization of gender and the body. My discussion of the body-politics in feminist poetry of the Vietnam era is both indebted to this cultural and political work and meant to foster a critical awareness of its historical situatedness, to illustrate some of the complex ways these discourses converged, overlapped, and reconfigured other cultural and political discourses of a period key to the emergence of contemporary feminism.

4

"Fragging the Chain(s) of Command": Mutilation and GI Resistance Poetry

Unknown Soldiers

In a 1969 issue of the underground newspaper *A Four-Year Bummer*, an untitled poem by an active-duty soldier stationed in Vietnam began

> When laughter ceases—loud—hideous laughter
> Comes the silence.
> Then the crying and screaming.
> The legless and the mind blown far into the midst of a
>   bomb;
> Consuming lifeless, headless babies with hysterical
>   women.

Signed "A Peace Lover," this anonymous poem ends by accusing "[m]en in business suits," depicted above the fray on "two hills," for such atrocities. The poem's final lines describe these businessmen:

> Feeling no pain
> Seeing no blood
> Losing no arms.
> They say, "Stay and Fight."
> I say, "Go to Hell."[1]

The poem structures an opposition characteristic of dissident soldier poetry written during the Vietnam War. Those who must experience war will be disfigured, mutilated, even destroyed; those who wage war from the safe distance of their offices remain whole, undamaged, unaffected. Those who have not suffered the psychic and *physical* trauma of combat ask others to endanger their bodies. The signifying chain of the poem's last lines indicts the "businessmen" for having felt no pain and witnessed no blood, and, more importantly, for remaining physically whole while the Vietnamese and American soldiers must bear the loss of limb, the mutilation of body. In the last line, the soldier refuses to participate in atrocity and thereby legitimate the opposition between whole and mutilated, metaphorical of the hierarchy of oppressor and oppressed. Indeed, his blunt imperative subverts this opposition by implicating violence to the "businessmen's" bodies, commanding them to the Hell the soldier refuses.

Produced covertly on the Chanute Air Force Base in Illinois, *A Four-Year Bummer* was an important example of the underground press that emerged around a widespread movement of dissident active-duty and veteran soldiers who opposed the Vietnam War and the military during the war. In 1969 more than sixty different newspapers like *A Four-Year Bummer* were being printed and distributed to active-duty soldiers throughout the country and on U.S. bases overseas. This underground press gave voice to numerous soldiers who opposed the Vietnam War and the military. The titles of these clandestine papers were often based in imaginative and subversive rearticulations of military and countercultural jargon. The Chanute paper's title, for example, is a pun on the acronym AFB (air force base), rearticulating military jargon as countercultural, subverting discipline with the polyvalent language of the drug culture (a bummer, a "bad trip," a drug-induced experience gone bad). Other examples included *About Face, As You Were, Eyes Left*, and *Left Face*. Such titles redeployed military commands as deliberately ambiguous code signaling political dissidence to their readers while ostensibly reassuring military authorities.[2] Such code was crucial considering how few democratic freedoms soldiers were granted in military life and the unusually high risks dissident soldiers took to print what could be considered mutinous literature. Through imaginative and densely intertextual recodings of their military culture, soldier-activists during the Vietnam War forged an important resistance to both the war and the ideologies of the war.

Such imaginative forms of resistance and the culture of dissent that the GI underground press fostered reflect on the very real corporeal traumas and extremities of soldier experience in the war. The poem by "A Peace Lover" appeared in a box alongside "Vietnam: A Personal View," by Sp/4 Mike Connell (ret.), which recounts the ambush of his patrol company after his first two months in Vietnam. According to Connell's account, his company suffered numerous casualties, but the battalion commander, "safe, high overhead in his observation helicopter," ordered them back into the field: "Let's go back in there and get a body-count!" One of Connell's platoon members, who lost a friend in the ambush, yelled back, "If you do, I'll shoot you out of the sky!" Connell explains how over time he came to see that "for the average Vietnamese the American army is an army of occupation. . . . For them, *We* are the Enemy!"[3] As in the "Peace

Lover" poem, the soldier sees himself at risk like the Vietnamese, while "management" remains safe. Both the "businessmen" and Connell's battalion commander seek a good body count. Both the poem and the prose narrative demonstrate how bodies *count* in Vietnam, and not merely as the abstract integers tallied by those who manage war. And in both, a soldier refuses orders, threatening the "chain-of-command," the hierarchy of law and order, with the destruction they have trained him to wage against dispossessed others.

Sp/4 Greg Laxer's poem "For My Still Imprisoned Comrades," in a 1971 issue of another GI Resistance paper, *The Bond*, celebrates antiwar soldiers imprisoned at Fort Leavenworth and also calls for the disruption of military order:

> every time a yellow infant explodes forth unto the
>   world, from the womb-darkness to greet the
>   sun,
> though besieged on every side by napalm-phosphorus-
>   defoliant
> another nail is driven into the coffin of capitalism
> . . . .
> comrades, do not despair, though the lackey-mindless
>   guards may taunt you unceasingly
> for the time is not far off when the bones of the
>   capitalist shall lie bleaching in the sun
> and up through the hollow eye-sockets shall push
>   flowers
> and the earth shall again bustle with the joy of life,
> most of the weapons will lie rusting, but some we shall
>   preserve to insure
> that never again does this class of bandits subjugate
>   our beings[4]

By representing the birth of a Vietnamese child as an explosion, Laxer subverts that tragic reality in which Vietnamese children were themselves exploded by the U.S. military; here the child's explosive birth signals the death of capitalism and its military—the child becomes a weapon for revolution. In the graphic images of the "capitalist's" rotting corpse in the last lines, the poet rearticulates mutilation so that, rather than the body of a Vietnamese or the soldier who must fight against his will, it is the body of the oppressor that is mutilated. As in the Connell narrative and the "Peace Lover" poem, resistance is articulated through representations of mutilation; by inverting the position of mutilated and mutilator, dissident soldiers sought to "frag" the chain of command.

"Fragging" is military argot for the assassination of officers and career soldiers ("lifers" in GI slang) by GIs. The word is derived from the term "fragmentation device," the grenades often used in such actions. As the U.S. military's goals in Vietnam became increasingly vague and meaningless to GIs after the 1968 Tet Offensive, and as soldiers increasingly began to see themselves as fodder for a cause they did not support or even understand, fragging became increasingly prevalent. According to U.S. army records, more than 300 fraggings resulting in 73 deaths and 500 injuries occurred from 1969 through 1970; by 1972, fraggings increased to 551, leaving 86 dead and over 700 injured.[5] Although fraggings were largely individual acts, large-scale and organized mutinies also proliferated in the final years of the war. The first reported mutiny of American troops in Vietnam was recorded in August 1969, when, after a long and painful push through the Songchang Valley near Da Nang, the "A" Company of the Third Battalion, 196th Infantry refused orders to continue farther down Nuilon Mountain. In 1970, CBS News televised live coverage of a refusal of orders by the soldiers of "C" Company of the Second Battalion, 7th Cavalry. Such "refusals" occurred in every year from 1969 to the last withdrawal of U.S. troops.[6] Connell's story of soldiers' willingness to frag U.S. military personnel rather than continue placing themselves and their fellow soldiers at risk reflected the widespread disintegration of discipline and morale throughout the military during the war.

In this chapter, I will deploy "fragging" as a metaphor for the discursive dis-incorporation of the ideological signifying "chain of command" that subjects the soldier as a seamless, impenetrable corporeality. A common element in the texts from the GI underground press quoted previously is an emphasis on mutilation. By insisting on the brutal fact of the human body's mutilation in the Vietnam War, these writers exemplify a common tactic in GI movement poetry. Such texts demand that readers face what Elaine Scarry has called "the incontestable reality of. . . the body in pain, the body maimed, the body dead and hard to dispose of.'"[7] In the two poems quoted, images of the body's mutilation carry considerable weight; often such images are the most detailed and graphic in GI poetry. By focusing on the mutilation of human bodies, dissident soldier-poets produced a counternarrative to the dominant (and dominating) narratives of the glory of war and the impenetrable body of the male soldier. Through this poetics of mutilation, dissident soldier-poets refuse the orders of dominant ideology, refuse to be complicitous in the production of war, and ultimately seek to rupture norms of masculinity in which corporeal totality and wholeness are produced as metonymic of U.S. victory in the Vietnam War. It is through images, tropes, and symbols of mutilation that this poetry paradoxically resists the war narrative that demands mutilation.

Throughout this chapter, I will use the term "GI Resistance" to designate the social phenomenon of soldier dissent during the war. The GI Resistance was a unique oppositional movement in American history. This movement, perhaps more directly than any other during the period, threatened to undermine, sabotage, and disintegrate the structures of the very institution that had secured U.S. global dominance since World War II, and it significantly endangered U.S. operations in Vietnam. In no other period of U.S. history had such a widespread and often well-organized movement of dissident soldiers emerged during a military conflict.[8] Several different GI and veterans' groups were actively engaged in dissidence during the war, some more organized than others, some working together in coalitions, some aligned with more established civilian leftist groups. The American Servicemen's Union (ASU), for example, was associated with the Trotskyite Worker's World Party (WWP) and focused primarily on organizing active-duty GIs as workers. The Vietnam Veterans Against the War (VVAW), on the other hand, tended to be less politically doctrinaire and included few active-duty GIs, although the group maintained close contact with them during the war. Although different in their approaches and structure, these groups shared many goals, including an end to the war, increased civil rights for soldiers, and an end to racism in the military.

I will also include as "GI Resistance" race-related activism in the military. African American soldiers were often ambivalent toward the established GI groups, but they also were often in the forefront of confrontations, stockade rebellions, refusal of riot control duty, and other actions that the organized groups used as a means of coalition-building among troops.[9] Antiracism was a powerful organizing force in the GI Resistance throughout the war. Dissident white soldiers, like civilian activists, strongly identified with African Americans as victims of a racist military's oppression, and they viewed black soldier rebellion as a model for active resistance. According to David Cortright, "Of all troops in Vietnam, the most rebellious were the blacks. As was the case throughout the armed forces, black GIs in Vietnam were militant leaders of the GI resistance, posing great problems for American commanders."[10] Radical, racially identified groups in the United States made important alliances with GIs. The Black Panthers, for example, regularly featured columns in their newspapers from soldiers and activists in the GI Resistance who analyzed the inherent racism of U.S. policies in Vietnam. A 1969 issue of *Black Liberator* featured one of the first articles on the GI Resistance.[11] Angela Davis, in prison at the time, wrote an article for the GI newspaper *Offul Times* that praised dissident GIs and prisoners: "Their beauty, their commitment, their strength are a threat to the interests of the rich, to racism, to wars which sacrifice human lives for profit and power."[12]

Women in the military during the war were much less likely to engage in oppositional activism and participate in the GI Resistance. Yet despite the overwhelming focus on men in historical, cultural, and literary studies of the war, more than eleven thousand women saw active military duty in Vietnam from 1962 to 1973, and the total number of American women working in Vietnam during the war has been estimated at between thirty-three thousand and fifty-five thousand, including both military and civilian.[13] The majority of active-duty military women served as nurses, and most nurses did not engage in active resistance to the war and/or the military.[14] The relative lack of female resistance in the military stems from the unique conditions women faced in the military during the war and the intensely masculinist culture of both the military and the GI movement. Women in the military were generally much more cut off from civilian activism and feminist support than women in college. Since most women in the military then were volunteers, their relationship to antiwar resistance was fraught with ambivalence. Moreover since the majority of women working in Vietnam were nurses, they were acutely aware that acts of resistance such as refusal of orders, strikes, or sabotage could endanger the very men they were helping. While male resistance could be directed at a disruption of war-making, for women who worked to keep U.S. male soldiers and, often, Vietnamese victims alive, resistance was much more problematic.

Furthermore, dissident activism could often result in military women being labeled as lesbians, which in turn could lead to brutal harassment or even discharge for homosexuality. This was further complicated by the conflicted relationship lesbians had to their status in the military. According to a report on United States Servicemen's Fund organizing by women, lesbians could not relate to GI Resistance politics because, as the report's authors noted, "the army is basically pretty good for them. . . . [T]hey are not in a position to move politically—they don't want to get kicked out of the army."[15]

These conditions were complicated by the entrenched masculinism of GI culture. Although many GI groups questioned gender roles and sought to analyze the interrelatedness of war, racism, and sexism, most GI groups and their papers served as alternative forms of male bonding to the authoritarian and oppressive forms perpetrated by the military. Since their military training had brutally enforced a violent, misogynist cathexis of masculine subjectivity, many dissident soldiers found it difficult to change such deeply inscribed gendering. As Tischler notes, "The male soldiers who rejected the war and who, in many cases, struggled to distance themselves from the most destructive aspects of the aggressive 'male' military ethos, nevertheless often developed their own bonds that excluded women." These

bonds were often expressed through ritual handshakes and a herme-
tic vernacular based on military combat jargon, which necessarily excluded women.[16]

Despite the overwhelming difficulties military women faced in
voicing opposition and/or organizing dissent, many were active. A
number of GI underground papers printed letters and articles by
women; these demonstrate "a growing awareness of their oppression
in the larger culture, dissatisfaction with their treatment within the
enlisted ranks, and a sense of futility about their ability to bring the
war to an end."[17] There is evidence that some enlisted women and
wives of military personnel marched in demonstrations with civilian
antiwar protesters, developed civilian feminist-style consciousness-
raising groups off base, and engaged in other acts of resistance. Tischler
cites a women's group at Fort Bragg, North Carolina, which organized study of "worker's history, third world history, and women's
history."[18] Like civilian feminists, these women also organized classes
in emergency first aid, auto mechanics, self-defense, and carpentry to
intervene in traditionally male-dominated skills and empower
women to be self-reliant.[19] There is evidence of an active-duty female
nurse threatening to "frag" her commanding officer. A medical tech-
nician wrote to *Fragging Action* that "one very hip sister threatened to
do in her C.O."[20] At Travis Air Force Base, California, a WAF resisted
the war by refusing to accept her transfer to the Philippines. At least
one military women's underground paper, *Whack!* (a pun on WAC),
was produced in 1971 at Fort McClellan, Alabama. And the masthead
of some predominantly male GI Resistance papers, including *Left
Face*, which was produced at Fort McClellan, read "Published by GIs
and WACs Against the War."[21] Such papers printed regular features
aimed at women, such as "Women's Rap" and articles about how
women could form support groups, resist sexism, and support an
end to the war.[22]

Although the general movement was dominated by men and often masculinist, many men in the GI Resistance were supportive of
women and the feminist cause. For example, a male soldier writing
for *A Four-Year Bummer* recognized the plight of military women on
his base: "The WAFs stationed at Chanute are continually oppressed
and discriminated against by the brass." The writer goes on to argue
that military sexism was deeply related to "the capitalist economy
of this country" and that such inequality "dehumanizes men and
women." *AFB*, which was affiliated with the American Servicemen's
Union, argued that "anything that divides people serves only the
pigs, whether it's racism or male chauvinism or inter-squadron ri-
valry."[23] Although the GI movement was overwhelmingly male-dominated, the contributions of women and their supportive male

colleagues in the GI Resistance press helped to forge a new awareness of women's issues among dissident soldiers.

What particularly makes the GI movement unique is its production and support of numerous underground papers.[24] GI Resistance groups published underground newspapers, organized small press companies, and developed a sophisticated network for the dissemination of their literature to soldiers throughout the country and in military bases around the world. By 1971, when Laxer's poem appeared, at least 144 different GI newspapers were being produced on U.S., European, and even Southeast Asian bases.[25]

Some papers were affiliated with nationally organized groups; *The Bond*, for example, was the journal of the American Servicemen's Union. Most newspapers, like *A Four-Year Bummer*, were less affiliated with any one national group and were primarily identified with a particular military installation. Such papers, however, reprinted national and international articles, poems, and artwork by GIs that helped foster a global network of GI dissent. Base papers often reached national and international audiences, as soldiers surreptitiously passed their copies on to other soldiers or took them to overseas bases, including bases in Vietnam. Some papers were produced overseas on or near American bases. Through this underground press network, GIs and veterans circulated personal narratives, essays, manifestos, art, and poetry. The GI Resistance press born of this activity served as a foundation for the development of the Vietnam-veteran literature that has helped shape recent American literature.[26]

As in Black Liberation and Women's Liberation movements, poets were usually in the vanguard of the movement, and poetry was an important medium of dissident expression in the GI press.[27] Many soldiers during the period seemed to consider poetry a genre inherently antagonistic to the rigid constraints of prose, especially a prose that had become so dangerously "jargonized" in military discourse. Lorrie Smith contends that for soldier-poets of the Vietnam War, "poetry remains free of the mass-market vortex which swallows almost all other forms of expression in America."[28] Soldier-poets of the war, moreover, have been prolific, publishing antiwar poetry from 1966 to the present and producing at least fifty books and about a dozen anthologies. Poetry by veterans has been circulated through VA hospital programs, veterans' support groups, and even the Internet.[29] Indeed, the range of poetic texts by soldiers and veterans of the Vietnam War is vast.[30] Since my study concerns activist-poetry produced during the war, this chapter will focus on soldier and veteran poems published before 1975.

The fact that active-duty soldiers published antiwar poems as part of an extensive culture of resistance against the military and the government during war makes their work unique in the history of war literature. Although twentieth-century history is replete with poetry by soldiers and veterans critical of war-making, the dissident nature of GI Resistance poetry, the fact that it sought not simply to critique "War" as a concept, but the U.S. military and the Vietnam War specifically, sets it apart from the canon of war poetry. Despite this, or perhaps because of it, GI Resistance poetry remains largely invisible in the history of radical literatures. Unlike the Black Liberation and Women's Liberation movements, the GI Resistance has gained little coverage in the histories and cultural studies of Vietnam-era America. The few references to soldier/veteran activism that presently exist in antiwar histories tend to be brief, often elliptical.[31] Admittedly, this has been partly due to the inaccessibility of the movement's literature; writers in the Black Liberation and Women's Liberation were often connected to colleges and universities, had access to mainstream publishing, and, with the establishment of Afro-American and Women's Studies programs, were able to ensure some measure of institutional accessibility to their literature. In comparison, the GI Resistance's extremely limited access to legal forums for dissent also limited the movement's ability to produce its literature with any consistency. Beyond the barely readable, highly ephemeral mimeographs and photocopies of the GI movement's underground papers, activist soldier poetry appeared in only very small presses.[32]

These conditions were compounded by the highly dangerous nature of GI Resistance organizing and activism. As Cortright has explained:

> Restrictions on a soldier's civil liberties are nearly absolute. Public assembly, distribution of literature, the wearing of political symbols—all such means of political expression are strictly forbidden on post. Indeed, there is very little a soldier can legally do anywhere. Even off-post demonstrations are prohibited if in a foreign country, if the serviceman is in uniform, or if his activities "constitute a breach of law and order." GIs who attempt something even so innocuous as a newsletter, [sic] risk arrest merely distributing it on base.[33]

Many of the dissident soldiers involved in producing the GI Resistance press and its literature were imprisoned during the war for their activities, given dishonorable discharges, or transferred to destabilize their ability to form a base for organizing. As Cortright continues, "Beyond these formal strictures, however, rank-and-file organizers are imperiled by extralegal harassment and punitive administrative measures—options easily available in an isolated and authoritarian bureaucracy such as the military."[34]

In addition, *agents provocateur* often infiltrated GI groups and sought to entrap members by inciting especially dangerous strategies or planting incriminating evidence against organizers. Harry Haines, recounting his experiences working on the GI paper *Aboveground* when he was stationed in 1969 at Fort Carson, Colorado, relates an incident in which an agent infiltrated the group and advocated setting fire to fort barracks. As Haines explains, these barracks were built during World War II and would burn down within a few minutes, inevitably killing GIs trapped inside. "It meant murder. It meant killing GIs, guys like us. . . . Our little band of dissidents was so potentially threatening that military intelligence actually risked the incineration of U.S. soldiers in order to discredit us!"[35] Haines also describes how printers for the GI press could be harassed by agents, the local police, or the FBI.[36] Although many militant civilian groups, perhaps most notably the Black Panthers, were subjected to infiltration and sabotage, the U.S. military's attempts to subvert GI Resistance often were more vociferous because soldiers had very few legal rights to organize and dissent.

The historical and critical neglect of the GI Resistance and its literature may also be attributed to the ways in which the dissident soldiers and soldier-poetry of the Vietnam War transgress a number of ideological and cultural norms. Not only did the dissident soldier directly challenge the military and the state, but soldiers were often stigmatized as "baby-killers" or dupes of the state, so that the civilian left found it difficult to forge effective alliances with soldiers. And like many soldiers during the war, dissident soldiers tended to come from working-class backgrounds with less access to postsecondary education than activists in the civilian left. The direct, seemingly uneducated, sometimes brutal approach of antiwar soldiers made their relations with the leftist intelligentsia problematic at best. Combat soldiers had experienced atrocities that civilians in the antiwar movement could only imagine, but soldiers had also sometimes committed atrocities, acts that often condemned them in the eyes of peace activists. Consequently, the cultural studies and histories produced about activism during the war—usually written by college-educated and middle-class former activists in the Vietnam-era civilian left—tend to marginalize the GI Resistance. The GI movement's virtual invisibility in American cultural history makes it necessary, therefore, to perform a bit of reconnaissance. By tracing the history and politics of the movement I hope to establish a context for a reading of mutilation in GI Resistance poetry and, thus, incorporate this lost movement of activist writers into the history of Vietnam-era oppositional culture.

Reconnaissance

Estimates of exactly how many active-duty GIs were involved in resistance activities vary widely and are hard to verify accurately, not only because of the military's reluctance to acknowledge dissent but also because of the movement's transient membership.[37] Figures also vary widely according to how one defines "resistance" and "dissent." If individual, noncollective acts of dissent are included, the numbers greatly increase. Matthew Rinaldi writes, "From January '67 to January '72 a total of 354,112 GIs left their posts without permission."[38] "Cincinnatus" cites figures showing that desertions in the army from 1967 to 1969 alone rose by more than 2,200 to a total of 39,234. Desertions increased dramatically after the 1968 Tet Offensive, rising in 1969 to 56,608, and in 1970 to 65,643. These figures do not include AWOLs who returned before they were listed as deserters, nor do they include cases of "malingering," in which soldiers repeatedly went on sick leave.[39] Although not all desertions were conscious acts of political resistance, these figures nevertheless indicate that a substantial number of troops literally rejected the war and their participation in it, and that such dissent had a powerful impact on military effectiveness.

Military antiwar resistance and activism occurred predominantly among enlisted personnel, usually of low rank, most often in the army and marines, branches that saw the most combat.[40] Evidence suggests that antiwar activism in the other branches was proportional to the degree of involvement in combat operations.[41] Even though relatively fewer soldiers saw combat in Vietnam than in other twentieth-century wars, the literature of the GI Resistance relies heavily on narratives and images of combat.[42] Combat duty tended to radicalize soldiers. As several studies have demonstrated, combat troops were more likely to come from economically and educationally disadvantaged backgrounds.[43] Studies have also shown that disproportionate numbers of minorities died in combat. By as early as 1965, African Americans accounted for 24 percent of all combat deaths in Vietnam. James William Gibson points out that "black men died in greater numbers than their proportion of the population."[44] Not surprisingly, as Black Power and other racial liberation movements gained momentum, minorities in the ranks often took the lead in oppositional activism. Because the draft also targeted the working class, many activists in the GI movement came from economically disadvantaged backgrounds.

Soldier opposition to the war can be traced to the earliest U.S. troop deployments in Vietnam. In a 1964 issue of *Negro Digest*, a piece entitled "Letter from an A.W.O.L. Soldier" both expresses early critiques of the war based in a racial analysis and epitomizes many key themes of later GI Resistance literature. Interestingly, the article also foregrounds political resistance and racial discourse as corporeal. Its first paragraph begins:

> I am a Negro, a G. I., and AWOL. Having lost some seventeen (17) pounds in weight after suffering a recurrent chronic back ailment, coupled with long-lasting headaches, generally feeling run-down and weak and not being able to get a long enough break to some-what arrest my condition, I then went over the hill (AWOL).

The writer situates the will to resist in the conditions of his body. The list of physical ailments he suffers is presented as just cause for his dissent, but it also illustrates how his body was made to feel un-healthy before he left the military. As the writer continues:

> After two weeks of rest and recuperation in seclusion, the headaches are gone and I've regained most of my weight. My chronic condition is somewhat relieved. During the idle hours of the past few days, I've had a chance to thoroughly analyze myself as an American Ne-gro soldier, and what I see amazes me.

Resisting, in the form of unauthorized leisure, leads to a healthier body, and furthermore, allows for a clearer self-analysis. The writer then goes on to recall how after the murders of four children in a Birmingham church in 1963, a white chaplain and an officer lectured him and other troops about the glories of U.S. democracy and how they should be proud to defend their country:

> I wondered to no end in complete amazement how white Democ-racy can deny a black man nearly all the rights they put him in uni-form to defend, while at the same time expect him to perform his duties ungrudgingly to a country and a system which seemingly strive to deprive him of his dignity. And I wondered silently if all the white people in America thought I should be willing to let them send me to Germany with an M-1 rifle in my hands to stand ready to guard the white German's freedom and liberty with my life; or will-ingly let them send me to Vietnam to perhaps die in defense of Viet-namese, and so that the Oriental there could live in freedom, when either a Vietnamese or a white German could come to the shores of "free" America, grasp from me the freedom which I went to his homeland and died for. He would then be more free than I who have lived here through 350 years of slavery, segregation, lynching, bombings, discrimination, patriotism and bravery through a Civil and other Wars. And still I would be the hopeless, rightless, citizen-less "nigger" at the bottom of the barrel. . . . Contented?

The writer recalls the brutality of his life in the South, the indignities he and his family routinely suffered through Jim Crow laws and the prejudice of whites. He concludes by asking: "If I am not yet ready for most of the human rights white people take for granted, how then have they arrived at the conclusion that I *am* ready to serve in their Army? . . . . Can I find the strength to serve a society which so boldly denies me most nearly all that which it says I'm OBLIGATED to preserve?"[45]

This article asks questions that would resonate throughout Black Liberation during the Vietnam era. The rising resistance of the Third World to the West captured the imagination of black culture by the mid-60s. An underlying assumption evident throughout the AWOL soldier's article is a *national* distinction between the white United States and African Americans; blacks, in other words, reside outside the nation. He describes the army as "their" (white people's) army, the society that denies the soldier his basic rights is a society he does not belong to; the country he is asked to serve is clearly different from the soldier's sense of his own country. Although the soldier expresses resentment that a Vietnamese might find freedoms the soldier himself cannot find in the United States, the black man figures himself as a victim of oppression in the same way that the Vietnamese is; both seek the freedom and basic rights that they have been denied. The sense of separateness this article expresses evokes the cultural nationalism that would become the dominant ideology motivating the Black Liberation of the late 60s and early 70s.

Furthermore, this separateness is literally inscribed in the body. The soldier believes his health is threatened by his service in the white army; he needs to separate himself from the dominant and dominating cultural apparatus in order to recover physically. More broadly, of course, the "fact" of his blackness places him outside the "nation." At the lecture he has earlier described, he notes "that there were few blacks in the class" and further states:

> Me, being a rather dusty Darkie, I'm sure the sick disgust was quite evident on my face. I wondered what the chaplain thought of my intelligence—if he thought I had any; if he really thought I'd be willing to lay down my life for second-class citizenship to prevent some enemy from taking it away from me? And finally, there being only a few blacks in class, if he was at all aiming his talk at us.[46]

Here it is the visible, epidermal mark of racial difference that constitutes belonging or not belonging to the nation, to being hailed as a subject of the chaplain's discourse. The color of his skin calls into question not only his humanity but also his subject-position within the ideology of U.S. democracy. Moreover, the soldier emphasizes his epidermal difference to signal the extent to which he rejects this ideology.

This text suggests that African American soldiers had begun challenging the ideology of American intervention into Southeast Asia at least a year before Lyndon Johnson sent the first marine battalions to Da Nang in 1965. By then, increasing numbers of individual soldiers would begin to publicly oppose the war. In November 1965, for example, Lt. Henry H. Howe, Jr., was court-martialed for carrying a sign in an El Paso, Texas, antiwar demonstration that read: "End Johnson's Fascist Aggression in Vietnam" and "Let's Have More than a Choice between Petty Ignorant Fascists in 1968." At his court-martial, Howe was charged with "disrespectful utterances toward public officials"; he was convicted in December, sentenced to two years hard labor, and dishonorably discharged.[47] A few months after Howe's court-martial, Cpl. John Morgan went AWOL from the marines and participated in a New York City peace rally where he announced his refusal to serve in Vietnam. He was arrested shortly afterward and court-martialed.[48]

Morgan had published poems in an antiwar poetry newsletter produced at the marine barracks in Camp Lejeune; that underground paper was already in operation by 1966. Shortly before Morgan's arrest in New York City, he wrote a poem, "The Second Coming," that appeared in a special 1966 joint issue of the New York alternative journals *The Gargoyle* and *Kauri* and later was reprinted in Walter Lowenfels's antiwar anthology *Where is Vietnam?* Like other GI Resistance poems, Morgan's articulates resistance through representations of mutilation that bear witness to the atrocities of the war while at the same time they subvert the relations of oppressor and oppressed that characterize the war. The poem is in three parts. Its first part envisions the apocalyptic birth of America as a monster. In the second part, Morgan portrays the collusion of church and state as interrelated arms of repression in the monstrous land that America has become:

> Dominus vobiscum.
> Dominus go frisk 'em.
> Shake 'em down, god, they might have
> something dangerous hidden in their
> ragged coats,
> these fire-headed youth scrambling under
> your shocked and wary eyes,
> these angry lambs whose only truth is now,
> and only sin is love.
> You fear their love,
>   and rightly
> for it is their very compassion
>   for the living

that will hang you on the cross of
your own making,
and leave your corpse rotting in
> tomorrow's air.
Sancti, sancti, sancti
the sheep of the streets
> with wolves in their bellies.[49]

Invoking the Latin of the Roman Catholic Church and Christian symbolism, Morgan represents church, state, police, and military as indissociable aspects of the same power. The "fire-headed youths," a Ginsbergesque image of the counterculture, are also associated with the Vietnamese. The opening lines evoke images of the military search of Vietnamese; American soldiers were taught that all Vietnamese were potential enemies, that they might be hiding weapons under their ragged clothes. Both the war resisters in America and the Vietnamese seek only peace but are harassed by the powers that seek to police their bodies. But the poem foretells a future when the "wolves" become food for the sheep, who rise up in the last lines to crucify the repressive powers on their own cross. Through images of impalement and devouring, the victims of oppression have become victors. In the third section, the poet prays for the deadly overthrow of the repressive powers:

I sing death to you, king.
My words like a common butcher's
knife slash through your ears.
. . . .
I call for the weeping sun and the
exploding air to find you cowering;
and carry you to the darkening fields
of your church,
for your own vultures to dip their
> savage beaks
> into the dust of your soul,
and shriek with untamed feeding in the
> roaring dawn,
until the calm of noon shall find flowers
> sprouting
again in
the canyons of America. (94–95)[50]

The imagery here is similar to that found in the Laxer poem, "For My Still Imprisoned Comrades," in which the "capitalist" body is disintegrated; here it is not decay but the mutilation caused by vultures eating the body that allows flowers to grow freely in the land.[51] Like the Laxer piece, and also like Connell's narrative, the poet seeks to place the power behind the war in the actual war, to experience "the exploding air" and "the darkening fields" that this power has created.

The first dissident soldiers to gain wide media attention and strong support from the antiwar movement were Pvt. Dennis Mora, Pvt. David Samas, and Pfc. James Johnson, also known as the Fort Hood 3. In June 1966 they refused to fight in Vietnam. Mora, of Puerto Rican descent, had been an active member of the W.E.B. DuBois Club in New York prior to being drafted. Samas was of Italian and Lithuanian descent.[52] Pfc. James Johnson, an African American, associated his people's struggles with those of the Vietnamese in a statement he read to the press:

> Now there is a direct relationship between the peace movement and the civil rights movement. The South Vietnamese are fighting for representation, like we ourselves. . . . Therefore the Negro in Vietnam is just helping to defeat what his black brother is fighting for in the United States. . . . Although he bears the brunt of the war, he will receive no benefits. . . . We gain absolutely nothing in Vietnam.[53]

The Fort Hood 3 case is often discussed in antiwar histories, primarily because at the time the civilian movement believed the case afforded opportunities for organizing resistance more broadly in the military. Several well-known civilian peace activists, such as A. J. Muste and David Dellinger, became involved in the case. Its failure to change the course of the war decisively, however, disillusioned pacifists and dampened their enthusiasm for mobilizing GIs. Although their history of antiwar activism offers some of the more extensive references to GI Resistance in the available antiwar histories, Nancy Zaroulis and Gerald Sullivan portray the Fort Hood 3 case's significance primarily in terms of its value to the Fifth Avenue Peace Parade Committee.[54] Zaroulis and Sullivan emphasize the "diligence of leaders in the Fifth Avenue Peace Parade Committee," a group led by Muste and Dellinger. The Fifth Avenue Committee, a coalition of pacifist groups such as Women Strike for Peace and SANE (Committee for a Sane Nuclear Policy) did help the Fort Hood 3 gain media attention, but the soldiers themselves had requested that the committee organize publicity.[55] Zaroulis and Sullivan's narrative displaces the soldiers' political activism and replaces it with a focus on the civilian pacifist organizing. The racial politics of the soldiers and Private Mora's association with the W.E.B. Du Bois Club prior to being drafted are elided in their account. Significantly, Muste and other older pacifist leaders had signed a statement on the eve of a 1965 peace march rejecting Communist groups, such as the Du Bois clubs, from participation because "the older peace people . . . wanted the world to know that they, at least, were not 'soft on Communism.'"

Younger pacifists refused to sign, and Muste later apologized for the statement, but pacifist antiwar historians, such as Zaroulis and Sullivan, reiterate this antiradicalism when they decontextualize the Fort Hood 3's activism.[56]

Antiwar historians often decontextualize early acts of dissidence among soldiers and portray them as isolated expressions when in fact, as Mora's political background and Johnson's black-power rhetoric suggest, there were important connections between military and civil forms of dissent. A culture of resistance within the military during the Vietnam War can be traced to the beginnings of large-scale U.S. troop involvement. A common notion among historians of Vietnam-era activism, however, has been that resistance within the military only became significant in the last years of the war. According to James R. Hayes, for example, "The formative years of the movement [1965–1967] were typified by a number of different individuals engaging in similar behaviors, i.e., protesting the war, but acting largely independent of each other with no real communication existing among them."[57] Yet *Veterans Stars and Stripes for Peace*, an antiwar paper distributed to GIs, claimed that thirty Vietnam veterans' groups for peace were already operating around the United States by late December of 1967.[58] Furthermore, in a 1967 history of antiwar movements, Joseph Conlin remarks, with some skepticism, that "[t]he government did not reveal the exact number of servicemen who quietly refused to obey orders that would ship them to Vietnam or officers who resigned over the war, although it maintained that such incidents of resistance were few."[59] Conlin also quotes several high-ranking officers who publicly expressed either profound reservations about policy in Vietnam or outright opposition to the war. It seems unlikely, then, given Conlin's attention to military dissent, that GIs could have "no real communications" about dissent among them.

These early signs of GI resistance suggest that dissent among troops was widespread, signifying crucial ruptures in the ideological consensus within the military at the earliest stages of the war. This contradicts most portrayals of the U.S. military as "normally" a cohesive totality, a representation that locates dissent as simply the late result of outside agitation or the lack of popular support. The unpopularity of both the war and the draft in American society, of course, had a great deal to do with the spread of troop dissent. Those who were drafted often came into the service with feelings of animosity toward military authority and the war. Many who enlisted quickly became disillusioned as they experienced the brutality of training and witnessed the seemingly senseless slaughter of Vietnamese. As Barbara Tischler writes, "For young people who had recently begun to question and challenge authority and to see this challenge as a legitimate exercise of popular political will, the reality of military life ran counter to their notions of the fundamental principles of American politics embodied in the Bill of Rights."[60]

The spread of dissent in U.S. society generally, countercultural attitudes against authority, and other civilian cultural forces certainly contributed to the spread of GI Resistance. It is important, however, to recognize how soldier dissent during the Vietnam War emerged from within the structure of the Vietnam-era U.S. military itself. Even before the civilian antiwar movement sought to organize GIs against the war, and while the civilian movement itself was relatively young, dissent can be discerned in the military. To isolate incidents such as the Fort Hood 3 case from the overall contexts of resistance among troops to the racism and class antagonisms fostered in the military and epitomized by the war seems to reaffirm a revisionist ideology of the war that, according to Harry W. Haines, identifies "television news coverage . . . civilian antiwar activists, or some other factor as the 'cause' of 'morale problems' among troops." Such an interpretation suppresses the political and historical implications of GI Resistance and its importance in oppositional struggle during Vietnam. As Haines further argues, "The hegemonic process whereby a discredited political elite re-establishes its ideological dominance has resulted in the positioning of the Vietnam veteran as a sign of consensus; discussions of antiwar soldiers go against the grain, because such discussions threaten the positioning of the Vietnam veteran as a sign—a witness—of ideological crisis."[61] A common means of rehabilitating the war has been to represent the troops as forming a single consensus on victory in Vietnam in the early years, only to be morally confused later by media attention to civilian activism. In conservative accounts, the war's loss is attributed to a kind of "infection" by a civilian counterculture of the military "corps." Political scientist Guenter Lewy, for example, represents dissent in the military as similar to an infection: "Growing permissiveness in American society and an increase in social pathology, such as a rising crime rate and widespread attitudes of disrespect toward authority and law enforcement, undoubtedly played an important role." As Gibson asserts, Lewy may be "correct in some ways," but his representation "sets up a 'pure' military that was subverted from without—drug pushers, radicals, and liberal news people all became a new set of foreign Others."[62] The military "corps" is also represented here as a healthy body until it was infected by pathological outsiders. The military's control of the media in the more recent war between the United States and Iraq can be read as an attempt to circumvent morale problems and enforce troop and public ideological consensus. Even in this war, however, signs of dissent can be discerned.[63]

To ignore acts or movements of resistance in the military is both to concede that the military constitutes a seamless whole and to ignore the contradictions in social formations that allow for critical intervention and new hegemonic forms.[64] Such historical blindness actually effaces resistance. By isolating and decontextualizing soldier resistance during the Vietnam War, leftist historians—like many in the civilian left during the period—continue to cast the soldier as either a brute "baby-killer" or a dupe of the system, erasing the dissident soldier as an agent within oppositional culture. In this way the rift between civilian radicalism and the GI Resistance has been perpetuated and sustained even in recent accounts of the Vietnam era.

The racial politics articulated by the Fort Hood 3 became explosive as the war dragged on, and as the percentages of minorities increased in the military with larger drafts, soldier resistance often erupted over race relations within the military. One of the first open acts of African American opposition to the war among troops occurred in July 1967 at Camp Pendleton, when two marines, William Harvey and George Daniels, organized a meeting that questioned black participation in a white man's war. When Harvey and Daniels sought to discuss this issue with the base commander, they were arrested and charged with insubordination and promoting disloyalty. They were subsequently sentenced to six and ten years.[65] The first soldier court-martialed for "fragging" was Pvt. Billy Dean Smith, an African American soldier who enlisted from Watts. Smith was tried for killing two white officers in 1967 after enduring months of harassment for having a "bad attitude." Typically, white officers read any black soldier's expression of black cultural nationalism as a "bad attitude." Numerous disciplinary actions were taken against African American soldiers for growing naturals, wearing Malcolm X buttons, displaying posters of Black Power leaders, or reading Black Power literature. Smith's trial for murder later became a rallying point in the GI Resistance, and his case was often contrasted in the GI press with the case of Lt. William Calley. The military's prosecution of Smith seemed to epitomize its inherent racism. When Smith was tried in 1972 and acquitted of murder but guilty of assault, he wrote an article, reprinted in the *Lewis McChord Free Press*, that argued the Vietnam War "was unjust and racially motivated." His article ended with a poem he wrote in prison, "Mr. Yes Sir," that expresses the same subversive oppositions evident in other poems from the GI Resistance:

Hey! Brothers, listen to what I have to say,
You say you want equal opportunity each and every day.
Well, how're you going to get this if you're not willing to fight
And stand up for what you believe in because you know it's right. . . .
He drafts you into the army, where you are strong and brave,

But if you happen to be Black, you wind up being a slave.
He sends you cross the waters to fight the Viet Cong,
But if you think on who caused the trouble, you'll find out that he's
the one.[66]

This poem advocates disrupting the chain of command, turning the guns on the war managers, just as does the Laxer poem quoted earlier. By exploiting the semiotics of African American cultural traditions in its references to the Middle Passage, the poem underscores the historical links between U.S. intervention in Vietnam and racism in America.

Smith's violent revolt against the military was repeated numerous times throughout the war. In 1969 the Pentagon confirmed 96 fragging incidents; by 1970 there were 209 confirmed incidents, and by 1971 the number went to 215. The Pentagon reported that 80 percent of fragging attacks targeted officers and noncommissioned officers; soldiers in the lower ranks rarely fragged each other. As James William Gibson points out, however, the number of incidents confirmed by the Pentagon is probably much lower than the reality. Gibson quotes one source who reasoned from Marine Criminal Investigating statistics that in 1969 at least 500 fragging incidents occurred.[67]

During the Vietnam War, soldiers who organized against the war or whose dissent was politically motivated risked considerable punishment, not only through court-martial but also through unofficially sanctioned forms of violence inflicted by officers and fellow soldiers. To put down a stockade rebellion at Fort Campbell, Kentucky, in 1968, for example, commanders ordered military police to shoot to kill.[68] Often, soldiers who resisted or who attempted to organize could be assigned especially hazardous duty.[69] Officers might restrict activist-soldiers to base or their quarters whenever an antiwar demonstration occurred in the area. To break up GI groups, members could be transferred to different bases or shipped overseas.[70] To isolate and destabilize a particularly troublesome soldier, the military might transfer him several times in a period of months, thereby making it almost impossible for him to form any relationships with fellow soldiers. Risking extreme punishment, injury, and even death, GIs who resisted the war faced challenges the civilian left rarely faced.[71] Unlike the civilian antiwar movement, the GI Resistance had little or no precedent of military antiwar activism from which to draw inspiration or to use as a guide in organizing.

The GI movements' relations with civilians were generally tenuous at best. Student activists, feminists, and pacifists tended to stereotype all soldiers as "the enemy" or as witless weapons of the state. The soldier's very body signified conformity, discipline, and violence:

rigid, straight postures, short hair (as opposed to the countercultural preference for long, "natural" hair signifying freedom), uniforms emblazoned with platoon patches showing guns, daggers, or thunderbolts. Young civilian antiwar activists, usually about the same age as soldiers, styled their bodies to signify their oppositionality (for example, long hair, slouching, pierced ears) and their rejection of conformity. When soldiers, whose bodies had been inscribed with the signs of militarism, began to reject the war and militarism, to oppose the cultural discourses that in some sense actually determined their identities as soldiers, the counterculture and the antiwar civilian left were more often than not confused and suspicious.

The effect of styling the body to signify opposition exemplifies a further difference between civilian and GI resistance. While civilians might have to endure cultural rejection for their oppositional appearance, the stakes for soldiers were often high. The expression of dissent through the soldier's bodily appearance could act as a catalyst for broader troop dissent; consequently, any soldier who attempted this risked imprisonment and punishment. According to David Cortright and Max Watts, battles between GIs and officers over hair length during the Vietnam War often became the seed for larger, broader revolts, as in the case of the "Berlin Brothers." In 1974, eight soldiers stationed in Berlin refused repeated orders to cut their hair. As military legal action was taken and the case proceeded, the soldiers became militant in their demands for a more humane military and in their rejection of military authority. Over twelve hundred soldiers in the Berlin area signed petitions in support of the "Brothers." The soldiers' defiance soon spread until a campaign against racism in the military took hold, leading to a sit-down by twenty-two soldiers of the 94th Artillery. The arrival of television crews and increased media attention prompted a military coverup and the eventual trial of the "Brothers," who received several months of jail in 1975.[72]

Civilian groups and GI Resistance groups made few attempts to form coalitions, and those that were created tended to be short-lived. After 1968, these alliances usually involved civilian antiwar movement and various radical group organizers either offering assistance and support to GI activists or actually infiltrating the military to organize from within.[73] The GI coffeehouses were an important means of supplying the GI movement with advice and support. Located off-base and run by civilians—often organizers for groups such as the Sociialist Workers Party (SWP) or the Young Socialist Alliance (YSA), as well as the antiwar movement—the coffeehouses served as places where dissident GIs could talk with civilians in the left, obtain personal and legal advice, and associate with other soldiers without military harassment. Cortright credits the coffeehouses with offering the first attempts to establish coherence and direction to GI dissidence.[74] The attempts of the coffeehouse movement to break down barriers between the primarily middle-class civilian activists and the GIs were nevertheless limited. Civilians could always go home, whereas GIs had to return to base or face imprisonment.

In many ways, despite its problematic relations with the civilian left, the GI Resistance threatened the machinery of the military and the state more than any other oppositional movement in the period. GIs understood that machine, had access to its workings, and knew how to sabotage it. Some have even argued that by 1970 the internal damage in the military caused by troop dissent may have been the determining factor that convinced the Pentagon to withdraw from Vietnam. Pete Rode, for example, a Vietnam veteran and research and policy director for the Urban Coalition, claimed in a 1991 editorial that "[b]y 1971, military officials were asking for a speedup of troop withdrawal [from Vietnam] to help cure the Army's internal problems."[75] Harry W. Haines writes that because of dissension, desertion, sabotage, fraggings, and other acts of insubordination, "[b]y 1970 American political and military leaders could no longer depend on U.S. troops to perform their mission in Vietnam."[76] The military's anxiety over the GI Resistance and dissent among the troops can be detected in the numerous military-sponsored studies of troop dissent and morale that appeared after 1969. Rinaldi quotes Col. Robert D. Heinl, who stated in a 1971 *Armed Forces Journal* article that "[s]edition, coupled with disaffection within the ranks, and externally fomented with an audacity and intensity previously inconceivable, *infests* the Armed Services." Rinaldi concludes, "Covered up whenever possible and frequently denied by the military brass, this upheaval was nevertheless a significant factor in the termination of the ground war."[77]

Collective resistance became more common and more effectively organized after 1967. Early in that year veteran Jeff Sharlet established *Vietnam GI*, the first underground paper that attempted to organize GIs against the war. This newspaper introduced many of the structural features characteristic of the later underground press that blossomed around the GI Resistance. It regularly ran letters from GIs and interviews with a GI either recently returned from the war or active in a recent protest against the war or the military. The paper was staffed by veterans who distributed it on bases around the country, thus making the paper the first effort to organize a nationwide resistance in the military.[78] Later in 1967, near Berkeley, Andy Stapp founded the first national organization for GI Resistance, the American Servicemen's Union. Stapp's paper, *The Bond: Voice of the American Service-men's Union*, published in Berkeley by a coalition of active-duty soldiers, veterans, and civilians until 1968 and then afterward in New York City, was nationally and internationally distributed; directed specifically to GIs, it claimed a circulation of more than one hundred thousand by 1971.[79]

After the Tet offensive of 1968, which demoralized the military, more and more soldiers refused service, deserted, went AWOL, organized resistance groups, disseminated underground newspapers on and around military bases, and began "fragging" officers and sabotaging supplies.[80] As collective forms of dissent expanded among GIs, national organizing networks for GI resistance emerged, although these tended to be decentralized and segmented.[81] The rise of collective dissent in the military coincided with dramatic increases in the number of drafts and active duty personnel, which reached a peak in 1968. At the same time, Black Liberation and other racial liberation movements had erupted in American culture.[82] After Tet, stockade rebellions arising over racial strife either among military prisoners or between prisoners and the military police became a growing concern for the U.S. military. Often resistance erupted over the assignment of riot-control duty to minority GIs, particularly in the summer of 1968 and throughout 1969.[83]

As the war lingered and casualties mounted, the GI Resistance expanded as a community and became a visible force on the general antiwar scene. Most histories that consider this movement at all often focus on this later period, which included such events as the Winter Soldiers hearings of 1971.[84] An unofficial war crimes hearing held by veterans, not active-duty GIs, at a Detroit Howard Johnson's, this action marked a culmination of many years of movement organization rather than the first significant appearance of soldier/veteran antiwar activism. Veterans also staged dramatic demonstrations, such as the Dewey Canyon III event, which drew thousands of veterans and focused the nation's attention not only on the atrocity of the war but also on the plight of the soldier as victim of class oppression. Dubbed "Operation Dewey Canyon III, a limited incursion into the country of Congress," the event entailed a week-long rally, camp, and lobbying of Congress by Vietnam Veterans Against the War (VVAW) from April 16 to April 23, 1971, to call attention to war crimes. The operation's name comes from Dewey Canyon I and II, illegal military operations in Laos that characterized for these veterans the criminality of the war. John Kerry's statement before the Senate Foreign Relations Committee during Dewey Canyon III demonstrates the rhetoric of the GI movement's emerging focus on the rights of soldiers:

Where is the leadership? We are here to ask where are McNamara, Rostow, Bundy, Johnson, and so many others? Where are they now that we, the men whom they sent off to war, have returned?. . . . [T]his Administration has done us the ultimate dishonor. They have attempted to disown us and the sacrifices we made for this country. In their blindness and fear they have tried to deny that we are veterans or that we served in Nam. We do not need their testimony. Our own scars and stumps of limbs are witness enough for others and for ourselves.[85]

Kerry's statement reflects a shift in perspective from antiwar protest to a focus on the civil rights of veterans of a war that no one in 1971 really wanted to take responsibility for. Evident in this statement is a representation of the soldier as a distinct class within American society deserving of equal rights; the rhetoric of veterans' rights began to emulate that of civil rights. Also significant is Kerry's invocation of the soldier's mutilated body as symbolic of his authority to speak about the war. The invocation of the soldier's authority based on a semiotics of his mutilated (masculine) body is a central rhetorical trope of Vietnam veterans' literature.

Such tropes of mutilation in GI Resistance literature resist the master narratives of the war. The mutilated body in Kerry's statement legitimizes his authority as a witness to the atrocities the U.S. military attempted to repress in its highly sanitized and jargonized accounts of the war, accounts that always deemphasized the "incontestable reality" of the human body. At official news briefings, the military portrayed American efforts as victories for the Vietnamese people. Using such terms as "antipersonnel device" to describe a grenade used to blow a human body into a bloodied mass of indistinguishable parts, or "pacifying" a village to describe the mass slaughter of Vietnamese through napalm and heavy bombardment, the military constructed a narrative of the war in which the human body was absent, thus dehumanizing its brutal effects. Dissident soldiers who came forward to testify to U.S. atrocities sought to foreground the bodies that the military sought to erase through discourse. Soldier-poets who rejected the war and its ideology incorporated in their poetry the physiological loss that the war cost the Vietnamese and U.S. soldiers and insisted on the mutilated body as paradigmatic of the Vietnam experience. Their obsessive display of wounds, dismemberment, and disfiguration expresses a radical critique of the militarism that produces such transgressions of the flesh. In the later years of the war, soldiers connected to the movement began publishing anthologies and individual volumes of poetry that reiterated the GI Resistance political discourse of the mutilated body. By reading this poetry and its representations of the human body, we can trace the disincorporations articulated by soldier poets of the Vietnam War.

Standard Operating Procedures:
Reading/Writing Mutilation

Graphic images of mutilation appear in most GI poems of the Vietnam era, but they are particularly significant in the anthology *Winning Hearts and Minds*, the first collection of dissident poems in U.S. history produced by soldiers during wartime.[86] According to W. D. Ehrhart, *Winning Hearts and Minds* is "a classic: the seminal anthology against which all future Vietnam war poetry would be judged." Privately funded, edited in a basement kitchen by three veterans active in the VVAW, the anthology appeared in 1972 as a culmination of the antiwar activism centered around the Winter Soldier hearings.[87] *Winning Hearts and Minds*, like other antiwar anthologies, was constructed as an act of resistance.[88] Its editors provide a detailed list of "ways this book of poetry can be properly utilized." The suggestions include reading the poems aloud at VFW meetings; distributing copies in the local community; acting out scenes from the poems in street theater; using the poems in fund-raising; putting the poems to music.

> Read it aloud
> Recopy it
> Dramatize it
> Give it as a gift
> And sing it!
> Poetry is a human gift.
>
> Use it.[89]

The anthology's editors, Jan Barry, Basil Paquet, and Larry Rottmann, were connected to GI antiwar activities. Barry was a founding member of VVAW, and Rottmann had been an editor of the VVAW newspaper *1st Casualty*. Initially, the anthology had been conceived as a VVAW project.[90] By 1972, VVAW had become the most prominent GI Resistance group through such highly publicized actions as the Winter Soldier hearings and other public hearings on the war. The VVAW consistently emphasized that the My Lai massacre was not an aberration in military conduct, but rather represented standard operating procedure. The emphasis in *Winning Hearts and Minds* on the atrocities of the war reiterated the VVAW line.

Mutilation infects *Winning Hearts and Minds* at almost every level. Its title not only reproduces the euphemism used by the Johnson administration to legitimate forced relocation of the Vietnamese—the uprooting of whole villages itself metonymic of the disfiguring of the nation—but it is also an image that, if read literally, evokes dismemberment, the separation of heart and mind, even as it emphasizes the reassembling, the "winning" of heart and mind. In a war where

brains and cardiomuscular organs were regularly blown apart by antipersonnel devices, the mutilation implicit in this title signifies the duplicity of U.S. policies in Vietnam, the masking of acts of violence by
moralistic euphemisms. In military jargon, "winning hearts and
minds" was often abbreviated as "WHAM," thus turning its intended
compassionate sentiment into an acronym that onomatopoeically represented the sound of the explosions that literally enacted U.S. policy.
The name of the veterans' group that published this book, 1st Casualty Press, further signifies mutilation, calling to mind an image of the
wounded, the Vietnam veteran as a casualty of an immoral war. It
also, of course, recalls Aeschylus's dictum that the first casualty in
war is truth, and thus evokes the problematic status of truth in any
representation of war, even in the eyewitness realism of this collection's poetry.

The first poem in *Winning Hearts and Minds* is actually an army
marching cadence, and it emblematizes the brutality of military training:

> I Wanna Go to Viet-Nam
> I Wanna Kill a Viet-Cong
> With A Knife Or With A Gun
> Either Way Will Be Good Fun
>
> Stomp 'Em, Beat 'Em, Kick 'Em In The Ass
> Hide Their Bodies In The Grass (WHAM, 1)

As a marching cadence that soldiers were forced to recite in unison
during training, these lines not only signify the brutality of the war,
but they also illustrate how the soldier was forced to express himself
as a brutal killer, a mutilator of human bodies. U.S. military culture is
rife with such violent verses. Soldiers in training are often taught to
chant lines that replicate the rhythms of whatever manual exercise is
being performed, which thus reinforces the psycho-physical relations
between their bodies' performance and the will to mutilate the bodies
of others. Common chants during the Vietnam War included, "VC,
VC kill, kill, kill. Gotta kill, gotta kill, gotta kill, cause it's fun, cause
it's fun"; or: "Marines are killers./We kill. We kill." Another common
march cadence was:

> I want to go to Vietnam
> Just to kill ol' Charlie Cong
> Am I right or wrong?
> Am I goin' strong?[91]

The third line in the cadence is a unique recognition of the sense of
moral ambivalence felt in American society about the war. But here
the question of right and wrong is destabilized by the question of

physical strength, stamina, and endurance. These chants exemplify how Vietnam-era military training indoctrinated the soldier to comprehend himself as a body that kills and mutilates other bodies; the soldier's identity becomes forcibly fused with the act of killing. On the same page just above the cadence quoted in *Winning Hearts and Minds* is a photograph of a sign for a Ranger base; it reads, "[I]f you kill for pleasure you're a sadist . . . if you kill for money you're a mercenary . . . if you kill for both you're a RANGER!!" By ironically opening their anthology with these illustrations of the brutality of military culture, the editors also signify that mutilation was central to their experience of the war and their training as soldiers. While the cadence proclaims that soldiers hide their victims' bodies, however, the anthology defies such standard operating procedures by making the bodies visible and exposing the "incontestable reality" of the war.

The military cultural discourse of these cadences represents a subject (the U.S. soldier) that radically transgresses the boundaries of normative behavior mapped out in the civil state. Paradoxically, however, the soldier-subject is at the same time the apparatus for maintaining and defending the boundaries, hegemony, and civil order of that state. More than violating the oxymoronic "rules of war" that nations have agreed to since the Geneva Convention, the acts represented in these epigraphs also signal a fundamental logical instability, which Elaine Scarry has shown to be characteristic of discourses of war. Insofar as the body of an individual manifests the state through various signs (such as gestures, posture, habits of dress), the individual's body can be said to be political. In refashioning the body's posture, gesture, or habits of dress to produce acts of murder, injury, and violence—acts that normally place a civil subject outside the laws of the state—the military "unmakes" the state as manifested in the body. Thus, even though an individual, a subject of the nation-state, enters the military to protect his or her country, this subject's body becomes "de-civilized" through military training; the subject's relation to the civil state becomes radically altered because the killing or injuring of another's body is outside the sanctioned behaviors of civilization. The soldier unlearns sanctions concerning how another person can be touched, how the fleshly boundaries of another person's body must not be violently penetrated.[92] The epigraphs of *Winning Hearts and Minds* signify how, in the Vietnam War, the normative boundaries of a civil subject's body had been so totally transgressed that those who supposedly were fighting for their country were, in fact, unmaking it. The epigraphs describe the mutilation that was standard in the Vietnam War, but they also signal a mutilation of the *civitas*, a dismemberment of the body politic.

Of the more than one hundred poems in this anthology, most

contain explicitly graphic images of mutilation. The following lines by DeWitt Clinton typify this:

> Dawn, perimeter intruders
> bleeding, aging,
> twenty-odd guerrillas
> stretched over barbed concertina
> the rat cleaned bones
> of splattered, fractured
> revolutionists.
> This morning's
> gold and orange and red
> glowed passively.
>
> Remembering . . . cool May showers.
>
> Smells of burnt flesh
> blood and powder
> penetrated
> into the minds
> and tears
> of those that were left.
> Black tubed artillery
> hurling red metal and smoke,
> shrapnel screeching
> in its arc of death,
> detonated for flesh ripping
> of Oriental skin.
>
> WHAT PANIC IN A MAN'S SOUL! (WHAM, 30–31)

These lines appear in the middle of the five-part poem "Spirit of the Bayonet Fighter," which traces the moral desolation of a soldier, from training, through his combat experiences, to his life back home. The vivid depiction of the physical horrors of war undercuts any abstract glories that cultures might attach to war. The "incontestable reality" of the Vietnamese bodies picked clean by rats renders their revolutionary cause irrelevant. Fragmentation devices indiscriminately rip the bodies of any Vietnamese regardless of political allegiance. The destruction of human flesh becomes so prevalent that it permeates the senses: thought and emotion become tainted with it. The one moment's recollection of "the world"—what GIs euphemistically called home, America, any place far from the horrors of war—intrudes for a brief phrase, out of joint and vacuous in the midst of carnage. The "re-membering" it attempts to enact is subverted by the break in the middle of the line, a gaping wound in the utterance. The line then gives way to the succeeding catalog of ghastly images and is rendered hopelessly sentimental in a world devoid of sense. As the capitalized line exclaims, the atavistic experience of combat seizes not only the body but the soldier's soul. Later in the poem, the soldier tries to adjust to attending classes even as the morning rush of students in hallways brings to mind the "acrid smell of contact,/diseased conflict,/ hot ripping metal." So tainted with the experience of witnessing war's massive destruction of human bodies, the soldier must relive his trauma when he is surrounded by bodies in the school hallways. The mutilated body has become an ever-present trope in his mind. It becomes figuratively "hard to dispose of," as Scarry has written; once having witnessed the atrocity of war, the soldier can never again see human bodies as normal. By poem's end the speaker asks for a blues song to honor this soldier's death; the speaker is unclear as to whether death resulted from a suicide, a common fate of traumatized Vietnam veterans, or whether the death referred to is symbolic of the death of the soldier's soul. Clinton's poem traces a narrative of degeneration, destruction, and moral decay prevalent in GI Resistance poetry. Throughout the poem any attempt to find a peaceful center, a stable moment of phenomenological coherence, is undercut by the intrusion of mutilation. The soldier, the icon of masculine potency, physical prowess, and heroism in American culture, is represented as disfigured, devastated, and pathological because he has encountered the reality behind the myth of American power and must carry that burden in his body.

The unrelenting ghastliness of many of the poems in this collection must be understood within the context of the politics of witnessing that GI Resistance promoted. Lt. William Crandell's "Opening Statement" at the 1971 Winter Soldier hearings repeatedly emphasizes that in testifying the soldiers seek to atone for their own complicity in the crimes of the war and to provide evidence of those crimes:

> We went to preserve the peace and our testimony will show that we have set all of Indochina aflame. We went to defend the Vietnamese people and our testimony will show that we are committing genocide against them. . . . We intend to tell who it was that gave us those orders; that created that policy; that set that standard of war bordering on full and final genocide. . . . We are ready to let the testimony say it all.[93]

The central role of testimony in the GI Resistance may also stem from patterns of social bonding among soldiers who have experienced combat. Combat soldiers tended to discuss avidly the details of their experiences in the field, "not so much for their intrinsic interest but, more importantly, to specify tactical procedures that may save lives in future encounters with the enemy."[94] The emphasis on testimony in the GI Resistance capitalized on the soldier's need to witness, and at the same time, gave his narrative ethically pragmatic meaning in the context of saving the country.

Studies have also shown that victims of traumatic experiences often exhibit a need to tell their story, and that, by bearing witness, trauma victims not only work through their experiences but feel a sense of survival. Kali Tal has written, "One of the strongest themes in the literature of trauma is the urge to bear witness, to carry the tale of horror back to the halls of normalcy and to testify to the truth of the experience."[95] Psychiatrist Robert Jay Lifton's research with Vietnam veterans demonstrates that antiwar veterans felt an acute need to tell their story so as to expose the meaninglessness and immorality of the war. According to Lifton, this need is bound up with a sense of mission and a sense of survival.[96] As Larry Rottmann, a GI poet and one of the editors of *Winning Hearts and Minds*, said in the Winter Soldier hearings:

> There is a question in many people's minds here. They say, "Well, why do you talk now?. . . ." I'm here, speaking personally, because I can't *not* be here. I'm here because, like, I have nightmares about things that happened to me and my friends. I'm here because my conscience will not let me forget what I want to forget.
>
> . . . .[A]fter a while, it gets to the point where you have to talk to somebody, and when I tried to talk to somebody, even my parents, they didn't want to hear it. They didn't want to know. And that made me realize that no matter how painful it was for me, I had to tell them. I mean, they had to know. The fact that they didn't want to know, told me they had to know.[97]

Rottmann's insistence that people know what he has witnessed, that the citizenry needs his testimony in order to understand the war, and that, further, such testimony is a moral and political responsibility, epitomizes the poetic style of the work in *Winning Hearts and Minds* and other GI Resistance poems. For GI poets, the war is never metaphor; mutilation is paradigmatic of the war experience, but the politics of the movement demands that its literature describe the witnessed details of that experience. In fact, a common motto in the GI Resistance press was to "tell it like it is."[98]

The sparse, often strangely matter-of-fact tones of most poems in *Winning Hearts and Minds* register the profound disillusionment and confusion soldiers felt toward their role in the war. Poems are often short declarative statements, adopting the speech patterns of the "grunt" for whom atrocity has become a commonplace. Despite the moral urgency of the anthology's antiwar agenda, its poems are rarely sentimental or histrionic. Larry Rottmann's "S.O.P." is typical:

To build a "gook stretcher," all you need is:
Two helicopters
Two long, strong ropes,
And one elastic gook. (WHAM, 53)

This piece, quoted in its entirety, reads like instructions from a drill instructor; the title emphasizes how such atrocity and racism are common in the U.S. military's prosecution of the war. "S.O.P." is the acronym for "standard operating procedure." Derived from official military language, the phrase and the acronym came to designate, in GI subcultural discourse, events or actions that, despite their absurdity or depravity, were nonetheless routine in the military. This use of the acronym satirizes military discourse for GIs, particularly those in the Resistance. Written in the voice of a soldier describing "standard operating procedure" to another soldier, this brief poem's flat, declarative tone ironically underscores the brutality it describes. The speaking soldier's use of the racist term "gook stretcher" perverts the concept of a stretcher, an object made to give comfort to the hurt body. Rottmann signals his own responsibility in the atrocity by not embellishing the poem, by not giving himself an out. As many GIs insisted throughout testimonies to war crimes in Vietnam, they all participated in atrocities.

Stan Platke's "Gut Catcher" is similarly matter-of-fact about the gore that has become an everyday experience in Vietnam. The poem opens by asking, "Have you ever seen/A gut catcher?"

There is no patent on them
They're makeshift
Depending upon the time
And place

I've seen ponchos used
And a pack
And a canteen cover
Or your hands

You catch the guts of your buddy
As they spill out of his body
And try to stuff them back in
But they keep sliding out

For a face blown in
For an eye blown out
For an arm blown off
For a body blown open
       . . . A gut catcher. (WHAM, 21)

Like the Rottmann poem, the tone of this piece is declarative and mimics military jargon in its description of makeshift equipment—a "gut catcher" for which "there is no patent." Other than the gruesome term that serves as the title, the poem is free of metaphorical language. The title, which at first seems to be jargon for military equipment, finally is revealed as a metaphor for a soldier's hands. The uselessness of the "gut catcher" is that it fails to stop death, fails to mend the body that has been sliced open. Throughout the war, GIs were forced to work with inadequate equipment, and much soldier literature focuses on how such equipment often endangered troops in battle.[99] The futility of using hands to stop human bodies from falling apart epitomizes the soldier's experience. This representation of mutilation delegitimates the war through its exposure of the brutal senselessness that produced such violence; the poem implies that such violence only signifies the moral emptiness of U.S. involvement in Vietnam.

The pervasiveness of mutilation in the soldier's life in Vietnam, its overwhelming and undeniable presence coupled with its negation of corporeal integrity, comes to frame subjectivity in many of the poems in this anthology. A poem by John Stulett, written only months before he was killed in action in 1971, epitomizes this. Entitled "Dick Nixon, I am Lt. John Stulett, U.S. Army, 1st Cav. Div.," the poem represents mutilation as normative in the Vietnam War.

> A soldier dies in the puddle as I write this line, a hiding child convulses
> as you read it. The Killing is our wound-up clock!! tick, tick tick,
> trickling away blood, beautiful arms, my drunk buddies and
>   beautiful slant eyes. (WHAM, 60)

In this poem, the soldier-speaker's experience is of a constant proliferation of body parts generated by the war's "crazed expenditure."[100] As Stulett states early in the poem, "Hands and eyeballs still fly off in all directions forever/from the unmercy of Viet Nam" (WHAM, 60). The Vietnam envisioned by the poem is an expanding vortex of body parts and mutilation. Repeatedly, the poet asks Richard Nixon, "What does it mean?"—until finally the "it," the death, mutilation, and moral depravity of the war, means nothing more than its own processes, its own display as spectacle; the dis-articulation and dismemberment of this spectacle defies meaning. John Stulett as a subject exists only as an I/eye, recording images of death and mutilation: "A soldier dies in the puddle as I write this line, a hiding child convulses/as you read it" (WHAM, 60). The assonance in these lines ("dies. . .I. . .write. . .line. . .hiding. . .child") underscores the wailing of humans caught in the violence of the war, the inchoate mourning and grief that defies language. Wherever Stulett turns his gaze he encounters mutilation: "men who blow out eyes by being slow! /. . . and a wrinkled man scratches his back up and down on a shrivelled hut—/he doesn't have any arms left" (WHAM, 61). The dying soldier, the hiding child, the armless man as objects define the boundaries of the I/eye who writes as subject. In the last line the soldier answers his own repeated question: "What does it mean?/I'm afraid to know" (WHAM, 61). Indeed "meaning" has become as "fragged" as the multiple images of body mutilation and fragments of half-articulated subjectivity in the poem; the lived experience of the soldier is finally a fear of knowledge, a fear of the inevitably horrible understanding that must fuse together the fragments of body parts and the death that the war produces. Although the poet addresses his "commander-in-chief" by announcing his name and rank, the official identity of a soldier, this identity finally can only be negotiated in the fragments of the body the poem catalogs. No images of the poet's body appear in the poem; it is as if the subject lacked any sense of his body in the overwhelming phenomenal experience of witnessing mutilation. Lacking coherence, the body can no longer function as the potent sign of masculine soldiery offered by dominant ideology; it becomes, instead, a contradictory, fractured, dis-membered sign revealing the incoherence of this ideology itself.

Just as the geography of Vietnam was a deterritorialized zone of incoherent signs for American soldiers, the human body existed in the war as a "fragged" object—the *corps sans organes*. Herman Rapaport appropriates this term from Gilles Deleuze and Felix Guattari's philosophy to describe the Viet Cong as analogous to a "schizoanalyst" of antipsychiatry. The United States insists on totalities, a seamless ideological structure, whereas the Vietnamese guerillas seemed able to exploit fragmentation to psychologically undermine the myth of U.S. military totality:

> [T]he "whole" body, that sexual and libidinized corps, is perceived by the third world as inherently castrated, and . . . for this reason it was so easy to terrify troops in the field by simply bringing up again a forgotten trauma, the lack of a phallus, the body as partial object. Enter the guerilla as schizoanalyst. Indeed, the "unity" which the Military Corps maintained was only another register of the rhizome, split down the middle by an all-or-nothing ideology, de-totalized and fragmented. The Vietnamese's ability to see the contradiction was to sight Vietnam, the Thousand Plateaus, within the metaphysical geo-psychography of the West, to have entered our paradigms only to overcode them with theirs, to liberate from within our *machine de guerre*, in true antipsychiatric fashion, the *corps sans organes*.[101]

The return of the repressed, the primal fear of castration, resonates throughout representations of mutilation in this anthology. According to Rapaport, "When 'Charlie' castrated the corpses of its enemy, it wasn't anything else but a sign pointing to the fact that dismemberment means a loss of sexuality, a ruining of Western man's acceptability as a man in the eyes of his peers."[102]

The literal castration depicted in Basil T. Paquet's "Basket Case" becomes paradigmatic of the vet's status in American culture, a culture that fetishizes the unity of its military "corps." A fourteen-line poem, "Basket Case" undermines the pastoral conventions of sonnet form with its brutal rendering of mutilated sexuality.

> I waited eighteen years to become a man.
> My first woman was a whore off Tu Do street,
> But I wish I never felt the first wild
> Gliding lust, because the rage and thrust
> Of a mine caught me hip high.
> I felt the rip at the walls of my thighs,
> A thousand metal scythes cut me open,
> My little fish shot twenty yards
> Into a swamp canal.
> I fathered only this—the genderless bitterness
> Of two stumps, and an unwanted pity
> That births the faces of all
> Who will see me till I die deliriously
> From the spreading sepsis that was once my balls.
>   (WHAM, 20)

The images of failed fertility (the "little fish" wasted in a "swamp canal," fathering only abstract sensations of bitterness and pity, the disease that replaces the scrotum) and the association of sex and violence in the image of the mine signaled by the internal rhyme (lust/thrust, thighs/scythes) convey the complicated relation to sexuality that the speaker experiences. In a society where the mutilated male cannot be sexual because mutilation is metonymic of a lack of phallic coherence, a sexual subject-position for the poem's speaker both marginalizes and transgresses the norm. He is at once male, by virtue of being a soldier, and not-male, by having lost the "equipment" that defines male-ness. As the old boot camp chant went: "This is my rifle, this [penis] is my gun, one is for fighting, one is for fun." The failure the soldier expresses in this poem is not only sexual but military, especially since sexual prowess/fertility/potency and military prowess are made almost indistinguishable in the training of Vietnam era soldiers.

As R. Wayne Eisenhart has noted, "The sexuality of the men [in basic training] was closely tied to the success or failure of the unit. Masculinity was affirmed through completion of the military function."[103] The personal narratives of Vietnam-era GIs are filled with accounts of the conflation of sexuality and military success. Commonly, drill instructors challenge the sexuality of recruits who cannot perform up to unit standards by calling them "faggots" and "girls." Eisenhart, himself a veteran of the war, recounts his own experiences in basic training, emphasizing that drill instructors only stopped challenging recruits' sexuality after they exhibited intensely violent aggressive outbursts.[104] The relationship between sexual identity and military prowess, sexuality and violence, as forged in the metaphorical link between phallus and rifle, is frighteningly illustrated by Eisenhart:

> While in basic training we were issued M-14 rifles. The breech of the weapon is closed by a bolt which is continually pushed forward by a large spring with considerable force. One night three men who had been censured for ineffectiveness in their assigned tasks were called forward in front of the assembled platoon, ordered to insert their penises into the breeches of their weapons, close the bolt, and run the length of the squad bay singing the Marine Corps Hymn.[105]

The punishment for "ineffectiveness" is meted out at the point in the male body most identified with military prowess and gendered subjectivity, the penis. This quasi-castration, and the simultaneous grotesque enlargement of the penis, brutally enacts the link between weaponry and phallus, sexuality and violence.

Indeed, violence becomes an integral aspect of the formation of subjectivity in the soldier. In a study of soldiers in the German Freikorps of the early twentieth century, Klaus Theweleit has argued that violence and pain serve to define the boundaries of the soldier's body and to enable him to construct an armor which will eventually constitute his sense of an ego:

> Since the "ego" of [soldier males] cannot form from the inside out, through libidinal cathexis of the body's periphery and identification, they must acquire an enveloping "ego" from the outside. My suspicion is that cathexis occurs as a result of coercion; it is forced upon them by the pain they experience in the onslaught of external agencies. The punishments of parents, teachers, masters, the punishment hierarchies of young boys and the military, remind them constantly of the existence of their periphery (showing them their boundaries), until they "grow" a functioning and controlling body armor, and a body capable of seamless fusion into larger formations with armorlike peripheries. If my assumptions are correct, the armor of these men may be seen as constituting their ego.[106]

The military training soldiers received during Vietnam literally inscribed the soldier-ego on the soldier's body through psychologically traumatic forms of corporal punishment. Those who effectively formed an "armor-ego" could become the "killing machines" that drill instructors demanded; they could envision themselves as impenetrable bodies, indestructible and totalistic. The soldier then knows himself, the boundaries of his ego, the condition of his subjectivity, by experiencing physical pain and containing it. As Theweleit puts it, "I feel pain, therefore I am."[107] Consequently, when GIs experienced forms of combat in Vietnam that bore little relationship to the logic of military training but followed instead the syncretic principles of guerilla warfare waged on the Vietnamese's own geographical and psychological terrain, and that favored the deterritorialized and the disfigured, the result was a radical disturbance in the soldier's subjectivity. By expressing this trauma, GI Resistance poetry also seeks to unmake the military training that has enforced the boundaries of subjectivity around the extremes of pain. The many appearances of castration images in this poetry signify politically insofar as they resist the military's archetype of the soldier-male as an impenetrable masculine totality for whom the phallus is the principal weapon.

The Paquet poem, like other representations of castration in Vietnam-era soldier literature, resonates powerfully with the military discourses inscribed on the soldier's body that make loss of the phallus equivalent to military failure and vice versa. The abject fear that the Vietnamese guerillas provoked in American soldiers by castrating corpses not only foregrounds the radically deterritorialized nature of combat in Vietnam but also signifies failure of the unit, the military, and, ultimately, the country. While such symbolism may operate to relegitimize masculinity—to blame the loss of the war, for example, on a lack of "balls" on the part of either the soldiers or the country— more often in GI Resistance poetry castration delegitimizes the military.[108] The Paquet poem, for example, achieves its impact in its representation of the soldier's body as the obverse of dominant cultural representations of the soldier. The macho braggadocio in the opening lines crumbles into the impotence of the final lines. The male body becomes monstrous, outside the symbolic order of phallic law, engendering only alienation and "unwanted pity."

Several GI Resistance poems use images of mutilation to symbolize the incoherence of the war and the inchoate state of abject fear and hopelessness many soldiers experienced in combat. Mutilation signifying castration renders the (male) soldier body meaningless in the symbolic order; the male body penetrated by fragments of grenades and mines, or high-velocity bullets, is transgressed in a way that defies language, that makes metaphor, symbol, and circumlocutions useless. The opening up of a body, the production of gashes and new orifices that exceed the limits of the body's coherence, defies dominant representations of the soldier as a seamless totality, an impenetrable masculinity, so that, rather than being the phallic penetrator, the soldier in Vietnam became the penetrated, inverting one of America's most powerful cultural symbols of the masculine.

In a poem by Ronald J. Willis that appeared in the GI Resistance paper *Gigline* in 1969, the penetration of the soldier's body is chillingly rendered in precise detail:

> Bullet has muzzle velocity, so great,
> 1235 feet per second
> and 1.2 seconds later it meets Steel Helmet
> who held up as well he might Bullet
> but Bullet's force was great and he
> was melting and vaporizing and
> spiritizing out tiny blobs of lead
> as Helmet gave in
> inward bulged the steel and
> on rushed Bullet 1.204 seconds
> after leaving Muzzle—
> jagged edges behind him he met
> Hair who held him up nowise in his Journey
> Skin gave way to mushroomed Bullet and
> Bones deformed at his will
> 671 feet a second he went as he tore
> vessels too surprised to bleed
> then Bullet nosed through soft gray-white stuff
> hardly hard as butter

This poem, ironically titled "Victory," anthropomorphizes the bullet, helmet, and body parts, while the human body the bullet has penetrated is rendered inert, inhuman, and barely discernible. Only military gear and body parts have any agency—the whole body hardly exists. This is the poem's paradox; the minutely detailed parts describe the destruction of a whole human body—but in the incoherence of the war, the whole person has no meaning, is an illegible sign, a cipher waiting to be tallied up in the body count. As the poem narrates the soldier's death, it represents the soldier's subjective memories as objects, similar to tissue or bone, that the bullet passes through:

> First he cut through the memory of Mom
> then a small gray dog
> through a first car, a wreck but the hell
> it ran
> through a huge area of scraped knees and
> pulled pigtails then
> a little bit of fear. . .

The poem proceeds through a catalog of thoughts and memories that define the human experiences of a man who is in the very process of being rendered inert, dead matter before the reader's eyes. The sentimentality of the images chosen to describe the soldier's memories is defused by the poem's focus on the agency of the bullet; the sentimental has been made senseless by the insensitive bullet. When the bullet finally explodes out of the other side of the soldier's head, the poem follows it to a tree where it lodges, "sitting there warmly—/duty done—/to map Hell where Paradise had been."[109] Alongside this poem in *Gigline* is a drawing of a helmet with a hole in it. When the poem was reprinted in a 1969 issue of *OM*, a graphic drawing of the limp body of a soldier, his exploded head thrown back against a rock, mouth gaping open, appeared on the same page. Underneath this drawing are lines from Sophocles: "Who is the slayer, who the victim? Speak."[110]

The exposure of the body's insides that results from mutilation or death, the penetration of the once-seamless whole body by a bullet or shrapnel, throws the whole notion of a stable subjectivity into question. If the boundaries that once guaranteed a distinction between inside and outside, subject and object, can be so readily transgressed, what defines the subject? The radical incoherence of subject and object relations that the soldier experiences when mutilated or witnessing mutilation calls forth a condition of abjection. According to Julia Kristeva, distinctions between Subject and Other are guaranteed by the sealed surfaces of the body; the violation of this seal by traumatic experiences, such as mutilation resulting in the ejection of material from the body, destabilizes the subject. The distinctions between subject and object no longer hold and a phobic state of abjection is experienced. As Kristeva describes it:

> The body's inside . . . shows up in order to compensate for the collapse of the border between inside and outside. It is as if the skin, a fragile container, no longer guaranteed the integrity of one's "own and clean self" but, scraped or transparent, invisible or taut, gave way before the dejection of its contents. Urine, blood, sperm, excrement then show up in order to reassure a subject that is lacking its "own and clean self."[111]

Several GI Resistance poems represent the expulsion of bodily matter as characteristic of the Vietnam experience and the collapse of subjectivity into the state of abjection. Paquet's "In a Plantation," for example, resembles the Willis poem "Victory" by representing how a bullet's penetration of a man's skull makes subjectivity meaningless:

> The bullet passed
> Through his right temple,

His left side
Could not hold
Against the metal,
His last "I am" exploded
Red and grey on a rubber tree. (WHAM, 12)

The force of a bullet entering the soldier's head ejects subjectivity; in this sense, the subject is only what can be contained within the flesh. The image challenges a Cartesian notion of subjectivity by insisting on the corporeal limits of being. The images of fertility, of the plantation and the rubber tree, that frame this poem seem to be similarly emptied of their symbolic content by the mutilation described; they can no longer adequately signify fertility and life but instead exist as inert natural material, just as the once sentient brain tissue blown against the tree exists only as inert, abject matter.

In Don Receveur's "night fear," the integrity of the soldier's "own and clean self" has been disrupted and rendered abject by the overwhelming phobia occasioned by a night patrol:

i heard my meatless bones
clunk together
saw the ants drink
from my eyes
like red ponies
at brown pools of water
and the worms in my belly
moved sluggishly
delighted. (WHAM, 15)

The soldier body here, rather than the impermeable totality represented in dominant narratives on war, is penetrated, infiltrated by what is "unclean," wholly Other. At the same time, however, what is wholly Other intimately infests the body that contains the subject so that the distinction between subject and object, self and other, collapses. This collapse is the Abject, the borderline experience.

Paquet's poem "They Do Not Go Gentle" rewrites the Dylan Thomas image of the willful individual's struggle against death as the convulsions of abjection devoid of any individuality or will.

The half-dead comatose
Paw the air like cats do when they dream,
They perform isometrics tirelessly.
They flail the air with a vengeance
You know they cannot have.
After all, their multiplication tables,
Memories of momma, and half their id
Lies in some shell hole
Or plop! splatter! on your jungle boots. . . . (WHAM, 3)

Similarly, W. D. Ehrhart represents the convulsive rage of the mutilated body in "The Sniper's Mark":

> He seemed in a curious hurry
> To burn up what was left
> Of the energy inside—
> A brainless savage flurry
> Of arms and legs and chest
> And eyes at once. (WHAM, 12)[112]

In both poems the spasms of death are represented as "brainless" bodily responses. The images are formed through a collection of body parts; the last two lines in the Ehrhart poem focus our attention on the "flurry" not of a unified body but of its parts, and the Paquet poem locates agency in the brain that has been blown out of the body's skull. The soldier's body has been emptied of meaningful content: it lacks identity, agency, or will; it is utterly foreign, alien, other. The representations of mutilated soldiers in these poems contradict normative images of soldiers as active, self-reliant, endowed with certainty of will and resolve.

The poetics of mutilation that GI Resistance poetry employs can also be linked to the central importance of the body count in the Vietnam War. Gibson shows how promotion, troop rewards such as rest and relaxation (R&R) leaves, and other perks in the military were dependent on the production of high body counts.[113] Gen. Julian Ewell, for example, rated military units according to a system of kill ratios and rewarded commanders of these units based on a ratio of allied to enemy killed. In Ewell's system of rewards, one Allied killed to fifty Enemy killed designated a unit as "highly skilled." The 25th Infantry Division conducted "Best of the Pack" contests that rated platoons in the division according to points earned for each body counted.[114] A soldier testifying to U.S. military atrocities in the war described how platoon leaders explained the body count: "Every dead Vietnamese body earns three days off for the soldier responsible for it."[115] Whether the Vietnamese body is VC, NVA, ARVN, or civilian is unimportant to the platoon leader. A poem by Don Receveur, "August 17, 1970," illustrates military managers' gruesome fetishization of the body as proof of military success. The poem focuses on the opening of a Vietnamese grave by U.S. soldiers:

> The bones showed
> disease yellow
> through the rags
> and the skull
> was covered with
> ants,

like medals
on a colonel's chest.
They told us
to.
They said it might
contain something
of military importance. (WHAM, 45)

The poem's style conveys the horror soldiers felt at carrying out orders contrary to their ethics; the desecration of a grave breaks taboos that guarantee the separation of living and dead, clean and unclean.[116] The image of the bones yellowed from disease and covered in rags suggests the poverty of the people American soldiers must kill. These soldiers must dig up the grave, however, not simply to desecrate it, but to provide the military with information—another body to count, evidence of American military superiority. Just as the ants devour the flesh on the body's skull, the medals on the colonel's chest, awards for the production of mutilation, are the signs of the military's devouring of human bodies.

The emphasis placed on the body count in military reward and advancement encouraged soldiers not only to produce needless slaughter to legitimate their role in Vietnam to the military managers but also to manufacture imagined numbers. One method was to count enemy dead more than once. According to a veteran, the "unwritten order" for body counts was that "for every dead one make it three."[117] Troops were eventually trained, as the body count became more important and the war progressed, to read a complex semiotics of body parts in order to produce numbers satisfactory to military management. The "inferential counting rule" became a standard operating procedure. This unofficial rule was used by a company "to infer numbers of enemy dead according to some found object or sign—an enemy weapon, a blood trail, a dismembered body part, or other mark of enemy presence. . . . Severed limbs signified a whole body for counting purposes."[118] While military managers sought to represent the war as a set of abstract numbers falling into debit and credit columns, ground troops were made either to produce these numbers directly—by opening fist-sized holes in the chest of a villager who did not understand the American commands to halt, for instance—or to infer these numbers from the macabre bits of bone and tissue cast aside by the war's destruction. Mutilation, in other words, was systemic in the discourse of the Vietnam experience for ground troops.

GI poetry may mimetically represent this systemic experience of mutilation in discourse through the visual arrangement of the text.

D. C. Berry's poetry, for example, is characterized by truncated, staggered lines that visualize disfigurement:

> The sun   goes
>   down
> a different way when
>
>   you
>
> are lungshot in a rice
> paddy and you
> are taking a drink of
> your own unhomeostatic
> globules each
>
> Time
>
> you swallow a pail
> of air   pumping like you
> were
>
> bailing out the whole
> world   throw
>   ing it in your leak
>   ing   collapsible lung
> that won't hold even
> a good quart   and on
> top of that   the sun
> goes down
>
>   Bang
> ing the lung completely
> flat.[119]

The gaps within lines, the severed gerunds, the staggered left margins, the awkward enjambment all mimic the disfigurations of a "lungshot" body. The rhythm structured in this broken text, moreover, replicates the broken speech of a soldier gasping for air as he dies. Don Receveur's "Eagle in the Land of Oz" employs similar techniques to replicate the "fragged" logic of soldiers in Vietnam:

> i was talking
> to a friend
> and i noticed
> a tin
> leg
>
>   hanging on his wall
>
> he said he
> got it

in cambodia

there had been
an air strike
on a

    n.v.a hospital

it had been on
one

    of the bodies

i thought of the
Tin Man of Oz
    who had no heart

      lions and tigers and bears. (WHAM, 48)

The single indented lines help foreground the immorality inherent in the friend's actions. U.S. troops were never authorized to cross over into Cambodia, and an airstrike on a hospital would have violated the Geneva Convention. By mutilating a corpse for his amusement, the friend becomes associated with the Tin Man, a heartless man-machine, the soldier-subject protected by armor, a collection of parts. The final line recalls the scene in *The Wizard of Oz* in which the idealistic and innocent Dorothy, the Scarecrow, and the Tin Man find themselves lost in a strange and forbidding forest. The speaker of the poem feels similarly lost in the forest/jungle of this incomprehensible war; but the pathological soldier who keeps a tin leg on his wall is also lost. The broken lines remind us of the broken body from which this soldier got the leg; beneath the vignette described in the poem is the mutilation that gives rise to its significance.

Although images of mutilation predominantly occur in GI Resistance poems as a means of representing the witnessed horrors of war, they also occur to represent states of mind. In "A Vet Raps to a POW," published in *The Bond*, Umojo Kwaguvu compares his experiences of combat on the ground to the relatively safe experience of a pilot who returns from a POW camp to a heroic welcome: "The war was under my feet, over my head,/stabbing my eyes, raping my ears, choking my throat,/and ripping my stomach."[120] Kwaguvu's psychological experience of war is represented as a mutilation of his body. Such imagery is particularly characteristic of poetry written after the war, when soldier-poets began to rely less on representing the immediate conditions of war and more on configuring the war experience into the broad historical patterns of American life. Describing the pain many veterans felt at not being able to communicate with loved ones about their experiences, or at the insensitivity exhibited toward them,

Basil T. Paquet represents words themselves as mutilating in "A Visit":

> "You don't look bitter,"
>   she said.
>   He thought,
> "Bitter is a taste,"
>   feeling her words
>   scrape across
>   memory's slow healing
> like a slow knife. (WHAM, 110)

John Balaban's 1974 poem "Mau Than" is a postwar reflection on his experiences in Vietnam, written to a Vietnamese friend he left behind. Its four sections find the speaker looking for whatever peace may be had after witnessing the atrocities of the war. In the opening lines of the final section, the poet describes waking up from a nightmare about the war:

> Out of the night, wounded
> with the gibberings of dogs,
> wheezing with the squeaks of rats,
> out of the night, its belly split
> by jet whine and mortar blast,
> scissored by the claws of children,
> street-sleepers, ripping their way free
> from cocoons of mosquito netting
> to flee the rupturing bursts
> and the air dancing with razors
> —out I came, to safe haven.[121]

He finds himself safe, far from the war, in Japan. The imagery used to describe the night, however, suggests that the atrocities he experienced in Vietnam form his metaphorical language. The night is represented as "wounded," "its belly split" and "scissored"; yet the scene described is not in Vietnam but in the "safe haven" of Japan. Balaban's imagery calls into question the notion that there can be any safe haven for anyone who has experienced the war.

The resistance to the master narratives of the war forged by tropes of mutilation in GI poetry parallels, paradoxically, what Homi K. Bhabha identifies as a form of resistance in postcolonial discourses. Paraphrasing Freud, Bhabha argues:

> The melancholic discourse, Freud says, is a plaint in the old-fashioned sense; the insistent self-exposure and the repetition of loss must not be taken at face value for its apparent victimage and passivity. Its narrative metonymy, the repetition of the piecemeal, outside the sentence, bit by bit, its insistent self-exposure, comes from a

mental constellation of revolt: "The melancholic are not ashamed and do not hide themselves, since everything derogatory they say about themselves is at bottom said about somebody else." This inversion of meaning and address in the melancholic discourse—when it "incorporates" the loss or lack in its own body, displaying its own weeping wounds—is also an act of "disincorporating" the authority of the Master.[122]

I do not mean by this comparison to suggest that the experiences of U.S. soldiers and veterans of the Vietnam War can be read *in place of* the oppression of colonized peoples and the discourses such peoples produce to address their experiences. I do, however, find Bhabha's reading of Freud's description of melancholia powerfully suggestive in the contexts of GI Resistance literature. Some comparisons between the melancholic, the colonized, and the antiwar soldier might prove productive and ultimately subversive in such contexts. Throughout the latter years of the war and well into the Reagan years, the Vietnam veteran occupied the role of a melancholic in American culture, being consistently figured as deficient, either physically or psychically. Lorrie Smith has suggested,

> In many ways, veterans of the Vietnam War share a similar position with women and ethnic minorities; mute, invisible, objectified by the dominant culture, blamed for circumstances which in fact have victimized them. Writers in this position necessarily find an authentic voice by resisting the cultural codes that define them as other, and they necessarily challenge prevailing literary norms.[123]

Indeed, while the place of the Vietnamese in the war has often been erased in U.S. cultural representations, GI Resistance poets have often demonstrated an acute sensitivity to the Vietnamese and their culture. Jan Barry's poems, for example, often focus on the people and the country of Vietnam. In "Memorial for Man in Black Pajamas" he mourns the murder of a Vietnamese poet by American soldiers:

> Trinh Vo Man was a poet
> in his own land a scholar
>
> . . .
> til the blue-eyed visitors
> came uninvited
> and shot him
>
> because a Man wearing
> black pajamas
> to them
> was just a slope, a dink, a gook
> was "Vietcong." (WHAM, 94)

John Balaban, who as a conscientious objector served during the war as a field representative for the Committee of Responsibility to Save War-Injured Children in Vietnam, has returned to Vietnam many times, collecting and translating Vietnamese poetry. As Jeffrey Walsh has pointed out, in American literature about the war, poets alone have "demonstrat[ed] a profound awareness of the structure and feeling of Vietnamese culture."[124]

Casting comparisons between the postcolonial and the GI Resistance poets also ventures a paradox—it serves to counter the colonialist narratives that U.S. militarism has brutally inscribed on history. The soldiers who were sent to *write* the mutilations of Vietnamese now are themselves seen as the mutilated; and their poetic tropes of mutilation turn and rearticulate this violence as an epistemic rupture of the colonialism that dis-figured those who experienced the war. Their poetry's melancholy obsessions with corporeal wounds, mutilations, and disfigurements foreground the uncanny return of the body politic's repressed, its own fragmentariness, its inability to cohere. As Bhabha suggests, the melancholic role can be oppositional. Just as the self-derogatory display of loss in the postcolonial narrative is also directed toward the colonial, the antiwar soldier's display of his own mutilated body enacts a "disincorporation" of the metanarratives in American culture that enabled citizens to support the war, send their children to kill others, and thereby produce the psychic and physical losses the GI poets display. When crippled veterans threw their Medals of Honor on the steps of the Capitol at the 1971 Dewey Canyon III demonstration, it contradicted cherished perceptions of the soldier's role in American society and epitomized the disturbing realities of the Vietnam War's effects on its young men. This moment drew attention not only to the veterans' loss but to America's as well.[125] As John Balaban's powerful poem, "After Our War," reminds us, the mutilations of the Vietnam War, the "weeping wounds," are our wounds:

> After our war, the dismembered bits
> —all those pierced eyes, ear slivers, jaw splinters
> gouged lips, odd tibias, skin flaps and toes—
> came squinting, wobbling, jabbering back.
> . . . .
> Since all things naturally return to their source,
> these snags and tatters arrived, with immigrant uncertainty
> in the United States. It was almost home.[126]

After the Vietnam War, the returned soldier would embody the disfiguration in American culture that the war had enacted. Furthermore, the Vietnam veteran became a cultural sign of the war's loss, of the greatest military defeat in American history.

GI Resistance poetry insists on the "incontestable reality" of mutilation to foreground the incoherence of the war and its atrocities. Images, tropes, and symbolic renderings of mutilation must be read as integral to the poetics of the GI Resistance, rather than, as some critics maintain, an aberrant deficiency of style. When they discuss it at all, however, critics tend to reject soldier poetry of the Vietnam War precisely on the basis of its insistence on the concrete reality of the mutilated body. Of those very few critics who have written on this, Philip D. Beidler's work has been exemplary. Until recently, Beidler's *American Literature and the Experience of Vietnam* offered the only extensive and insightful treatment of this poetry, and its approach to the imaginative literature of the war has become a standard reference in the nascent field of Vietnam studies.[127] Yet Beidler's critique of the early soldier poetry (exemplified by *Winning Hearts and Minds*) reproduces a critical perspective that has served to marginalize GI poetry. He argues that GI poetry is characterized by

> a somewhat predictable division between what might be best described as a dogged concreteness, an attempt to render the experience of the war in all its brute sensory plenitude, and what could be called notes toward a new mythic iconography, attempts to devise new images for a new experience, so to speak, images fierce and unsettling in their bitter originality of imaginative invention.[128]

By privileging the "mythic" and a "bitter originality of imaginative invention" over "dogged concreteness" and "brute sensory plenitude," Beidler's critique reiterates New Critical values. Poetry that can be read as universal, that transcends historical contingencies, is privileged and valued as legitimate poetry. Beidler's critique of GI Resistance poetry's "dogged concreteness" echoes the assessment put forward in Jeffrey Walsh's *American War Literature 1914 to Vietnam*. In his brief survey of soldier-poetry of the Vietnam War, Walsh characterizes it as "conventionally 'realistic.'" Walsh argues that "[w]hat clearly is lacking" in the poems of *Winning Hearts and Minds* "is an available artistic mode of a sustained kind, an extended formal utterance or discourse in which the war's distinctive technical nature as well as its moral nature can be realised." He compares GI poetry unfavorably to the poetry of Wilfred Owen, who "exploit[ed] as a working tradition the language of certain Romantic poets, such as Keats and Shelley. . . . Such a resonant literary language supplied Owen with locutions in which he could speak compassionately, bitterly and ironically in turns and write poetry counteractive to the dead rhetoric of slogan makers and politicians."[129] Walsh's critique fails to recognize how "the working tradition[s]" that GI poetry exploits may stem from a set of cultural traditions vastly different from those available to

Owen. Similarly, Beidler's critique does not consider how a "dogged concreteness" might be essential to the poetry of soldiers insistent on bearing witness to the atrocities of the Vietnam War. As Adi Wimmer has argued, the critical neglect of GI Resistance poetry stems from "standard *New Criticism* fare—ignoring the message of an implicit moral vision."[130] By measuring poetry of the Vietnam War against the received values of a critical ideology rooted in pre-Vietnam culture, an ideology that favors ambivalence, irony, complexity, and the displacement of direct political discourse, Walsh and Beidler legitimate a canon established in such a way as to exclude work like GI poetry. Cary Nelson has argued, "The canon as it now exists serves as much to prevent (or at least to discourage) us from reading certain kinds of texts—particularly texts marked as disruptively political—as to ensure that what we have judged to be the best literature will continue to be read."[131] The reiteration of New Critical injunctions against the engagement with historical necessity in poetry acts as what Fredric Jameson has called "strategies of containment."[132] By appealing to the "mythic," critics like Beidler and Walsh seek to cast what are essentially "local" interpretive codes as universal codes. Anything that does not correspond to the preestablished criteria of mythic in this view can, thus, be critically contained as deficient.

The locutionary language, ambivalence, and irony favored by New Critical standards of poetry runs counter to the political imperatives of GI Resistance literature, which favors renderings of direct experience, testimony over analysis, in order to "bring the war home" to readers. Elaine Scarry has argued that locutionary languages commonly deployed in cultural discourses on war (including those derived from discourses valorized in the traditional literary canon) enable cultural groups to wage war, an event singularly unique in its insistence on the production of injury and death: "war . . . requires both the reciprocal infliction of massive injury and the eventual disowning of the injury so that its attributes can be transferred elsewhere, as they cannot if they are permitted to cling to. . .the human body."[133] According to Scarry, injury can be disowned by a number of different rhetorical devices. It can be disowned through omission; soldiers are trained to believe that their goal is the defense of their country, their fellow soldiers, their honor, when in fact, as Scarry demonstrates, the central goal of any soldier in combat is to out-injure his opponent. Injury can disappear through metaphor as redescription; tanks, armaments, and forts can be said to be killed or crippled, whereas human bodies killed or injured can be described as neutralized or liquidated, adjectives more descriptive of chemicals and metals. Injury can be described as the "cost" of victory; but, in fact, injury is the product of war, and a major portion of the technology of war is designed to produce mutilation.[134] Metaphorical, locutionary discourses, by aestheticizing war and the "incontestable reality" of its atrocities, contribute to a "covering up" of the war. In GI Resistance poetry, however, the obsessive display of the "weeping wounds" of the bodies mutilated by the war disincorporates the narrative devices that seek to disown injury. As Scarry maintains, "the perpetuation of war would be impossible without the disowning of injury."[135] By emphasizing how the body's mutilation is the central event of war, GI Resistance poetry seeks to intervene in the ideological perpetuation of war. Direct statement and graphic representation by GI poets bear witness to the story about the war the military and the state did not want told.

I do not mean, however, to endorse GI poetics to the exclusion of all other poetic responses to the Vietnam War; clearly the range of antiwar poetries produced on the war provides ample evidence against any narrowly prescriptive view. I believe it is important, nevertheless, to recognize how the critical marginalization of GI Resistance poetry reflects less some objectively evident lack of literary merit in this work than the ideologically and historically situated reading practices favored by New Criticism. As Paul Lauter has argued, "[T]he central issue is not [which poetry] is 'better' but what we mean by 'better'. . . . such standards of judgment, which shape the canon, [are] rooted in assumptions derived from class and caste about the techniques, qualities, and especially the function of art."[136]

W. D. Ehrhart characterized the poems in *Winning Hearts and Minds* as "artless . . . . lacking skill and polish, but collectively they had the force of a wrecking ball."[137] This force, the violence of GI poetry, is its resistance, its obsessive vision of the ideological contradictions of a war of attrition, the trauma of a genocidal conflict. The artlessness of this poetry can actually be read in some sense as expressive of GI subcultural style. Barbara Tischler, in her study of GI Resistance underground papers, writes:

> [M]any of the GI papers opted for the direct, often unedited but authentic, voice of the soldier. . . . The practice of not "correcting" contributions, even for grammar or spelling, was common. The idea that GI antiwar papers presented the views of their readers *as they were* . . . was an article of faith with many editorial staffs that regarded form as subordinate to content.[138]

In a subculture that opposed the academy, the "brass," and the rhetorical jargon of official ideology and discourse, authenticity was paramount, realism a politically essential style. Although the emphasis on concrete realism may seem "un-poetic" by academic standards, for a movement intent on testifying to the atrocity of U.S. military policies in Vietnam—atrocity too often, as in the case of Lt.

William Calley and the My Lai massacres, covered up, silenced, or repressed in official narratives—such realism offered a means of resistance and counternarrative.

Rather than a deficiency in literary style, then, mutilation in GI poetry functions politically to undercut American culture's myths of war's glory. Representations of mutilation in GI poetry also bear witness to the traumatic experiences of combat in the Vietnam War. The mutilated body comes to represent the incoherence of dominant ideology, the deterritorialized body politic, and ultimately the castration of a masculinist military. The mutilated body as a sign also registers complex psychosexual contradictions in the subjectivity of the soldier constructed by military discipline and through his experience in Vietnam. In these (dis)figurations the body appears as the Abject, excremental, not only in the obvious sense as waste, but as economic and/ or political excess, transgressive, discarded. Throughout GI literature, enlisted men are referred to by officers and DIs as "grunts" who live in a "world of shit." The soldier is perceived as a meaningless excess of military economy, waste expelled in a war designed to support the larger "corps."[139] In the overwhelming phenomenal experience of military life and combat during the Vietnam War, where identity was constantly negotiated between the physiological extremes of injury and safety, life and death, between intense, chaotic firefights that flared up and out in minutes and long days of boring routines, the soldier's relation to the human body, both his own and others', became all-encompassing. Through the rigors of training he is forcefully interpellated as a soldier, whose subjectivity is linked to his ability to be a soldier, to master his body and thus keep it safe. What the Vietnam War taught so many U.S. soldiers, however, was that their bodies were never safeguarded by the myth of U.S. military dominance but were instead always open to penetration and disfigurement.

Read within their cultural contexts, the poems of the GI Resistance come to represent a profound challenge to the hegemonic narratives of the war. They resist the tendency to impose mythic patterns on the incoherent, unincorporable text of the war. As Smith has written, GI poetry "resist[s] the 'received cultural imagining' of the Vietnam War thematically," while representations in other genres tend to elide contradictions by rearticulating the war into "the grandiose, heroic, or redemptive narrative patterns of earlier wars" leaving the deeply rooted assumptions and premises of American culture and its foreign policies unexamined.[140] By insisting on the "incontestable reality" of war's tragic effect on the human body, GI Resistance poems "frag" the discursive chains of command that produced and continue to mythologize the Vietnam War.

Conclusion

As this book has demonstrated, many of the pressing social and political struggles of the Vietnam era were engaged in the poetry of activists. Poetry was an important vehicle of political expression in the oppositional culture of the 60s, and activist poets were prolific, publishing and disseminating a dense array of texts that document key social struggles of the period. Yet today almost none of this vital and once widely available literature survives in any but the most obscure and hard-to-access forms: in microfilm collections, out-of-print books, and special collections. How has this literature virtually disappeared from literary history? It may be that this disappearance stems from U.S. poetry criticism's disdain for radical activist poetry. Literary criticism of the post-Vietnam era has given virtually no attention to the activist poetry of the Vietnam era. This is especially puzzling when one considers how the major trends in criticism, theory, and cultural studies since the war have been deeply inscribed by the radical activist politics of the Vietnam era.

Discussion of 60s poetry today almost invariably focuses on a handful of the most established poets—typically writers who were students of other recognized poets, who have won the major literary prizes, whose work is published by the mainstream press and most well-known literary journals, and who have taught in the writing workshops that proliferated among colleges and universities in the late 60s. This canon of 60s poetry, limited to a few names such as Robert Bly, W. S. Merwin, James Merrill, and John Ashbery, gives very little sense of the diversity of poetic production in the period. Most literary histories, critical studies, and anthologies of post-1945 poetry accord no place to the hundreds of activist poets of the Vietnam era.[1] And despite the fact that virtually every major poet publishing in the Vietnam era wrote about the political conflicts of that period, the academy's representations of post-1945 poetry cast these concerns with politics as a marginal, aberrant diversion from a broader, transhistorical literary tradition. Politically committed poems are usually dismissed as unfortunate excesses of the period. Further, because these studies only discuss major poets, who, with a few exceptions, tended to focus their political engagement in the antiwar movement, activist poetry of the period tends to be equated with antiwar poetry. Few of the major histories and studies discuss or even acknowledge poetry written in the contexts of the Black Liberation or Women's Liberation movements. Poetry written in the contexts of other movements, such as the GI Resistance, American Indian Movement, Chicano Movement, and Gay Liberation, remains largely unexamined.[2] Contemporary poetry continues to be regarded by U.S. literary criticism as a genre antithetical to activism, outside the contingencies of social and historical struggle, and inappropriate for the expression of partisan, tendential views.

As part of his survey of twentieth-century poetry, David Perkins, for example, generalizes 60s concerns with activism in a passing reference: "Beatniks, drugs, communes, feminism, gay liberation, black pride and power, Zen, and other manifestations of cultural eclecticism, and the protest against the war in Vietnam had an impact on the subject matter and style of poetry." Perkins suggests that such factors might have played some role in the rejection of "closed" form and the New Criticism, but he goes on to assert that "the most immediate reason for the reaction against the New Criticism was, I believe, its acceptance within the classroom."[3] In other words, the 60s revolution in poetic sensibilities can be reduced to an agonistic contest between professors and their students. Black activism, feminism, and protest against the Vietnam War are not only reduced to blips on the cultural screen but also trivialized. Perkins implies that the move toward "open" form in poetry amounts to little more than youthful immaturity, or simply student disrespect for their professorial elders.

While Perkins's history largely eschews engagement with cultural history, even recent accounts that focus on the cultural dimensions of 60s poetry tend to devalue the role of social activism. In his book devoted to the "psycho-political" tenor of 60s poetry, Paul Breslin declares, "From 1965 onward, the war in Vietnam was the central political issue in American life, whether one supported it or opposed it. Among intellectuals and writers, the opposition was, by the late sixties, almost universal."[4] Despite this assertion, Breslin primarily refers to poets' opposition to the war only to castigate them for their naiveté. He criticizes writers such as Denise Levertov and Robert Duncan for idealizing the Viet Cong, romanticizing Vietnamese life, and too simplistically condemning the United States.[5] Similarly, Charles Altieri's readings of both Bly and Levertov acknowledge the "social concerns caused by the war in Vietnam" but offer no account of how these poets' activism shaped their work.[6] Although he suggests that the social activism of 60s poetry made "rethinking the metaphysical situation" possible and plausible, he attacks Levertov's antiwar poetry as representing "the most basic weaknesses of the contemporary aesthetic."[7]

Robert von Hallberg concedes that in the late 60s "the Vietnam war became the one overarching political subject," but argues that this led to "many variations of a single poem," which ultimately lacked "refinement."[8] Von Hallberg represents the central political conflicts motivating poetry of the 60s as antagonisms between intellectuals; this view necessarily privileges writers affiliated with higher education. When von Hallberg claims that higher education constituted "most of the audience for contemporary poetry," he implicitly considers only poetry produced in writing workshops and academic settings as legitimate.[9] This is evident in the writers he chooses to discuss in his chapter entitled "Politics": Robert Bly, Richard Wilbur, Robert Lowell, Mark Strand, George Oppen, James Wright. As I have demonstrated, the production, dissemination, and reception of political poetry in the Vietnam era went far beyond these names. Furthermore, von Hallberg's discussion of political poetry is limited to how it compares to canonized poetic standards and traditions. Levertov's "To Stay Alive," for example, is dismissed as an example of the failure of Poundian aesthetics.[10] While Levertov's poetry should be read in relation to Pound's paratactical methods and Olson's projective verse, it might also prove productive to read "To Stay Alive" within the contexts of such activist traditions of expression as leaflets, broadsides, and rally chants. Although all three critics give compelling readings of the poets they discuss, and von Hallberg and Breslin develop sophisticated analyses of some cultural contexts in 60s poetry, they all cling to the notion, inherited from the antiradical backlash of the New Critics, that tendential, partisan poetry is necessarily "bad" poetry. For all three, however, "bad" is defined purely in terms of a set of aesthetic criteria informed by certain world views. The result is that, even though activist poetry played an important role in the cultural history of the Vietnam era, such work is either marginalized or beneath remark—truly an "underground" literature, a poetry buried by an ideologically conservative literary criticism.

This is not to suggest, however, that only critics such as Perkins, Breslin, and von Hallberg, associated with a still-dominant New Critical tendency in poetry studies in the United States, have contributed to the burial of Vietnam-era activist poetry. Even avowedly leftist critics have marginalized this literature. Again the tendency has been to reiterate a modernist aversion to poetry that explicitly expresses its politics, a position that allows leftist critics to evoke a Frankfurt

School modernism compatible with the hegemonic New Critical tastes of poetry criticism in the United States.[11] Indeed, despite the so-called radicalization of the academy since the 80s, there has been little attempt to reconceptualize the ideological assumptions underwriting the marginalization of 60s political poetry. This is particularly ironic given that in recent years a number of critics have worked to recuperate the political literature of earlier periods.

Cary Nelson's work is in many ways emblematic of the institutional silence on 60s activist poetry from this leftist perspective. In *Repression and Recovery*, he makes the compelling point that

> no texts are merely erased from our memory in a neutral and non-ideological fashion. There are no innocent, undetermined lapses of cultural memory. The possibility of their erasure may initially be set in motion by their being stigmatized or scandalized (whether as outrageous, trivial, or inferior), and the scandal itself—even if it is no longer linked to exemplary texts, often remains in place as part of the institutional structure of what we do remember.[12]

Yet Nelson's own work is curiously complicitous with the process of erasure and forgetting he critiques. In his chapter on antiwar poetry of the Vietnam era in *Our Last First Poets*, Nelson reasserts the ideologically constituted aesthetic criteria of the canon when he notes that "the great majority of published Vietnam poems are flat, predictable, and not likely to survive."[13] He criticizes Ginsberg's "Wichita Vortex Sutra" for being too historically situated, too of the moment—a critique that is based on the notion that poetry must be historically disentangled, universal, transhistorical.[14] As many critics have argued since the 40s, much of the same criticism could be applied to the proletarian poetry of the 30s. In his more recent work on proletarian poetry, Nelson's views of 60s poetry seem to have remained the same. In celebrating the antiwar poems of William Vaughn Moody, for example, Nelson contrasts them with 60s antiwar poetry:

> Moody manages to see the common soldier as a victim of the culture's ideology, rather than as a figure of evil. That was a distinction, notably, that neither the poets writing about the Vietnam war in the 1960s and 1970s nor the left in general was able to make. In well-known antiwar poems by poets like Robert Bly, Galway Kinnell, Denise Levertov, and others the ordinary soldier is almost always a figure of unqualified evil.[15]

Such a view can be supported by regarding only the most canonized 60s antiwar poetry and overlooking GI Resistance poetry and many Black Liberation poems written in sympathy with soldiers. By not applying the theories and evaluative criteria that inform his rethinking of proletarian poetry to an understanding of Vietnam-era activist poetry, Nelson risks contributing to the erasure of this literature from history. The absolutely necessary recuperation of activist 30s poetry that Nelson's *Repression and Recovery* attempts is, to some extent, undercut by his inability to regard 60s activist poetry as having a similar historical validity.

Criticism's dismissal of Vietnam-era activist poetry contributes to a historical amnesia that the academy inculcates in its students, an amnesia made manifest in the editing of teaching anthologies.[16] Practically none of the many activist poems of the 60s appear in teaching anthologies published in the post-Vietnam era. Many politically engaged writers who were major voices in 60s poetry, such as Carolyn Rodgers, Larry Neal, Marge Piercy, Don L. Lee, Dudley Randall, and Robin Morgan, are absent from these anthologies. Even the 60s activist poetry of writers such as Levertov, Ginsberg, and Bly, who have been mainstays of the post–World War II canon, has been edited out of their careers in the teaching anthologies.[17] Most teaching anthologies claim to represent both quality and historical depth, the best work in the various periods covered. Their contents are typically arranged chronologically by author and within an author's *oeuvre*. The absence of activist poetry from the post-1945 sections of such anthologies strongly suggests to their readers that such work is neither characteristic of the period nor of high enough quality. Although space limitations clearly vex any editing project, the reasons typically given for excluding activist poetry from teaching anthologies invoke aesthetic rather than material concerns. In the third (shorter) edition of the *Norton Anthology of American Literature* (1989), the introduction to the section "American Poetry Since 1945" notes the importance of protest poetry and the involvement of poets in the antiwar effort but dismisses this poetry as aesthetically and historically insignificant. "Some poetry of the late 1960s," the editors claim, "had the insistence, urgency, and singlemindedness of political tracts. But the more enduring effect of political protest on poetry was to make a broader, more insistent range of voices available to verse; poems dramatized individual predicaments, stressing the underlying angers and desires that also issue in political action."[18] Insistence, urgency, and singlemindedness are regarded as detrimental to good poetry; to transgress genre and read like a political tract makes for bad poetry. What endures is something "broader" and more "individual."

While the Norton anthology editing practices have always been fairly conservative, the suppression of 60s activist poetry is more surprising in a candidly progressive, multicultural teaching anthology, such as the groundbreaking *Heath Anthology of American Literature*. Although it emerged out of the activism of the Modern Language Association's Radical Caucus and the heated debates within the academy over the politics of canonicity, the Heath anthology still contains very few activist poems from the 60s. Even though the anthology, admirably, collects once-forgotten activist poems from the nineteenth century and the proletarian period, the 60s poetry of, for example, Carolyn Rodgers, A. B. Spellman, W. D. Ehrhart, Basil T. Paquet, Robin Morgan, and Marilyn Lowen is missing. In fact, most of the poets in the anthology who were writing and active during the Vietnam era have few of their poems from the period represented. The selection of Denise Levertov's work is typical of this: as in the Norton anthologies, the Heath anthology includes her work from the 50s until the early 60s and then skips to her post–Vietnam-era work. This pattern is repeated in the selections of other poets, such as Allen Ginsberg, Robert Lowell, Gary Snyder, and Gwendolyn Brooks.[19]

As Nelson points out, erasures from the canon often begin with the institution's stigmatization of a particular style, movement, or topic. Perhaps because many of the leading critics and writers working today were educated and held their first academic posts in the politically fractious Vietnam era, and perhaps because many of them lent their youthful enthusiasm to various oppositional causes only to suffer the painful disenchantments of the 70s with Watergate, the slow withdrawal of troops, and the insidious undermining of the left by the government, explicitly political poetry of this period reflects on their own personal investments and histories; thus, it may seem naive to them. It is almost as if 60s activist poetry has become something of a scandal in the academy. The language many critics use suggests that they look on this literature as embarrassing—as many critics once may have looked on 30s activist poetry. Now, in a post-Vietnam, postmodern era, critics look with a jaundiced eye on the tendential, partisan poetry of their youth, even though the recuperation of such poetry from earlier historical periods and in postcolonial contexts continues apace. The arguments that many scholars working with proletarian, abolitionist, and anticolonialist literatures have been making is that the academy needs to rethink the ideological assumptions of its evaluative criteria to appreciate politically didactic literature. As I have tried to demonstrate in this book, the same argument should be made about the academy's understanding of Vietnam-era activist poetry. Although this literature may haunt the "baby boom" generation that is currently hegemonic in the academy, after more than twenty years it seems time to acknowledge that 60s activist poetry has played an important role in U.S. literary and cultural history.

Held against the standards of an aesthetic that favors linguistic complexity, formal innovation, and emotional and moral complexity, with its ambivalences and indecisions, much Vietnam-era activist poetry obviously fails. The United States, however, is one of the few countries to regard such standards as sacrosanct, as somehow extra-political and, therefore, transcendent of ideological stance. Yet as many critics of the canon and postcolonial literature have shown, it is precisely this notion that is most ideologically situated. It is on the basis of such ideology that poetry criticism in the United States continues to deny the existence and legitimacy of a vast range of poetries produced in the United States under conditions of resistance, struggle, and oppression. Throughout the world, especially in nations fraught with social strife and oppression, poets are the acknowledged legislators—Ernesto Cardenal, Roque Dalton, Claribel Alegría, Agostinho Neto, Christopher Okigbo, Dennis Brutus, and Mahmud Darwish have become revered by their people as simultaneously poets and partisans to their causes. Aesthetics and activism go hand in hand. There are, needless to say, vast differences between such poetry and poetry written in the United States during the Vietnam era. Yet the point is not to apply a politically engaged aesthetics to the poems of the *campesino* and a disengaged aesthetics to the U.S. poet writing against the Vietnam War, racism, and sexism. What I hope my book has shown is that any critical project must be politically engaged, and that it is not only in the Third World that poetry can be, to quote Barbara Harlow, "an arena of struggle."[20]

Although it remains vitally important to develop a poetics proper to the contexts of Vietnam-era activism, I have merely sought to demonstrate in this book the historical significance of this literature, to recuperate it from its "underground" status, and highlight some ways it might illuminate our understanding of the social struggles of this period. Even if its literary "quality" as defined by standard New Critical analysis often seems lacking, Vietnam-era activist poetry remains an important site for contestations over the meaning of identity that have indelibly shaped the cultural politics of our present moment. The "transfiguration of blackness" that occupied much of Black Liberation poetics articulated key interventions in U.S. racial discourses. Not only has the meaning of black corporeality undergone massive changes in the United States largely as a result of the cultural activism of Black Liberation, but the cultural work of this movement continues to inspire a new generation of African American artists. By overlapping the politics of reproductive rights, anticolonialism, and a critique of the Vietnam War and U.S. militarism, many Women's Liberation poems developed a unique dissolution of the hegemonic boundaries between private and public, personal and political. At its epistemological roots, these poetic strategies expressed an emergent cultural discourse that came to dominate feminism until the late 80s. The grim portrayals by GI Resistance poets of the war's atrocities gave voice to a profound disturbance in the masculinism that has underwritten U.S. militarism. In the graphic, brutal imagery of this poetry we find both a compelling historical testimony to the war's moral emptiness and the signs of a crisis in masculinity that has haunted the nation ever since the war's end. Moreover, 60s activist poetry's insistence on corporeality as the site of its struggles signifies an important development in late twentieth-century culture: the understanding that bodies and political ideologies, hearts and minds, are inextricably linked and determine our lived experiences.

My focus on discourses of corporeality in Vietnam-era resistance poetry and oppositional cultures has sought to foreground some ways in which the politics of identity, war, colonialism, and human rights—the politics that have tended to characterize contemporary struggles—traversed each other, inscribed and reinscribed, and interpenetrated each other in imaginative renderings of the body. The fact that attention to corporeality has become since the 80s an important phenomenon in literary and cultural studies and that this attention has vital roots in the cultural, social, and political work of Vietnam-era activism urges a reexamination of corporeality in this period. Further, it points to the ways in which "the body" continues to be thought of as a site of political and social struggle. The recognition of this becomes even more urgent under the shadow of AIDS. Since the mid-80s, a growing number of the performance poets who mark the cultural vanguard of contemporary literary practice have placed their bodies on the line to combat the malignant complacency that heteroculture has manifested toward this plague. The work of such performers as Ron Athey, Karen Finley, and others has brought us back to the contested spaces where public meets private in the body. And in an era in which the body politic has rarely been so hysterical about its health, when sex itself becomes viewed as an enemy of this body, and when the public articulates this in its fears of the bodies of others, study of the politics of corporeality seems especially pressing.

Many activist poets of the Vietnam era imagined the politically engaged self through their bodies, as bodies at risk, in danger, at war over issues and causes. As one activist poet recently told me, her political activism always came from the heart rather than the mind, something *felt* in the gut.[21] Acting on this intimate, sensate experience, it was through the empathetic need to render imaginatively a vision of corporeality, an understanding of those tangible, tender textures of human experience as also the terrain for their struggles for liberation and social justice, that activist poets sought to bridge the gap between public and private, heart and mind, and bring the war home. Perhaps it is in these gestures, at once fervent, often dogmatic, and also sensuously human, that the euphemism "hearts and minds" comes to find its deepest resonance in the history of the Vietnam era.

Notes

Introduction

1. Precisely when "winning hearts and minds" came to be linked with the U.S. intervention in Vietnam is unclear. There is some evidence that, in fact, the use of the phrase as a euphemism for the pacification program in Vietnam originated with Col. Edward Lansdale in the early 60s.

Of course, the metaphor has a long history in Western thought. It has been suggested by Samuel Freeman that in the speech I have cited, Johnson was paraphrasing an even earlier use of the metaphor from John Adams's description of the American Revolution: "The Revolution was effected before the war commenced. The Revolution was in the minds and hearts of the people." *Dictionary of the Vietnam War*, ed. James Olson (New York: Peter Bedrick Books, 1987), 194–195.

2. Johnson's speech cited the electrification of rural Vietnam as an example of the moral righteousness of U.S. efforts. Prior to this statement, Johnson described the Rural Electrification Administration's (REA) efforts as humane: "Tonight, an REA team is in South Viet-Nam at my request, talking and planning and working with the officials there, to find ways to bring the healing miracle of electricity to that poor, war-torn countryside where the per capita income is $50 a year, and where the average person's span of life is 35 years." The actual agenda of pacification, of course, had much more cynical goals in mind. *Public Papers of the Presidents of the United States: Lyndon B. Johnson, 1965*, Book 1: January 1 to May 31, 1965 (Washington, D.C.: United States Government Printing Office, 1966), item 230: 499, 498.

3. In a 1967 press conference, Robert Komer pointed out, "Some call this [pacification] chiefly a matter of providing protection or continuous local security in the countryside. Others call it the process of winning hearts and minds. For my money both descriptions are pretty good." Quoted in Frances Fitzgerald, *Fire in the Lake: The Vietnamese and the Americans in Vietnam* (New York: Vintage, 1972), 454.

4. The tensions between militarization and pacification are, however, much more complex than my brief summary suggests. Westmoreland actually supported pacification reservedly in 1966 and was later placed in charge of implementing it. Yet Westmoreland was most enthusiastic about search-and-destroy operations and increased firepower. Privately, he scoffed at the concept of "winning hearts and minds," believing that the South Vietnamese were too ignorant to effectively take charge of their own rebuilding and that the only way to win their

loyalties was through the exercise of sheer military power. See Larry Cable, *Unholy Grail: The US and the Wars in Vietnam, 1965–1968* (London: Routledge, 1991); Thomas W. Scoville, *Reorganizing for Pacification Support* (Washington, D.C.: Center for Military History, U.S. Army, 1982); David W. Barrett, *Uncertain Warriors: Lyndon Johnson and His Vietnam Advisers* (Lawrence: University Press of Kansas, 1993); and Neil Sheehan, *A Bright Shining Lie: John Paul Vann and America in Vietnam* (New York: Random House, 1988).

5. See R. W. Komer, *Bureaucracy at War: U.S. Performance in the Vietnam Conflict* (Boulder, Colo.: Westview Press, 1986).

6. Scoville, *Reorganizing for Pacification Support*, 3. Scoville casts the dichotomies as "security versus development or, put another way, military versus civil." Critical histories of the U.S. war in Southeast Asia have made clear that "security" was not really at issue. I believe "intervention" carries a more specific sense here.

7. Vince Gotera has recently discussed the "warrior against war" as one of the unique paradoxes of the Vietnam era legacy. See *Radical Visions: Poetry by Vietnam Veterans* (Athens: University of Georgia Press, 1994).

8. Conspicuously absent from such reckoning, of course, are the millions of Southeast Asians devastated by twenty years of American intervention. Indeed, when Johnson made the May 1965 speech cited previously, the United States had just completed one of its Rolling Thunder bombing raids on North Vietnam, executing more than 500 airstrikes. My dating here begins with the first determinant efforts on the part of the United States to intervene in Southeast Asia, in 1955, and ends with the fall of Saigon, in 1975.

9. Even though both words in the phrase describe body parts, "mind" (rather than "brain") has a much less organic and corporeal connotation than "heart."

10. By "corporeality" and the "corporeal" I mean a general phenomenological notion of bodiliness rather than any fixed essential concept of "the" body. I derive my use of this concept from Elizabeth Grosz, *Volatile Bodies: Toward a Corporeal Feminism* (Bloomington: Indiana University Press, 1994).

11. See Andreas Huyssen, *Across the Great Divide: Modernism, Mass Culture, Postmodernism* (Bloomington: Indiana University Press, 1989); Fredric Jameson, *Postmodernism, or the Cultural Logic of Late Capitalism* (Durham, N.C.: Duke University Press, 1990); and my introduction to *The Viet Nam War and Postmodernity* (Woodbridge, Conn.: Burning Cities Press, forthcoming).

12. It is important to note here that "politics of identity" is a distinctively post–Vietnam era concept. While "identity" and "subjectivity" had some currency during the 60s, "self" and "personal politics" tended to predominate as preferred terms. The emergence of a discourse of identity politics as the hegemonic articulation of oppositional cultural struggle can perhaps be situated in the Combahee River Collective's 1977 statement. This often cited statement argued that U.S. social relations should be understood as interconnected axes of oppression based on race, class, gender, and sexuality. The "politics of identity" that Combahee articulated would become central to contemporary discourses of multiculturalism. See Combahee River Collective, "A Black Feminist Statement," *Capitalist Patriarchy and the Case for Socialist Feminism*, ed. Zillah R. Eisenstein (New York: Monthly Review, 1979), 362–372. Also see Cherríe Moraga, *Loving in the War Years* (Boston: South End Press, 1983), 132–133.

Since the terms "identity" and "subjectivity" as they have been articulated in post–Vietnam era oppositional cultural politics stem directly from the liberation and "personal politics" of the 60s, my use of these terms throughout this book is meant not to dehistoricize them but, rather, to stress their cross-historical resonance.

13. Barbara Harlow, *Resistance Literature* (New York: Methuen, 1987), 28–29.

14. Ibid., 33.

15. Anne E. Zald and Cathy Seitz Whitaker assert that in 1972 "the total underground press circulation may have been as high as 3,000,000 with an estimated readership of 18,000,000," and that "the one consistent theme among the various political and cultural emphases" of underground newspapers was a strong opposition to the Vietnam War and the draft. "The Underground Press of the Vietnam Era: An Annotated Bibliography," *Voices from the Underground*, vol. 2, *A Directory of Sources and Resources on the Vietnam Era Underground Press*, ed. Ken Wachsberger (Tempe, Ariz.: Mica Press, 1993), 2.

16. In this context I consider "professional writer" to mean a writer whose primary work is literary writing, who publishes regularly in the literary journals and publishing houses recognized by the academic community, who regularly participates in readings and lectures, who usually has a college or university appointment teaching writing workshops, and/or has been recognized by the community of writers. Obviously, this designation lacks consistency and stability across time. Many writers I might consider "professional" now (such as Nikki Giovanni, Robin Morgan, and W. D. Ehrhart) were, during the Vietnam era, primarily less "professionals" and more "activists" emerging as professionals. And many who were considered part of the community of "professional" writers during the 60s and whose work bears consideration (such as Walter Lowenfels and Paul Goodman) dropped out of this community by the end of the period. I will insist on the distinction, however, to indicate how poetry was popularly written during the 60s and to show that a cultural study of 60s poetry must look beyond the narrow canonical boundaries that have been delineated around the works of such poets as Robert Bly, John Ashbery, Denise Levertov, and Allen Ginsberg— not to dismiss the considerable cultural work of such writers, but rather to engage an "underground" perspective on 60s poetry—a view beneath the surfaces into the buried social archives.

17. Len Fulton, *The Directory of Little Magazines and Small Presses*, 3rd ed. (El Cerrito, Calif.: Dustbooks, 1967), ii.

18. The sole exceptions I am aware of are David Cortright, *Soldiers in Revolt: The American Military Today* (Garden City, N.Y.: Doubleday, Anchor, 1975), and Harry W. Haines, ed., *GI Resistance: Soldiers and Veterans Against the War*, special issue *Viet Nam Generation* 2, no. 1 (Spring 1990).

19. Cary Nelson, *Repression and Recovery: Modern American Poetry and the Politics of Cultural Memory, 1910–1945* (Madison: University of Wisconsin Press, 1989).

20. Paula Rabinowitz, *Labor and Desire: Women's Revolutionary Fiction in Depression America* (Chapel Hill: University of North Carolina Press, 1991).

21. See Barbara Harlow, *Barred: Women, Writing, and Political Detention* (Hanover, N.H.: University Press of New England, 1992), and *Resistance Literature* (New York: Methuen, 1987). Also see James C. Scott, *Domination and The Arts of Resistance: Hidden Transcripts* (New Haven, Conn.: Yale University Press, 1990).

22. Maria Damon, *The Dark End of the Street: Margins in American Vanguard Poetry* (Minneapolis: University of Minnesota Press, 1993).

23. The one book-length study on antiwar poetry of the Vietnam era remains James F. Mersmann, *Out of the Vietnam Vortex: A Study of Poets and Poetry*

Against the War (Lawrence: University Press of Kansas, 1974). This study, however, focuses mainly on antiwar poems by canonical poets.

24. Dominick LaCapra, introduction to *The Bounds of Race: Perspectives on Hegemony and Resistance* (Ithaca, N.Y.: Cornell University Press, 1991), 3.

1. Bodies, Poetry, and Resistance

1. See especially Michel Foucault, *The Archaeology of Knowledge*, trans. A. M. Sheridan Smith (New York: Vintage, 1972), and *The History of Sexuality*, vol. 1, *An Introduction*, trans. Robert Hurley (New York: Vintage, 1978, 1980).

2. As Jana Sawicki has noted, "[F]or Foucault, discourse is ambiguous and plurivocal. It is a site of conflict and contestation." *Disciplining Foucault: Feminism, Power, and the Body* (New York: Routledge, 1991), 1.

3. See especially Michel Foucault, *Discipline and Punish: The Birth of the Prison*, trans. Alan Sheridan (New York: Vintage, 1977, 1979), and *The History of Sexuality*, vol 1.

4. Michel Foucault, "Technologies of the Self," in *Technologies of the Self: A Seminar with Michel Foucault*, ed. Luther H. Martin, Huck Gutman, and Patrick H. Hutton (Amherst: University of Massachusetts Press, 1988), 18; emphasis added.

5. For a detailed analysis of the various beliefs and attitudes toward proper style in black cultural nationalism, see William Van Deburg, *New Day in Babylon: The Black Power Movement and American Culture, 1965–1975* (Chicago: University of Chicago Press, 1992), 192–204, 248–272, and passim.

6. In one extreme example of this, Alice Echols notes how the Westside Group of Chicago, a feminist group that at one time included Shulamith Firestone, Naomi Weisstein, Heather Booth, and Vivian Rothstein and was active during the late 1960s, attempted to interest radical women in a "uniform" that would signify their resistance to consumerism. Echols writes, "Besides raising awareness of women's oppression and creating solidarity among radical women who wore it, Rothstein argued that the uniform 'is un-cooptable by the fashion industry unlike our previous uniforms of sandals, turtlenecks, and long hair.'" Echols further notes that "Rothstein suggested that those who feared that a uniform would erode individuality were merely dupes of consumerism." *Daring to Be Bad: Radical Feminism in America, 1967–1975* (Minneapolis: University of Minnesota Press, 1989), 68. Along with such measures, many feminists believed that women should not shave their legs or armpits and should keep their hair short to signify their commitment to Women's Liberation.

7. Foucault, *History of Sexuality*, 1:95–96.

8. See Ernesto Laclau and Chantal Mouffe, *Hegemony and Socialist Strategy: Towards a Radical Democratic Politics* (London: Verso, 1985).

9. Based on their readings of Foucault's theories of discourse, Laclau and Mouffe assert that articulation can be considered "any practice establishing a relation among elements such that their identity is modified as a result of the articulatory practice. The structured totality resulting from the articulatory practice, we will call *discourse*." Ibid., 105. Emphasis in original.

10. Quoted in Walter Kalaidjian, *American Culture Between the Wars: Revisionary Modernism and Postmodern Critique* (New York: Columbia University Press, 1994), 266, n. 9.

11. According to Michèle Le Doeuff, images "are not, properly speaking, 'what I think,' but rather 'what I think with,' or again 'that by which what I think

is able to define itself.'" Quoted in Elspeth Probyn, "This Body Which is Not One: Speaking an Embodied Self," *Hypatia* 6, no. 3 (Fall 1991): 115.

12. Ibid., 116–117.

13. For an analysis of the "discourse of enclosure" in medieval English culture and its role in mediating gender, see Shari Horner, *Enclosed Subjects: Reading and Writing Women in Early Medieval England* (Minneapolis: University of Minnesota Press, forthcoming). Also see Thomas Laqueur, *Making Sex: Body and Gender from the Greeks to Freud* (Cambridge, Mass.: Harvard University Press, 1990), who describes a "one-sex" model of the body that persisted from the classical age through much of medieval Christianity.

14. Quoted in Arthur Synnott, *The Body Social: Symbolism, Self and Society* (London: Routledge, 1993), 7.

15. Quoted in ibid., 24.

16. Ibid., 25.

17. Quoted in ibid., 25; emphasis in original.

18. See Scott Lash, "Genealogy and the Body: Foucault/Deleuze/Nietzsche," *Theory, Culture, and Society* 2, no. 2 (1984): 10 ff. Lash argues that, unlike Foucault and Deleuze, who conceive of the body as an abstract concept, for Nietzsche the body enacts the materiality of knowledge.

19. Ronald Fraser et al., *1968: A Student Generation in Revolt* (New York: Pantheon, 1988), 82.

20. Jean-Paul Sartre, *Being and Nothingness*, trans. Hazel E. Barnes (New York: Washington Square Press, 1956, 1992), 404, 428–430.

21. Simone de Beauvoir, *The Second Sex*, trans. H. M. Parshley (New York: Vintage, 1952, 1974), xviii, 33.

22. Judith Butler, *Gender Trouble: Feminism and the Subversion of Identity* (New York: Routledge, 1990), 12. "The theory of embodiment informing Beauvoir's analysis is clearly limited by the uncritical reproduction of the Cartesian distinction between freedom and the body. Despite my own previous efforts to argue the contrary, it appears that Beauvoir maintains the mind/body dualism, even as she proposes a synthesis of those terms."

23. Bryan Turner argues that contemporary history has brought about the development of a "somatic society": "We might define the somatic society as a social system in which *the body, as simultaneously constraint and resistance, is the principal field of political and cultural activity.* The body is the dominant means by which the tensions and crises of society are thematized; the body provides the stuff of our ideological reflections on the nature of our unpredictable time." *Regulating Bodies: Essays in Medical Sociology* (London: Routledge, 1992), 11–12; emphasis added. Although Turner locates this new social system in the events of the 1980s, I believe its emergence can be situated in the post–World War II years.

24. Van Deburg, *New Day in Babylon*, 51–53

25. Stephen Henderson, "'Survival Motion': A Study of the Black Writer and the Black Revolution in America," in *The Militant Black Writer in Africa and the United States*, Mercer Cook and Stephen Henderson (Madison: University of Wisconsin Press, 1969), 65.

26. Fredric Jameson writes that "'Marcuse' virtually becomes the name for a whole explosive renewal of Utopian thinking and imagination" in the 60s. *Postmodernism, or, The Cultural Logic of Late Capitalism* (Durham, N.C.: Duke University Press, 1991), 160.

27. Paul Robinson, *The Freudian Left: Wilhelm Reich, Geza Roheim, Herbert Marcuse* (Ithaca, N.Y.: Cornell University Press, 1969, 1990), 183.

28. Quoted in ibid, 194. The article quoted is "Existentialism: Remarks on Jean-Paul Sartre's *L'Être et le néant* (1948).

29. Frantz Fanon, *The Wretched of the Earth*, trans. Constance Farrington (New York: Grove Press, 1968), 211.

30. See Fanon's radical examination of this dilemma in Frantz Fanon, "The Fact of Blackness," chapter 5 of *Black Skin, White Masks*, trans. Charles Lam Markmann (New York: Grove, 1967), 109–140.

31. Malcolm X, *Malcolm X Speaks: Selected Speeches and Statements*, ed. George Breitman (New York: Pathfinder Press, 1965), 169.

32. Quoted in Fred Powledge, *Free at Last?: The Civil Rights Movement and the People Who Made It* (Boston: Little, Brown, 1991), 305; emphasis in original.

33. Quoted in Clayborne Carson, *In Struggle: SNCC and the Black Awakening of the 1960s* (Cambridge, Mass.: Harvard University Press, 1981), 101; emphasis added.

34. Walt Whitman, *The Complete Poems*, ed. Francis Murphy (London: Penguin, 1986), 128. For more on Whitman's body politics, see Michael Moon, *Disseminating Whitman: Revision and Corporeality in Leaves of Grass* (Cambridge, Mass.: Harvard University Press, 1991). One of Moon's important arguments is that Whitman's *Leaves of Grass* "attempt[s] to revise predominant conceptions of the bodily" (4). As I will argue, activist poetries of the 1960s are similarly invested in revising corporeality. M. Jimmie Killingsworth has noted that Whitman's glorification of the body stems from the prevalent nineteenth century view that "considered health to be a matter that involved the whole self—the physical, moral, and psychological being." *Whitman's Poetry of the Body: Sexuality, Politics, and the Text* (Chapel Hill: University of North Carolina Press, 1989), 14.

35. See Paul Breslin, *The Psycho-Political Muse: American Poetry since the Fifties* (Chicago: University of Chicago Press, 1987), 1–21; and Robert von Hallberg, *American Poetry and Culture, 1945–1980* (Cambridge, Mass.: Harvard University Press, 1985).

36. Killingsworth, *Whitman's Poetry of the Body*, 2–10.

37. Marjorie Perloff, *Radical Artifice: Writing Poetry in the Age of the Media* (Chicago: University of Chicago Press, 1991), 20. Despite the implications of the book's title, Perloff never discusses the Vietnam War as media event or context for leftist radical discourse. Although she offers a rich account of avant-garde writers, such as David Antin, it is interesting to note that she overlooks these writers' political activism. David Antin, for example, wrote several war-related poems in the late 1960s and early 1970s.

38. Donald E. Pease, "New Americanists: Revisionist Interventions into the Canon," *boundary 2* 17, no. 1 (Spring 1990): 24.

39. I cite 1963 as an initial moment in the emergence of the war into U.S. culture for several reasons: the Buddhist riots in Hué begun in 1963 attracted widespread media coverage and sparked a national debate; the TV images of Buddhist monks self-immolating during these riots became one of the first defining images of the Vietnam era. Further, in November 1963 South Vietnamese President Ngo Dinh Diem was assassinated, signifying to many the cynicism of the U.S. involvement in Vietnam. President Kennedy's assassination later in November delegitimated the state for many young Americans. By December 31, more than 16,000 U.S. military personnel were stationed in Vietnam, an increase of

more than 5,000 from the year before. In that same year, the murder of Medgar Evers and the bombing of the 16th Street Baptist Church in Birmingham marked turning points in Civil Rights activism; the frustration many African Americans felt in the face of these events presaged the rising militancy of SNCC.

40. The first official intervention in Vietnam began in late 1949, when Truman sent military advisers to aid the French and the Bao Dai regime.

41. The 1964 Gulf of Tonkin Resolution, however, gave President Lyndon Johnson unprecedented powers to circumvent the congressional, constitutional process. By 1975 this undeclared "war" had involved 2.5 million U.S. soldiers. It killed 58,135 of those soldiers in combat along with 35,000 U.S. noncombatant civilians. It wounded 303,616 more soldiers, 33,000 of whom were paralyzed. According to a 1982 report, 110,000 more died from "war-related" problems after returning to the United States—of those, 60,000 were suicides. It caused the deaths of over 1.9 million Vietnamese, 200,000 Cambodians, and 100,000 Laotians. The war left 3.2 million Vietnamese, Cambodians, and Laotians wounded and made more than 14.3 million more refugees by its end. According to one account, between 1965 and 1973 about one out of every thirty Indochinese was killed by the war. Reese Williams, ed., *Unwinding the Vietnam War: From War into Peace* (Seattle, Wash.: The Real Comet Press, 1987), 7–8.

42. Fredric Jameson, "Periodizing the 60s," in *The 60s Without Apology*, ed. Sohny Sayres, Anders Stephenson, Stanley Aronowitz, and Fredric Jameson (Minneapolis: University of Minnesota Press, 1984), 178.

43. In his study of U.S. films of the 60s, David E. James has argued that:

> For the last half of [the 60s] the war in Vietnam was the largest single determinant of other economic, social, and cultural developments in the United States, eventually becoming the master metaphor by which they were understood. As the imperial state declared itself in the ghettos, in the streets of Chicago, and on the campuses of the rest of the country, albeit with less ferocity than in the villages of Vietnam, Blacks and war protesters came to feel themselves to be fighting alongside the Vietnamese people in the same war of liberation.

James goes on to point out, "When Black Power's equation of the struggles of domestic minorities with that of the Vietnamese expanded to include other marginalized groups, then the notion of a unified Third World could stand in place of the largely absent class analysis, and acts of resistance against the state, especially as they became more violent in the Weatherman period, could be thought of as parallel to the Vietnamese resistance rather than simply ancillary or subordinate to it." *Allegories of Cinema: American Film in the Sixties* (Princeton, N.J.: Princeton University Press, 1989), 195–196.

44. Jameson, "Periodizing the 60s," 180.

45. James, *Allegories of Cinema*, 196.

46. Van Deburg, *New Day in Babylon*, 154.

47. Malcolm X made several comparisons in his speeches and statements between African American oppression and the U.S. intervention in Vietnam. SNCC's opposition to the war led to meetings with Ho Chi Minh and North Vietnamese leaders. The Black Panthers explicitly expressed solidarity with Ho Chi Minh and the National Liberation Forces of Vietnam. African American women often linked black feminist politics to opposition to the war. See Gerald Gill, "From Maternal Pacifisim to Revolutionary Solidarity: African-American Women's

Opposition to the Vietnam War," in *Sights on the Sixties*, ed. Barbara L. Tischler (New Brunswick, N.J.: Rutgers University Press, 1992), 177–195.

48. It has been often shown that women played critical roles in organizing opposition against the war. The Jeanette Rankin Brigade demonstration of 1968, for example, was an all-women's protest against the war. Not only did women organize against the war, but their work in the antiwar movement contributed to the formation of Women's Liberation. See Sara Evans, *Personal Politics: The Roots of Women's Liberation in the Civil Rights Movement and the New Left* (New York: Vintage, 1979), and Echols, *Daring to Be Bad*. In one important case of antiwar organizing giving rise to Women's Liberation, the feminist underground paper *off our backs* was started in late 1969 with four hundred dollars collected to start a GI coffeehouse.

2. *"The Transfiguration of Blackness"*

1. LeRoi Jones, "Black Art," *Black Fire: An Anthology of Afro-American Writing*, ed. LeRoi Jones and Larry Neal (New York: William Morrow, 1968), 302. Hereafter cited in the text as BF.

Although Jones officially changed his name to Imamu Amiri Baraka not long after this anthology was published, and has often changed his name throughout his career (Leroi, Ameer, and so on), whenever I discuss his work, I will use the name he favored at the time of its publication.

2. David L. Smith, "Amiri Baraka and the Black Arts of Black Art," *boundary 2* 15, no.1/2 (1986/87), 239.

3. William J. Harris, *The Poetry and Poetics of Amiri Baraka: The Jazz Aesthetic* (Columbia: University of Missouri Press, 1985), 68–69.

4. LeRoi Jones, "Balboa, The Entertainer," *The Dead Lecturer* (New York: Grove Press, 1964), 10. Hereafter cited in the text as DL.

5. Williams formed a small, armed cadre to defend Civil Rights activists in North Carolina, and after a gun battle with whites who had attacked nonviolent Civil Rights demonstrators, he and his family went into exile in 1959, first to Canada and then to Cuba.

6. Quoted in Abby Arthur Johnson and Ronald Maberry Johnson, *Propaganda and Aesthetics: The Literary Politics of African-American Magazines in the Twentieth Century* (Amherst: University of Massachusetts Press, 1979, 1991), 178.

7. Larry Neal, "The Black Arts Movement," *Visions of a Liberated Future: Black Arts Movement Writings*, ed. Michael Schwartz (New York: Thunder's Mouth Press, 1989), 66.

8. Smith, "Amiri Baraka," 238–239. I will often refer generally to African American poetry during this period as "Black Liberationist" to signify its distinctive appeals to cultural nationalism based in models of Third World liberation struggle. "Black Arts" poetry I will take to refer specifically to works produced by those poets associated with Amiri Baraka's Black Arts Repertory Theatre/School or with the various branches of this group (such as the Detroit Black Arts group). I will use "Black Aesthetic" to refer to the aesthetic, critical, and philosophical perspectives of black writing during the Vietnam era.

9. Ahmed Alhamisi, "The Black Narrator (At a Symposium for Afro-Americans)," *Black Poetry: A Supplement to Anthologies Which Exclude Black Poets*, ed. Dudley Randall (Detroit: Broadside Press, 1969), 39–40 (lines 1–7, 15–16, 19–23, 27–31, 34–37).

10. Judith Butler, *Bodies That Matter: On the Discursive Limits of "Sex"* (New York: Routledge, 1993), 2–3. Although Butler's theory of materiality and corporeality focuses on their relations to "sex," her ideas could be fruitfully applied to both "race" and what I am conceiving of as "political identity." "Blackness" in Black Liberationist cultural discourses is not only signified by one's beliefs and activism for black self-determination; it is also signified by the *look* of the body: natural hair, posture, walk, and so forth.

11. Stephen Henderson, " 'Survival Motion': A Study of the Black Writer and the Black Revolution in America," in Mercer Cook and Stephen Henderson, *The Militant Black Writer in Africa and the United States,* (Madison: University of Wisconsin Press, 1969), 67; emphasis added.

12. Stephen Henderson, *Understanding the New Black Poetry: Black Speech and Black Music as Poetic References* (New York: William Morrow, 1973), 7; emphasis in original.

13. Henderson and many of the other writers of the Black Aesthetic never consider how one may have African ancestry and be a descendant of slaves and yet not have the corporeal features commonly recognized as "black." In part, this reflects the problematic nature of light complexion in African American cultural history. The Black Aesthetic and Black Liberation were, in many ways, an assertion of an African American constituency historically marked as the underclass because of their darker complexion. Yet this does not contradict the critical point here that corporeality underwrites the theoretical project of the Black Aesthetic.

14. Perhaps Malcolm X stated this most powerfully in one of his sermons. "And when we say 'black,' we mean everything not white, brothers and sisters! Because *look* at your skins! We're all black to the white man, but we're a thousand and one different colors." *The Autobiography of Malcolm X,* with assistance of Alex Haley (New York: Ballantine, 1973), 201.

15. Frantz Fanon, *Black Skin, White Masks,* trans. Charles Lam Markmann (New York: Grove Weidenfeld, 1967), 11; emphasis added.

16. Ibid., 165.

17. Fanon uses this term in describing white science's efforts to "make it possible for the miserable Negro to whiten himself and thus to throw off the burden of that corporeal malediction." Ibid., 111.

18. Butler, *Bodies That Matter,* 3.

19. See Michael Omi and Howard Winant, *Racial Formation in the United States: From the 1960s to the 1980s* (New York: Routledge and Kegan Paul, 1986). I discuss Omi and Winant at some length later in this chapter. Barbara Jeanne Fields, "Slavery, Race and Ideology in the United States of America," *New Left Review* 180 (1990): 95–118, argues that "race" in the United States is an ideological construction that resulted from slavery and not, as is often believed, an objective truth that enabled slavery to exist in the first place.

20. Diana Fuss, *Essentially Speaking: Feminism, Nature and Difference* (New York: Routledge, 1989), 75.

21. See especially the 1963–1964 speeches in *Malcolm X Speaks: Selected Speeches and Statements,* ed. George Breitman (New York: Grove, 1965).

22. Although I have qualified the internationalist perspectives of the late 60s to early 70s as a "new" dynamic in African American oppositional activism, their novelty is relative to the immediate historical contexts. Garveyism of the early twentieth century was strongly inflected by an internationalism that bears striking resemblances to Black Liberationist discourses, and W. E. B. Du Bois's political

philosophies were consistently internationalist. As a hegemonic form of African American activism in the late twentieth century, however, Black Liberation's consistent emphasis of a Third-Worldist and national liberation approach marks both the unique historical contingencies for its development and its departure from post–World War II Civil Rights activism.

23. The phrase "the fact of blackness" comes from the title of the fifth chapter in Fanon, *Black Skin, White Masks*.

24. Although Truman signed an executive order calling for an end to segregation in the military in 1948, it took more than ten years to complete this order. See Howard Zinn, *A People's History of the United States* (New York: Harper, 1990), 441.

25. According to Philip Foner, the median income of nonwhite workers was 41 percent of the white median in 1939; by 1950 it had risen to 60 percent. Manning Marable, *Race, Reform, and Rebellion: The Second Reconstruction in Black America, 1945–1990*, 2nd ed. (Jackson: University Press of Mississippi, 1991), 16.

26. Ibid., 16, 13–17.

27. W.E.B. Du Bois, *The Souls of Black Folk* (New York: Vintage Books, The Library of America, 1990), 3.

28. Walter White, "Has Science Conquered the Color Line?" *Negro Digest*, December 1949, 37; emphasis added.

29. Ibid., 38; emphasis in original.

30. A "cure" for dark skin color has, in fact, been sought since as early as the eighteenth century. In 1792, Dr. Benjamin Rush, one of the "Founding Fathers" of the United States, presented a paper that argued that "the 'color' and 'figure' of blacks were derived from a form of leprosy. He was convinced that with proper treatment, blacks could be cured (i.e. become white) and eventually assimilated into the general population." Omi and Winant, *Racial Formation*, 148, n. 2. Cosmetic "whitening" products, such as Dr. Fred Palmer's Skin Whitener, have long been marketed to African American consumers. Frantz Fanon noted this: "For several years certain laboratories have been trying to produce a serum for 'denegrification'; with all the earnestness in the world, laboratories have sterilized their test tubes, checked their scales, and embarked on researches that might make it possible for the miserable Negro to whiten himself and thus to throw off the burden of that corporeal malediction." *Black Skin, White Masks*, 111. White's article might also be read within the contexts of the African American historical trope of "passing." Interestingly, White himself was so light skinned that he was known to walk through whites-only sections of the South unnoticed.

31. For more on White's role in the Renaissance, see Charles W. Scruggs, "Alain Locke and Walter White: Their Struggle for Control of the Harlem Renaissance," *Black American Literature Forum* 14 (1980): 91–99. By 1947 Walter White had gained control in the NAACP and aligned it firmly to the right. Marable writes that White "attempted to identify the struggle for black equality with the anticommunist impulse." Marable also notes, "The African-American leaders who emerged in the years after the Great Depression developed a strategic alliance with the Democratic Party and the administration of Franklin Roosevelt, which oriented the black electorate's behavior for the remainder of the century. Two pivotal figures who were architects of this alliance were Walter White, national secretary of the NAACP, and educator Mary McLeod Bethune. White had been instrumental in the creation of the Fair Employment Practices Committee during World War II, and was responsible for the NAACP's legalistic and gradualistic approach to achieve desegregation." *Race, Reform, and Rebellion*, 22, 249.

32. Quoted in Scruggs, "Alain Locke and Walter White," 93.

33. As Manning Marable has noted, social, political, and economic gains for the black working and middle classes "seemed to many to provide the basis for an entirely new political relationship between blacks and whites." *Race, Reform, and Rebellion*, 17.

34. Omi and Winant, *Racial Formation*, 17. Myrdal's study, underwritten by the Carnegie Commission, was supported by several major figures in social thought in this period, including Walter White.

35. William L. Van Deburg, *New Day in Babylon: The Black Power Movement and American Culture, 1965–1975* (Chicago: University of Chicago Press, 1992), 55. In *Shadow and Art* (1964), Ralph Ellison responded to Myrdal's book by asking "can a people . . . live and develop for over three hundred years simply by *reacting*? Are American Negroes simply the creation of white men, or have they at least helped to create themselves out of what they found around them? Men have made a way of life in caves and upon cliffs, why cannot Negroes have made a life upon the horns of the white man's dilemma?" Quoted in Lawrence W. Levine, *Black Culture and Black Consciousness: Afro-American Folk Thought from Slavery to Freedom* (New York: Oxford University Press, 1977), 293.

36. Quoted in Houston A. Baker, Jr., *Blues, Ideology, and Afro-American Literature: A Vernacular Theory* (Chicago: University of Chicago Press, 1984), 70. Emphasis Baker's.

37. Baker, *Blues, Ideology*, 68–70. Baker goes on to suggest that writers like Davis and Sterling Brown during this period "inscribe a Darwinian 'naturalness' in their critical prescriptions by suggesting American and English literary forms as *evolved* ones. Presumably, integrationism holds that structurally peculiar *Negro* forms are trapped in an evolutionary backwater." Emphasis in original.

38. David Theo Goldberg, "The Social Formation of Racist Discourse," *Anatomy of Racism* (Minneapolis: U of Minnesota Press, 1990), 306.

39. Of the collection's 226 poems, only 26 specifically mention race or racial issues or use the images of "black" and "dark" in their titles. Even fewer follow in the Renaissance tradition of drawing on black vernacular expressive forms, and often these elide the specificities of African American experience. Marcus B. Christian's " 'Go Down Moses!' " (34), for example, refashions the black spiritual as an allusion to the fall of Berlin and the victory of the Allies. Beatrice Murphy, ed., *Ebony Rhythm: An Anthology of Contemporary Negro Verse* (New York: The Exposition Press, 1948).

40. Most of the poems follow Anglo-American poetic traditions, using English ballad stanzas, iambic meters, and established rhyme patterns. Very few use dialect, and of those that emulate a black musical form, the spiritual is predominant. Lawrence W. Levine has argued that secular song, such as the blues, has been often associated with working class culture in black culture. Further, Levine notes how often skin color was interrogated in blues and other secular songs. See *Black Culture and Black Consciousness*.

41. Preface to *Ebony Rhythm*, np; emphasis added. Hereafter cited in the text.

42. J. Saunders Redding, "American Negro Literature," in *Within the Circle: An Anthology of African American Literary Criticism from the Harlem Renaissance to the Present*, ed. Angelyn Mitchell (Durham, N.C.: Duke University Press, 1994), 111; emphasis added.

43. Charles I. Glicksberg, "Negro Poets and the American Tradition," *Antioch Review* 6 (1946): 246.

44. Edward Bland, "Racial Bias and Negro Poetry," *Poetry* 63 (March 1944): 333; emphasis added.

45. J. Saunders Redding, "The Negro Writer—Shadow and Substance," *Phylon* 11, no. 4 (Winter 1950): 373.

46. Hugh M. Gloster, "Race and the Negro Writer," *Phylon* 11, no. 4 (Winter 1950): 369, 370–371; emphasis added.

47. Margaret Walker, "New Poets," *Phylon* 11, no. 4 (Winter 1950): 350.

48. According to Richard Dwyer, "white power secures its dominance by seeming not to be anything in particular. . . . This property of whiteness, to be everything and nothing, is the source of its representational power." "White," *Screen* 29 (Fall 1988): 44, 45. Also see George Lipsitz, who quotes Dwyer and follows by stating, "As the unmarked category against which difference is constructed, whiteness never has to speak its name, never has to acknowledge its role as an organizing principle in social and cultural relations." "The Possessive Investment in Whiteness: Racialized Social Democracy and the 'White' Problem in American Studies," *American Quarterly* 47 (September 1995): 369.

49. Frank Marshall Davis, foreword to *47th Street* (Prairie City, Ill.: Decker Press, 1948), 3, 5. Davis had been better known in the 30s as one of the "protest" poets. His *I Am the American Negro* (Chicago: Black Cat Press, 1937) takes a stance toward racial justice which, in significant ways, presages the politico-poetic discourses of Black Liberation.

50. Allen Tate, preface to *Libretto for the Republic of Liberia*, by Melvin B. Tolson (1953; reprint, London: Collier-Macmillan, 1970), 10–12; first emphasis mine.

51. In contrast to what I am suggesting about the binary opposition between form (body) and content (mind), see Amitai Avi-ram, "The Unreadable Black Body: 'Conventional' Poetic Form in the Harlem Renaissance," *Genders* 7 (Spring 1990): 32–46. Avi-ram argues that conventional form in black poetry has been misread as conservative due largely to an overly simplistic understanding of poetic form's relation to the body.

52. As Levine points out, skin color has always been a site of contestation within African American communities. Although lighter color has commonly been considered of greater value, Levine notes many cases where it has lesser value. Further, he cautions against the simplistic view that whiteness is always the most valued color. The popularity of tanning and skin-darkening products among whites belies this view. "It would be inaccurate to speak of a monolithic American ideology concerning color." *Black Culture and Black Consciousness*, 290.

53. See Thomas J. Sugrue, "Crabgrass-Roots Politics: Race, Rights, and the Reaction against Liberalism in the Urban North, 1940–1954," *Journal of American History* (September 1995): 551–578. Also see, in the same issue, Arnold R. Hirsch, "Massive Resistance in the Urban North: Trumbull Park, Chicago, 1953–1966," 522–550; and Gary Gerstle, "Race and the Myth of the Liberal Consensus," 579–586.

54. In 1950 only 9 percent of all U.S. households had TV; in 1954 this figure rose to 54 percent; and by 1960 it had jumped to over 87 percent. Cobbett S. Steinberg, *TV Facts* (New York: Facts on File, 1980), 142.

55. Adolph Reed, Jr., "The 'Black Revolution' and the Reconstitution of Domination," in *Race, Politics, and Culture: Critical Essays on the Radicalism of the 1960s*, ed. Adolph Reed., Jr., Contributions in Afro-American and African Studies, no. 95 (New York: Greenwood, 1986), 69.

56. The 1955 open-coffin funeral of young Emmett Till, a Chicago boy who was murdered in Mississippi for speaking to a white woman, was covered by the popular black press as well as by the national press. The photo of Till's mangled corpse in *Jet* became an early icon in the Civil Rights movement. As the television documentary of Civil Rights activism, *Eyes on the Prize*, explained: "A generation of black people would remember the horror of that photo." "Awakenings (1954–1956)," *Eyes on the Prize*, dir. Henry Hampton (Alexandria, Va.: PBS Video/Blackside, Inc., 1987).

57. Marable, *Race, Reform, and Rebellion*, 50.

58. As Marable notes, "For some white sociologists and cultural historians, the decade under Eisenhower and Cold War had seemed a sterile and vacuous period of social conformity. . . . For black America, however, this conservative cultural description does not apply. In the creative arts, in literature, in intellectual work, there was a significant outpouring of energy, talent and hope for the future." Ibid., 45.

59. Robert Allen, *Black Awakening in Capitalist America: An Analytic History* (Trenton, N.J.: Africa World Press, 1990), 40.

60. *Malcolm X Speaks: Selected Speeches and Statements*, ed. George Breitman (New York: Grove Weidenfield, 1965), 48–50. Malcolm X articulates similar positions in almost every speech and statement included in this collection.

61. Other prominent African American leaders of the early 60s who espoused a Third-Worldist revolutionary position included Harold Cruse, who stated in a 1963 article for *The Liberator*: "We American Negroes exist in essentially the same relationship to American capitalism as other colonials and semi-colonials have to western capitalism as a whole." Quoted in Allen, *Black Awakening in Capitalist America*, 175.

62. *Malcolm X Speaks*, 169; 157 ff.

63. Quoted in Van Deburg, *New Day in Babylon*, 1.

64. See Henry Louis Gates, Jr., "Talkin' That Talk," in *"Race," Writing, and Difference*, ed. Henry Louis Gates, Jr. (Chicago: University of Chicago Press, 1985, 1986), 402–403; and Omi and Winant, *Racial Formation*. Also see Fuss, *Essentially Speaking*, 81–86, for a critique of Gates's reading of "blackness."

65. Kobena Mercer, "'1968': Periodizing Politics and Identity," in *Cultural Studies*, ed. Lawrence Grossberg, Cary Nelson, and Paula Treichler (New York: Routledge, 1992), 430.

66. Quoted in Clayborne Carson, *In Struggle: SNCC and the Black Awakening of the 1960s* (Cambridge, Mass.: Harvard University Press, 1981), 101, emphasis added.

67. Hoyt Fuller, "Towards a Black Aesthetic," in *The Black Aesthetic*, ed. Addison Gayle, Jr. (Garden City, N.Y.: Doubleday, Anchor, 1971), 7–8.

68. Bigsby, *The Second Black Renaissance*, 50. Bigsby also reminds us that "for all its distinctiveness," the period from 1964 to 1970 epitomized by the Black Arts movement, "was part of a development in black writing which had begun with Richard Wright and which had continued throughout the 1950s, 1960s, and 1970s." Ibid., 3. In particular, as Bigsby's title suggests, the Vietnam era constitutes a reemergence of radicalism, nationalism, militancy, and cultural productivity characteristic of early twentieth-century African American history.

69. New York City police closed BARTS in 1966, charging that its members concealed weapons on its premises. See Amiri Baraka, *The Autobiography of LeRoi Jones/Amiri Baraka* (New York: Freundlich, 1984).

70. All these groups can be seen as directly stemming from groups of the late 50s and early 60s, such as the Umbra Workshop. Lorenzo Thomas helped initiate the Black Arts Center in Houston, Tom Dent went on to work in the Free Southern Theatre, which later became BLKARTSOUTH, and Askia M. Touré became involved in the beginnings of the Detroit Black Arts group. See Michael Orlen, "The Umbra Poets' Workshop, 1962–1965: Some Socio-Literary Puzzles," in *Belief vs. Theory in Black American Literary Criticism*, ed. Joe Weixlmann and Chester J. Fontenot, vol. 2 of *Studies in Black American Literature* (Greenwood, Fla.: Penkevill, 1986), 177–224.

71. The integrationist posture evident in *Negro Digest* from the 40s to 50s contrasts significantly with its cultural politics during the mid-60s under Hoyt Fuller's tenure as editor. The magazine had ceased publication after 1951, but John H. Johnson, its publisher, revived it in June 1961. Up until 1965, *Negro Digest* was "[i]n intention and tone . . . integrationist." By 1964, Fuller began introducing works by militant black writers who advocated the belief that literature should play a political role in the black struggle. Fuller's own essay in the June 1964 issue, "Ivory Towerist vs. Activist: The Role of the Negro Writer in an Era of Struggle," asserted the important relationships between political action and black writing. After the September issue, which featured a report on "The Negro Writer in the U.S.: Assembly at Asilomar" and included photos of both black and white writers, pictures of white writers never appeared again in the magazine. Under Fuller, *Negro Digest* increasingly endorsed black cultural nationalism and rejected integrationism. Throughout this period, the magazine would become the major forum for the black aesthetic of the 60s. Fuller gave space to LeRoi Jones (Amiri Baraka), Larry Neal, Carolyn Rodgers, Nikki Giovanni, and other important spokespersons of the new literary movement; by 1970, Fuller had become an Afrocentric cultural nationalist and renamed the magazine *Black World*. For a more detailed discussion of *Negro Digest*'s role in the post–World War II era, see Johnson and Johnson, *Propaganda and Aesthetics*.

72. Johnson and Johnson, *Propaganda and Aesthetics*, 170.

73. For important documents on the Black Aesthetic see: Addison Gayle, Jr., ed. *The Black Aesthetic* (Garden City, N.Y.: Doubleday, Anchor, 1971); Floyd B. Barbour, ed., *The Black Seventies* (Boston: Porter Sargent, 1970); Houston A. Baker, Jr., ed., *Black Literature in America* (New York: McGraw-Hill, 1971); Sherry Turner, "An Overview of the New Black Arts," *Freedomways* 9, no. 2 (Spring 1969): 156–163; Carolyn M. Rodgers, "Black Poetry—Where It's At," *Negro Digest*, September 1969, 7–16; Ameer Baraka (Leroi Jones/Amiri Baraka), "The Black Aesthetic," *Negro Digest*, September 1969, 5–6; Carolyn M. Rodgers, "Uh Nat'chal Thang—The WHOLE TRUTH—US," *Black World*, September 1971, 4–14; Geneva Smitherman, "The Power of Rap: The Black Idiom and the New Black Poetry," *Twentieth Century Literature* 19, no. 4 (October 1973): 259–274. These are just a few of the many articles published during the Vietnam era articulating the Black Aesthetic. Other major statements can be found in Larry Neal, *Visions of a Liberated Future: Black Arts Movement Writings*, ed. Michael Schwartz (New York: Thunder Mouth's Press, 1989); Jones and Neal, eds., *Black Fire*; and Abraham Chapman, ed., *New Black Voices: An Anthology of Contemporary Afro-American Literature* (New York: New American Library, Mentor, 1972). Stephen Henderson's work, especially in " 'Survival Motion,' " and *Understanding the New Black Poetry: Black Speech and Black Music as Poetic References* (New York: William Morrow, 1973), is often cited and provides one of the more analytical articulations of the Black Aesthetic.

For more recent overviews and critical analyses of the Black Aesthetic see: Henry Louis Gates, Jr., "Preface to Blackness: Text and Pretext," in *Afro-American Literature: The Reconstruction of Instruction*, ed. Dexter Fisher and Robert B. Stepto (New York: Modern Language Association, 1979), 44–69; and more recently, his "African American Criticism," in *Redrawing the Boundaries: The Transformation of English and American Literary Studies*, ed. Stephen Greenblatt and Giles Gunn (New York: Modern Language Association, 1992), 303–319; Jennifer Jordan, "Cultural Nationalism in the 1960s: Politics and Poetry," in *Race, Politics, and Culture: Critical Essays on the Radicalism of the 1960s*, ed. Reed, 29–60; and Houston A. Baker, Jr., *Blues, Ideology, and Afro-American Literature: A Vernacular Theory* (Chicago: University of Chicago Press, 1984). For black feminist critiques of the Black Aesthetic see bell hooks, *Ain't I A Woman: Black Women and Feminism* (Boston: South End Press, 1981), and Michele Wallace, *Black Macho and the Myth of the Superwoman* (New York: Verso, 1990).

74. In fact, many writers involved with militant left black activism in this period were cited by the white media and law enforcement as principal instigators of black revolt. Perhaps the most famous instance of this was Amiri Baraka's arrest and trial for his involvement in the 1967 Newark riots. Baraka was initially sentenced to three years in prison for his alleged involvement on the basis of his poem "Black People!" Judge Leon W. Kapp at the sentencing proceedings cited "Black People!" as a "diabolical prescription to commit murder and to steal and plunder." Quoted in Van Deburg, *New Day in Babylon*, 180.

75. Gates, "African American Criticism," 309.

76. Van Deburg, *New Day in Babylon*, 188.

77. Eldridge Cleaver, *Soul on Ice* (New York: Delta, 1968), 125.

78. Quoted in Marable, *Race, Reform, and Rebellion*, 86.

79. *Freedomways* 7, no. 1 (Winter 1967), 7; no. 2 (Spring 1967).

80. *Freedomways* 7, no. 4 (Fall 1967): 286. Begun in 1961 by black and white Marxists, *Freedomways* continues quarterly publication. In its early years it was edited by W.E.B. Du Bois and his wife, Shirley Graham. Although it was not an official publication of the Communist party, many of its supporters were members of the party. According to Johnson and Johnson, *Freedomways* "is historically important partly because it dramatized the clash between Marxism and black nationalism." They note that, although the names of editors and contributors have changed over the years, it has remained Marxist in approach. "Thus, the journal largely steered clear of the new nationalistic literature and discussions of the black aesthetic, even though it occasionally published some of the emerging young poets." *Propaganda and Aesthetics*, 228, n. 32. Although Johnson and Johnson are correct in noting the magazine's Marxist orientation, I believe they overemphasize the division between this orientation and black cultural nationalism. Although consistently inflected by party-influenced Marxism, the magazine featured perspectives in its articles and poetry that could be found in many of the important black liberationist periodicals of the era.

81. *Black Vanguard* 5 (1968): not paged.

82. Van Deburg, *New Day in Babylon*, 147.

83. Ibid., 99.

84. Numerous studies have been published bearing out these assertions. For more on the Project 100,000, see Lisa Hsiao, "Project 100,000: The Great Society's Answer to Military Manpower Needs in Vietnam." *Vietnam Generation* 1, no. 2 (Spring 1989): 14–37.

85. Van Deburg, *New Day in Babylon*, 99.

86. Gwendolyn Patton, "Black People and War," *Liberator*, March 1966, 31.

87. Van Deburg, *New Day in Babylon*, 96.

88. Malcolm X, *February 1965: The Final Speeches*, ed. Steve Clark (New York: Pathfinder, 1992), 150.

89. Orde Coombs, ed., *We Speak As Liberators: Young Black Poets* (New York: Dodd, Mead, 1970), 1. Hereafter cited in the text as WSAL.

90. In *The New Black Poetry*, ed. Clarence Major (New York: International Publishers, 1969), 141.

91. Introduction to *Vietnam and Black America: An Anthology of Protest*, ed. Clyde Taylor (Garden City, N.Y.: Doubleday, Anchor, 1973), xx. Hereafter cited in the text as VBA.

92. Gates, "African American Criticism," 309.

93. Quoted in Van Deburg, *New Day in Babylon*, 184.

94. Ibid., 179; emphasis added.

95. Amilcar Cabral, "Identity and Dignity in the Context of the National Liberation Struggle," *Return to the Source: Selected Speeches*, ed. Africa Information Service (New York: Monthly Review, 1973), 64–65. Cabral also argues that "[national liberation] struggles are preceded by an increase in expression of culture, consolidated progressively into a successful or unsuccessful attempt to affirm the cultural personality of the dominated people, as a means of negating the oppressor culture. . . . if imperialist domination has the vital need to practice cultural oppression, national liberation is necessarily an act of *culture*." "National Liberation and Culture," *Return to the Source*, 43. Before his assassination by Portuguese agents in 1973, Cabral was Secretary-General of the African Party for the Independence of Guinea and the Cape Verde Islands.

96. Marable, *Race, Reform, and Rebellion* , 107.

97. Gabriel Kolko, *Anatomy of a War: Vietnam, the United States, and the Modern Historical Experience* (New York: Pantheon, 1985), 49–50. An American edition of Ho's *Selected Writings* was published through a popular press in the mid-60s and was widely read by resistance activists.

98. See *The Black Panthers Speak*, ed. Philip S. Foner (Philadelphia: J. B. Lippincott, 1970), 4–6.

99. Sandy Robinson, "I HAD TO BE TOLD," *Journal of Black Poetry* 16 (Summer 1972): 34.

100. Carl Black, "No More," in *Jump Bad: A New Chicago Anthology*, ed. Gwendolyn Brooks (Detroit: Broadside Press, 1971), 80.

101. Emory, "On Revolutionary Art," *The Black Panther*, 20 June 1967, 1.

102. Ericka, "Revolution," *The Black Panther*, 5 October 1968, 14.

103. Raymond Washington, "Freedom Hair," in *New Black Voices*, 388. Texts from this collection will hereafter be cited in the text as NBV.

104. Sharon Scott, "Oh—-Yeah," in *Jump Bad*, 177.

105. Sharon Scott, "For Both of Us at Fisk," in *Jump Bad*, 181–182.

106. Van Deburg, *New Day in Babylon*, 51–53.

107. "Mantan" was the name of an African American character portrayed as a "Steppin Fetchit" stereotype in Charlie Chan movies.

108. Raymond Patterson, "Riot Rimes," in *Soulscript: Afro-American Poetry*, ed. June Jordan (Garden City, N.Y.: Doubleday, Zenith, 1970), 108.

109. Lebert Bethune, "To Strike for the Night," in *The New Black Poetry*, ed.

Clarence Major (New York: International Publishers, 1969), 27–28. Poems from this collection will hereafter be cited in the text as NBP.

110. Prentiss Taylor, "Tony," *Journal of Black Poetry* 16 (Summer 1972): 49.

111. Etheridge Knight, "2 Poems for Black Relocation Centers," in *Broadside Treasury*, ed. Gwendolyn Brooks (Detroit: Broadside Press, 1971), 82–83.

112. Michael Harper, "Debridement," in *Debridement* (Garden City, N.Y.: Doubleday, 1972, 1973), 67, 101

113. Suliaman El Hadi, "Ho Chi Minh," in Jalal Nuriddin and Suliaman El Hadi, *The Last Poets: Vibes From the Scribes, Selected Poems* (London: Pluto Press, 1985), 69–71.

114. Editor's note, *Vietnam and Black America*, ed. Taylor, 301.

115. Peter X, "BLACK!! Who Me?" *Black Vanguard* 5 (1968): 3.

116. Askia Muhammed Touré, "Extension (for Imam El Hajj Heshaam Jabeer and Leroi Jones)," in *Understanding the New Black Poetry*, ed. Henderson, 304.

117. Black Liberationists often pointed to the high number of Jewish landlords in major urban centers in the North, most notably in New York City, as an example of how Jewish Americans profited from blacks. Antisemitism was often manifested in the struggles for community control in New York during the 60s. Of course, the fact that Jewish Americans and members of other ethnic groups did own more property than blacks in New York City is the result of complex sociohistorical forces that many in the black movement had not adequately theorized.

118. Nikki Giovanni, "The True Import of Present Dialogue Black vs. Negro (For Peppi, Who Will Ultimately Judge Our Efforts)," in *Black Arts: An Anthology of Black Creations*, ed. Ahmed Alhamisi and Harun Kofi Wangara (Detroit: Black Arts Publications, 1969), 117. This poem originally appeared in Giovanni's book *Black Talk, Black Feeling* (1968).

119. Although antisemitism appears in twentieth-century black writing as early as W.E.B. Du Bois, the rising acceptance of Black Muslim philosophies in the 60s directly contributed to Black Liberationist antisemitism. Israeli-Arab conflict in the 60s also exerted some influence in Black Liberationist perceptions of Jews. As Clayborne Carson has noted, the pro-Palestinian line taken by SNCC during the 1967 Six-Day War served to exacerbate the antagonisms in African American and Jewish American relationships during the Vietnam era. Many Jewish Americans felt betrayed and threatened by SNCC's stand; because many Jews had supported the Civil Rights movement, they had expected support for Israel from blacks. SNCC activists, on the other hand, felt the Jewish community's reaction offered more evidence to support the antisemitism already festering in the movement. *In Struggle: SNCC and the Black Awakening of the 1960s* (Cambridge, Mass.: Harvard University Press, 1981), 266–269. For a Jewish perspective on relations between blacks and Jews in this period, see Jonathan Kaufman, *Broken Alliance: The Turbulent Times Between Blacks and Jews in America* (New York: Scribner's, 1988), especially 136–138. Kaufman also sees the 1967 Six-Day War as a factor in the breakdown of coalitions between blacks and Jews.

120. I thank Maria Damon for pointing out to me that this poem refers specifically to the Baroness Nica de Koenigswarter, with whom Thelonius Monk spent his last years, and in whose home Charlie Parker died.

121. Theodore, "You Are the Black Woman," *Liberator*, March 1969, 13.

122. The Daniel Moynihan report on the African-American family published in 1967 epitomized the institutionalization of these stereotypes as national policy.

See discussions of Moynihan's positions in Omi and Winant, *Racial Formation*, 18–21.

123. Orlen, "The Umbra Poets' Workshop," 209. Orlen reports, however, that Reed changed his allegiances several times in this period, moving between a militant nationalist line and a more multicultural line. Friends of Reed's have commented that this exemplified his mercurial and contentious nature more than any firm ideological belief. Ibid., 210. It is interesting to note that Julius Lester, one of the principal spokespersons and poets of the movement, converted to Judaism.

124. bell hooks, *Ain't I A Woman: Black Women and Feminism* (Boston: South End Press, 1981), 98. hooks points out, however, that Wallace "fails to understand that the 60s black movement did not merely eradicate many of the barriers that prevented inter-racial dating; it led to numerous social and economic gains for black people."

125. Ibid., 98, and 92 ff.

126. See, for example, Reed, "The 'Black Revolution' and the Reconstitution of Domination," 61–95.

127. For examples of important attacks on the Black Aesthetic, see Gates, "Preface to Blackness: Text and Pretext"; Michele Wallace, *Black Macho and the Myth of the Superwoman* (1979; reprint, New York: Verso, 1990); and Jordan, "Cultural Nationalism in the 1960s: Politics and Poetry," 29–60.

128. Omi and Winant, *Racial Formation*, 93.

129. Ibid., 38–39.

130. Ibid., 93.

3. *"The Territory Colonized"*

1. Throughout my study, I will use the terms "Women's Liberation" or "women's movement" generically to refer to the various feminist groups that emerged during the mid-60s. Although this may risk effacing critical distinctions between the multiply articulated groups organized as feminist in the Vietnam era, I hope it will also reveal alliances and resemblances. As Alice Echols notes, by the 1968 Sandy Springs conference, feminists had begun using the term "Women's Liberation" widely "because it was in the leftist vernacular of 'liberation movements.'" *Daring to Be Bad: Radical Feminism in America 1967–1975* (Minneapolis: University of Minnesota Press, 1989), 53. By regarding feminism as "Women's Liberation," I call attention to the broader viability of the oppositional vernacular that links feminism with both Black Liberation and antiwar activism within a historical context shaped by the nation's engagement in war with a Third World nation.

2. Quoted in Sara Evans, *Personal Politics: The Roots of Women's Liberation in the Civil Rights Movement and the New Left* (New York: Vintage, 1980), 42.

3. The release of the commission's report made a front-page story in the *New York Times* and was the topic of a special segment on NBC's *Today Show*. *The Feminine Mystique* was an immediate bestseller in 1963, selling over three million copies.

4. Carmichael quoted in Echols, *Daring to Be Bad*, 31. According to Mary King, however, Carmichael's comment may have been taken out of context and given far too much weight by feminists. King claims Carmichael's remark was a self-parodic allusion to the sexual headiness of the Freedom Summer days. See Echols, *Daring to Be Bad*, 31. Sara Evans points out that even though the Hayden-

King paper went mostly unnoticed at the meeting, it marked a moment when black and white women shared a common critique on sexual discrimination within the movement. *Personal Politics*, 87–88.

5. For further discussion of how the gendering of race played out in Black Liberationist cultural discourse, see the discussion in chapter 2 of this book. Also see Ruth Frankenberg, *White Women, Race Matters: The Social Construction of Whiteness* (Minneapolis: University of Minnesota Press, 1993).

6. Echols, *Daring to Be Bad*, 27.

7. Ibid., 42. At times the sexism of the male-dominated New Left broke out in blatantly misogynist reactions to women's calls for equality and liberation. When Marilyn Webb attempted to speak before the 1969 Counter-Inaugural Demonstration in Washington, D.C., organized by the National Mobilization Committee to End the War in Vietnam, several men in the audience chanted "Take it off!" and "Take her off the stage and fuck her!" Rather than attempt to control the unruly crowd, David Dellinger, one of Mobe's chief organizers of the event, tried to remove Webb and other women from the stage. Echols, *Daring to Be Bad*, 117.

8. Ibid., 33–34. "Prefigurative politics" is Echols's term. Interestingly, Echols points out that Tom Hayden was the first to call for a "re-assertion of the personal" in 1962. "By expanding political discourse to include the subject of personal relations, new leftists paved the way for feminists to criticize marriage, the family, and sexuality." Ibid., 28–29.

9. Evans, *Personal Politics*, 108, 112.

10. Susan Bordo, *Unbearable Weight: Feminism, Western Culture, and the Body* (Berkeley: University of California Press, 1993), 16.

11. Feminist activists throughout history, of course, have constructed forms of "body-politics." As Paula Rabinowitz has demonstrated, women writers of the 30s "recognized the female body as one contradictory site of sexual, gender, race, and class conflict in American society, and they used this understanding to rechart the terrain of literary radicalism." *Labor and Desire: Women's Revolutionary Fiction in Depression America* (Chapel Hill: University of North Carolina Press, 1991), 61. Rabinowitz also suggests that the marginalization of 30s women's radicalism in contemporary feminist history stems from the "tendency of both Marxist and feminist theories to assign primacy to one category of difference—class on the one hand, gender on the other." Ibid., 4. It is this tendency to essentialize and privilege gender that characterizes Vietnam-era feminism's body-politics.

12. Robin Morgan, *Monster* (New York: Vintage, 1972), 85.

13. See the selection from Gramsci's Prison Notebooks, "The Formation of Intellectuals," *The Modern Prince and Other Writings*, trans. Louis Marks (New York: International Publishers, 1987), 118–125.

14. Echols writes, "The idea that revolutionary consciousness emanates from 'the perception of oneself as one of the oppressed' would prove central to the emergence of the women's movement, but in 1966 [when Black Power became dominant] the new left embraced the idea in ways that further marginalized women." *Daring to Be Bad*, 37.

15. Webb quoted in ibid., 115; ibid., 3. It should be emphasized, however, that biological essentialism does not characterize all feminist discourse in Women's Liberation. As Echols points out, radical feminists tended to critique gender as a socially constructed term. Ibid., 6. The distinctions between radical and cultural feminists' positions on biological essentialism, however, are rarely absolute during the Vietnam era. A reading of radical feminist documents often

shows that despite an overt constructionist view of gender, traces of biological essentialism are manifest. See ibid., 188.

16. Addams et al. quoted in ibid., 44; ibid., 44.

17. Evans, *Personal Politics*, 190.

18. For an analysis of the discourse of control in feminism, see Irene Diamond and Lee Quinby, "American Feminism and the Language of Control," in *Feminism and Foucault: Reflections on Resistance*, ed. Irene Diamond and Lee Quinby (Boston: Northeastern University Press, 1988), 193–206.

19. Barbara Burris, "The Fourth World Manifesto," in *Radical Feminism*, ed. Anne Koedt, Ellen Levine, and Anita Rapone (New York: Quadrangle/New York Times Books, 1973), 322–323; 325; 326; 330. The byline of this paper reads "In agreement with Kathy Barry, Terry Moore, Joann DeLor, Joann Parent, Cate Stadelman."

20. Ibid., 334–335; emphasis added.

21. Echols, *Daring to Be Bad*, 245; ibid., 6. Echols later writes, "After 1975, a year of internecine conflicts between radical and cultural feminists, cultural feminism eclipsed radical feminism as the dominant tendency within the women's liberation movement, and as a consequence, liberal feminism became the recognized voice of the women's movement." Ibid., 243.

22. Judith Brown, "Toward a Female Liberation Movement," in *Voices from Women's Liberation*, comp. and ed. Leslie B. Tanner (New York: Signet, 1970), 410; emphasis added.

23. Echols, *Daring to Be Bad*, 62–65.

24. Michael Omi and Howard Winant, *Racial Formation in the United States: From the 1960s to the 1980s* (New York: Routledge and Kegan Paul, 1986), 47–48.

25. Robin Morgan, "Taking Back Our Bodies," in *The New Woman's Survival Sourcebook*, ed. Kirsten Grimstad and Susan Rennie (New York: Knopf, 1975), 33. Emphasis in original.

26. Ibid., 33; emphasis added.

27. Many feminists conflated forms of racial oppression with those of gender oppression. Roxanne Dunbar, for example, argued that pornography was analogous to the lynching of blacks. Echols, *Daring to Be Bad*, 165. Evans points out that the term "male chauvinism" commonly used by feminists during the Vietnam era was appropriated from the black struggle's term "white chauvinism." "It was prompted by women's perceptions in the wake of the civil rights movement that their oppression had many parallels to that of blacks." *Personal Politics*, 120.

28. When the issue of lesbianism within the women's movement erupted at the second Congress to Unite Women (1970), the nation-based paradigm became instrumental in the articulation of sexuality as the principal arena for political struggle. The Radicalesbian position paper, "The Woman-Identified Woman," "redefined lesbianism as the quintessential act of political solidarity with other women. By defining lesbianism as a political choice rather than a sexual alternative, Radicalesbian disarmed heterosexual feminists." Echols, *Daring to Be Bad*, 217. As one article in a 1971 issue of *The Furies* argued, "Lesbianism is not a matter of sexual preference, but rather one of political choice which every woman must make if she is to become woman-identified and thereby end male supremacy." Rita Mae Brown, a prominent voice for the lesbian insurgency within the women's movement, declared, "You can't build a strong movement if your sisters are out there fucking with the oppressor." Quoted in Echols, *Daring to Be Bad*, 232. Ac-

cording to Echols, "For the Furies, 'coming out' became the feminist equivalent of 'picking up the gun,' the barometer of one's radicalism." Ibid., 233. In these instances, the rhetorical strategies parallel the aspects of nationalism outlined by Omi and Winant. Interestingly, the nation-based paradigm of struggle reappears in the recent political phenomenon of Queer Nation.

29. Kobena Mercer, "'1968': Periodizing Politics and Identity," in *Cultural Studies*, ed. Lawrence Grossberg, Cary Nelson, and Paula Treichler (New York: Routledge, 1992), 433.

30. See documents from the Panthers' newspaper in *The Black Panthers Speak*, ed. Philip Foner (Philadelphia: J. B. Lippincott, 1970).

31. Mercer, "'1968,'" 434.

32. Ibid., 426.

33. Jan Clausen, *A Movement of Poets: Thoughts on Poetry and Feminism* (Brooklyn, N.Y.: Long Haul Press, 1982), 2.

34. Ibid., 5. Clausen argues that poetry may have become so popular among women because, as a form of writing, it allowed for interruptions, it was cheaper to publish, and fit more easily into "such contexts as the anthology, the newspaper, or the open reading." Ibid., 11–12.

35. Ibid., 12. According to Clausen, whether in readings or in anthologies, "'I am woman' was the core revelation sought or expressed." Ibid., 13.

36. Alicia Suskin Ostriker, *Stealing the Language: The Emergence of Women's Poetry in America* (Boston: Beacon Press, 1986), 92.

37. Howe and Bass's construction of a feminist canon might reflect their individual tastes, but it is important to recognize how their choices were informed by the politics of Women's Liberation and reiterate the prevailing modes of discourse in women's poetry of the Vietnam era. Howe writes in her foreword, "Much, if not most, of the poetry in this volume follows the revival/renewal of the women's movement in the mid-sixties." Howe also explains that in collecting poems she and Bass read "back issues of women's movement magazines and newspapers" to get a sense of what was current in women's poetry. *No More Masks!: An Anthology of Poems by Women* (Garden City, N.Y.: Doubleday, Anchor, 1973), xxix, xxvii. *No More Masks!* became an immensely popular and influential anthology, leading during this period to the publication of other feminist anthologies that also support Ostriker's claims. Anthologies I surveyed include *Psyche: The Feminine Poetic Consciousness*, ed. Barbara Segnitz and Carol Rainey (New York: Dial Press, 1973); *Mountain Moving Day: Poems by Women*, ed. Elaine Gill (Trumansburg, N.Y.: Crossing, 1973); *The Women Poets in English*, ed. Ann Stanford (New York: McGraw-Hill, 1972); *Rising Tides: 20th Century American Women Poets*, ed. Sharon Barba and Laura Chester (New York: Washington Square Press, 1973); and *We Become New: Poems by Contemporary American Women*, ed. Lucille Iverson and Kathryn Ruby (New York: Bantam, 1975).

38. Simone de Beauvoir, *The Second Sex* (New York: Vintage, 1974), 164.

39. Bordo, *Unbearable Weight*, 17.

40. Ruth Rosen, "The Day They Buried 'Traditional Womanhood': Women and the Politics of Protest," *Vietnam Generation* 1, no. 3/4 (Summer/Fall 1989): 210.

41. Susan Schweik makes this point in her study of women's poetry of World War II. See Schweik, *A Gulf So Deeply Cut: American Women Poets and the Second World War* (Madison: University of Wisconsin Press, 1991).

42. See Herbert Marcuse, *One-Dimensional Man: Studies in the Ideology of Advanced Industrial Society* (Boston: Beacon Press, 1964), 10. Here Marcuse considers

how the "Self (Ego) transposes the 'outer' into the inner" through a process of introjection. This "implies the existence of an inner dimension distinguished from and even antagonistic to the external exigencies—an individual consciousness and an individual unconscious *apart from* public opinions and behavior. The idea of 'inner freedom' here has its reality: it designates the private space in which man may become and remain 'himself.'" Also see Marcuse, *Eros and Civilization: A Philosophical Inquiry into Freud* (Boston: Beacon, 1955, 1966).

43. Adrienne Rich, "Tear Gas," in Adrienne Rich, *The Fact of a Doorframe: Poems Selected and New, 1950–1974* (New York: Norton, 1984), 198–200.

44. Susan Sherman, "Lilith of the Wildwood, of the Fair Places," *RAT*, May 3–June 1 1971, 28.

45. Sandra McPherson, "Pregnancy," in Howe and Bass, *No More Masks!*, 312. Hereafter cited in the text as NMM.

46. Alta, "Living in a Country at War/1968 Verson," *It Ain't Me Babe*, September 23, 1970, 10. Although pregnancy is never specifically named in this poem, the poem appeared together with two other poems by Alta, "First Pregnancy" and "Miscarriage."

47. Quoted in Echols, *Daring to Be Bad*, 54.

48. Kathie Sarachild also points out that this image was practically a "stock symbol" in the antiwar movement. The predominantly male editors of the underground press "adored Third World women with guns 10,000 miles away" but "still preferred 'Women for Peace' to 'Women's Liberation' at home." "Taking in the Images: A Record in Graphics of the Vietnam Era Soil for Feminism," *Vietnam Generation* 1, no. 3/4 (Summer/Fall 1989): 236–238. Emphasis in original.

49. I studied numerous titles and issues from the period, including: *Ain't I a Woman, Alice, Aphra, Big Mama Rag, Chrysalis, Everywoman, Female Liberation Newsletter, The Feminist Voice, The Furies, Goodbye to All That!, Herself, Hysteria, It Ain't Me Babe, Majority Report, No More Fun and Games, off our backs, Remember Our Fire, The Rising Tide, The Second Wave, Sisters, Tooth and Nail, Up from Under, Velvet Glove,* and *Women.*

50. Echols, *Daring to Be Bad*, 83–84. Sidebars to a reprint of Kathie Sarachild's "Consciousness-Raising: A Radical Weapon" cite Mao Zedong's model of the training of revolutionary cadres. One sidebar's quote from Mao's "On Practice" links revolutionary consciousness to corporeal phenomenology: "All knowledge originates in perception of the objective external world through man's physical sense organs." Another quotes William Hinton's *Fanshen* (1966): "This meeting was held . . . in an effort to educate the young revolutionary cadres in the fundamentals of class relations and class consciousness. . . ." Kathie Sarachild, "Consciousness-Raising: A Radical Weapon," in *Feminist Revolution*, ed. Kathie Sarachild and Redstockings (New York: Random, 1978), 146, 149.

51. See Gabriel Kolko, *Anatomy of a War: Vietnam, the United States, and the Modern Historical Experience* (New York: Pantheon, 1985), 51–55.

52. Echols, *Daring to Be Bad*, 185.

53. Ibid., 86. The emulation of Algerian women calls to mind not only Pontecorvo's film but also Frantz Fanon's celebration of the female subversiveness of Muslim women in "Algeria Unveiled." Burris, however, attacks Fanon's article as inherently patriarchal. See "The Fourth World Manifesto," 342–349.

54. Marilyn Lowen Fletcher, "A Chant for My Sisters," in Robin Morgan, ed., *Sisterhood is Powerful: An Anthology of Writings from the Women's Liberation Movement* (New York: Vintage, 1970), 559–560. Hereafter cited in the text as SIP.

55. Dien Bien Phu is the Vietnamese site of a famous battle and siege that ultimately brought about the surrender of the French in 1955. It was a stunning victory for the Vietnamese forces, particularly because it demonstrated the ability of guerilla tactics to outwit a technologically sophisticated First World military.

56. "Brandy French" (pseud.), "A Womb on Strike," *It Ain't Me Babe*, September 4–17, 1970, 15.

57. This feminist group used the acronym WITCH variously to stand for: Women's Independent Taxpayers, Consumers, and Homemakers; Women Interested in Toppling Consumption Holidays; Women Incensed at Telephone Company Harassment; Women Infuriated at Taking Care of Hoodlums; and Women's International Terrorist Conspiracy from Hell. WITCH staged a number of demonstrations noted for their theatricality; their strategy was to capitalize on the media's increasing need for sensationalism in the often carnivalesque atmosphere of 60s activism.

58. Adrienne Rich, "Vietnam and Sexual Violence," in Adrienne Rich, *On Lies, Secrets, and Silence: Selected Prose 1966–1978* (New York: Norton, 1979), 109; emphasis added. This article originally appeared in a 1973 issue of *The American Poetry Review*.

59. U.S. cultural representations of the Vietnam War have been noted by feminist critics for deploying these same hierarchies to justify the U.S. role in Vietnam. See, for example, Susan Jeffords, who argues that "an important way to read the [Vietnam] war, perhaps the most significant way when we think about war itself, is as a construction of gendered interests. . . . [T]he arena of warfare and the Vietnam War in particular are not just fields of battle but fields of gender, in which enemies are depicted as feminine." *The Remasculinization of America: Gender and the Vietnam War* (Bloomington: Indiana University Press, 1989), xi.

60. Robin Morgan, "Freaks," in Morgan, *Monster*, 22.

61. Diane Wakoski, "In Gratitude to Beethoven," in *Psyche: The Feminine Poetic Consciousness*, ed. Barbara Segnitz and Carol Rainey (New York: Dial Press, 1973), 206. Hereafter cited in the text as *Psyche*.

62. For examples, see Linda Williams, *Hard Core: Power, Pleasure, and the "Frenzy of the Visible"* (Berkeley: University of California Press, 1989); Walter Kendricks, *The Secret Museum: Pornography in Modern Culture* (New York: Viking, 1987); Rosalind Pollack Petchesky, "Foetal Images: The Power of Visual Culture in the Politics of Reproduction," in *Reproductive Technologies: Gender, Motherhood, and Medicine*, ed. Michelle Stanworth (Minneapolis: University of Minnesota Press, 1987), 57–80.

63. Kendricks, *The Secret Museum*, 221.

64. "Society of the spectacle" is Guy Debord's term for the situation in late capitalism when images and representations have become the dominant commodity. *Society of the Spectacle* (Detroit: Black and Red, 1977, 1983).

65. Laura Mulvey, Annette Kuhn, and Luce Irigaray all argue "that visualization and objectification as privileged ways of knowing are *specifically masculine* (man the viewer, woman the spectacle)." Petchesky, "Foetal Images," 84.

66. Fredric Jameson, "Periodizing the 60s," *The 60s Without Apology*, ed. Sohnya Sayres, Anders Stephanson, Stanley Aronowitz, and Fredric Jameson (Minneapolis: University of Minnesota Press, 1984), 187, 188, 190.

67. For Michel Foucault, Jeremy Bentham's eighteenth-century prison model of the Panopticon serves as a metaphor for modern power. A building

divided into backlit cells circumscribing a tower with windows on each cell, the Panopticon provides the warden with total visibility of each inmate. The effect of the design, according to Foucault, is to "induce in the inmate a state of conscious and permanent visibility that assures the automatic functioning of power." Foucault argues, "Panopticism is the general principle of a new 'political anatomy' whose object and end are not the relations of sovereignty but the relations of discipline." *Discipline and Punish: The Birth of the Prison,* trans. Alan Sheridan (New York: Vintage, 1979), 195–228. The object of this discipline is the individual human body.

68. Susan Bordo, "The Body and the Reproduction of Femininity: A Feminist Appropriation of Foucault," in *Gender/Body/Knowledge: Feminist Reconstructions of Being and Knowing,* ed. Alison M. Jaggar and Susan R. Bordo (New Brunswick, N.J.: Rutgers University Press, 1989), 17. Interestingly, Bordo connects these twentieth-century developments with the growth in the number of cases of such psychopathologies as agoraphobia among women in the 1950s and early 60s.

69. I use the term "bio-power" in the sense that Foucault described it in his *The History of Sexuality,* vol. 1, *An Introduction,* trans. Robert Hurley (New York: Vintage, 1980), 139 ff. Foucault argues that power operates through disciplines of biology, medicine, sociology, and anthropology, which by monitoring and operating on human bodies enable the regulation and management of individuals and populations in societies.

70. Barbara Ehrenreich and Deirdre English, *Complaints and Disorders: The Sexual Politics of Sickness* (New York: The Feminist Press, 1973), 5.

71. Ostriker, *Stealing the Language,* 133.

72. Ibid., 78.

73. Liz Yorke, *Impertinent Voices: Subversive Strategies in Contemporary Women's Poetry* (London: Routledge, 1991), 49.

74. Clausen, *A Movement of Poets,* 13.

75. Sylvia Plath, "Lady Lazarus," in Sylvia Plath, *The Collected Poems,* ed. Ted Hughes (New York: Harper and Row, 1981), 246.

76. Plath, "Tulips," ibid., 160.

77. Anita Rapone, "The Body is the Role: Sylvia Plath," in *Radical Feminism,* ed. Anne Koedt, Ellen Levine, and Anita Rapone (New York Times Books, Quadrangle, 1973), 407, 411. The article originally appeared in a 1971 issue of *Notes from the Third Year.*

78. Jacqueline Rose, *The Haunting of Sylvia Plath* (Cambridge, Mass.: Harvard University Press, 1992), 123.

79. Anne Sexton, "You, Dr. Martin," in *Selected Poems of Anne Sexton,* ed. Diana Wood Middlebrook and Diana Hume George (Boston: Houghton Mifflin, 1988), 9. Hereafter cited as SPAS.

80. Anne Sexton, "The Firebombers," in *The Complete Poems* (Boston: Houghton Mifflin, 1981), 308.

81. May also reports that a study of over four thousand Americans conducted in 1957 "found that the reliance on expertise was one of the most striking developments of the postwar years." *Homeward Bound: American Families in the Cold War Era* (New York: Basic Books, 1988), 27.

82. See Dr. Naomi Weisstein, "'Kinder, Kuche, Kirche' as Scientific Law: Psychology Constructs the Female," in Morgan, ed., *Sisterhood is Powerful,* 228–245; Mary Jane Sherfey, "A Theory of Female Sexuality," in ibid., 245–256; Nathalie Shairness, "A Psychiatrist's View: Images of Women—Past and Present,

Overt and Obscured," in ibid., 257–274; Betsy Warrior, "Sex Roles and Their Consequences," in *Voices from Women's Liberation*, comp. and ed. Tanner, 243–252; Shulamith Firestone, *The Dialectic of Sex: The Case for Feminist Revolution* (New York: Morrow, 1970), 46–80.

83. May, *Homeward Bound*, 14.

84. See Paul Breslin, *The Psycho-Political Muse: American Poetry since the Fifties* (Chicago: University of Chicago Press, 1987); Arthur Lerner, ed., *Poetry in the Therapeutic Experience* (New York: Pergamon Press, 1978); and Kara Provost, "Poetry, 'Therapy,' and 'Confession': The Work of Anne Sexton" (paper presented at the annual meeting of the Midwest Modern Language Association, Kansas City, Mo., 1990).

85. Carol Bergé, "Chant for Half the World," in *In a Time of Revolution: Poems from Our Third World*, ed. Walter Lowenfels (New York: Random House, 1969), 5–8.

86. *Where is Vietnam?: American Poets Respond*, ed. Walter Lowenfels (Garden City, N.Y.: Doubleday, Anchor, 1967), 84; emphasis added. Hereafter cited in the text as WV.

87. Nguyen Cao Ky, an air marshal in the Army of the Republic of Vietnam (ARVN), led the military government formed in 1965 following a series of U.S.-backed regimes, which in turn followed President Ngo Dinh Diem's 1963 assassination. According to Gabriel Kolko, Ky was instrumental in the massive drug trade in South Vietnam that flourished after 1965. *Anatomy of a War*, 363.

88. Although Adnan is Lebanese, I cite this poem because it appeared in Walter Lowenfels's popular and important antiwar anthology *Where is Vietnam?* Adnan also associated herself with the emerging feminist movement in the 60s, while living in New York and Paris.

89. Vicki Pollard, "Producing Society's Babies," in *Voices from Women's Liberation*, ed. Tanner, 194. This article originally appeared in a 1969 issue of *WOMEN: A Journal of Liberation*.

90. Mary Daly, *Gyn/Ecology: The Metaethics of Radical Feminism* (Boston: Beacon Press, 1978), 226.

91. Adrienne Rich, "The Theft of Childbirth," in *Seizing Our Bodies: The Politics of Women's Health*, ed. Claudia Dreifus (New York: Vintage, 1977), 153; emphasis added.

92. Patricia Giggans, "Two Poems," *Aphra* 3, no. 3 (Summer 1972): 32–33.

93. Helen Sorrells, "To a Child Born in Time of Small War," in *The Women Poets in English: An Anthology*, ed. Ann Stanford (New York: McGraw-Hill, 1972), 238–239.

94. Dotty LeMieux, "The war is still on somewhere," *Women*, Fall 1970, 6. This poem was first published in the Harvard 1970 yearbook alongside a poem by Jean Tepperman. LeMieux was not a student at Harvard, however, and she was unaware that the poem had been reprinted in *Women*. Personal communication to author, July 24, 1995.

95. Carol Driscoll, "The Abortion Problem," ibid., 7.

96. Rosen, "The Day They Buried 'Traditional Womanhood,'" 213.

97. Ibid., 214.

98. As Elaine Tyler May has written, "These activists were among the first postwar middle-class whites to organize against the social and political status quo." *Homeward Bound*, 218. May further points out that a number of the strike's leaders were feminists who had worked for women's rights during the 40s and

50s. For more on WSP, see Amy Swerdlow, "Motherhood and the Subversion of the Military State: Women Strike for Peace Confronts the House Committee on Un-American Activities," in *Women, Militarism, and War: Essays in History, Politics, and Social Theory*, ed. Jean Bethke Elshtain and Sheila Tobias (Savage, Md.: Rowman and Littlefield, 1990), 7–28. Swerdlow points out that the 1961 WSP demonstration was "the largest female peace action of the twentieth century." Ibid., 9. She notes, however, that the fifty thousand figure claimed by WSP and accepted by the press may be inaccurate and that no more than twelve thousand women may have actually participated. Ibid., 25, n. 5.

99. May, *Homeward Bound*, 219. Swerdlow claims that WSP's performance before HUAC helped to discredit the committee and led to its eventual downfall. She quotes Charles DeBendetti as saying, "WSP activists challenged for the first time the House Un-American Activities Committee's practice of identifying citizen peace seeking with Communist subversion. . . . The open disdain of the WSP for HUAC did not end the Congress's preference for treating private peace actions as subversive. But it did help break the petrified anticommunism of Cold War American politics and gave heart to those reformers who conceived peace as more than military preparedness." "Motherhood and the Subversion of the Military State," 8, 25, n. 4.

100. WSP lobbied in Washington, D.C., for a diplomatic solution to the war in 1964, and in January 1967, WSP led a march of twenty-five hundred women on the Pentagon. When they were denied a meeting with Secretary of Defense Robert McNamara, a number of them chanted and pounded on the building's main doors. Several WSP women slipped past guards and caused disturbances throughout the building.

101. Firestone, *The Dialectic of Sex*, 81.

102. Quoted in Echols, *Daring to Be Bad*, 55. This was a response to the Jeanette Rankin Brigade antiwar protest in Washington, D.C. A coalition of women's groups opposed to the Vietnam War, the Brigade named itself after the first woman elected to Congress, the only member of Congress to vote against United States intervention in World Wars I and II. Firestone criticized the Brigade's demonstration, saying, "They came as wives, mothers and mourners; that is, tearful and passive reactors to the actions of men rather than organizing as women to change the definition of femininity to something other than a synonym for weakness, political impotence, and tears." Although Betty Friedan added her name to a Brigade petition, she was quoted as saying, "I don't think the fact that milk once flowed within my breast is the reason I'm against the war." Quoted in Echols, *Daring to Be Bad*, 56.

103. Quoted in Sarachild, "Taking in the Images," 239.

104. Quoted in Echols, *Daring to Be Bad*, 113. As Echols points out, there was a great deal of controversy over Firestone's suggestion at the 1969 Seneca Falls feminist conference that "pregnancy is physically debilitating and inevitably oppressive." Corrine Coleman objected to Firestone's views, calling them "barbaric." Quoted in ibid., 112.

105. Echols describes how Jane Alpert's 1973 manifesto "Mother Right: A New Feminist Theory" marked the ascendance of cultural feminism and a shift away from Third World– inspired concepts of feminist radicalism. *Daring to Be Bad*, 247–259.

106. Linda Gordon, *Woman's Body, Woman's Rights: Birth Control in America*, rev. ed. (New York: Penguin, 1990), 391. Gordon also points out that population

control arose out of very different political interests than Margaret Sanger's birth control movement of the early twentieth century. Yet Planned Parenthood "married the two, in a union in which the birth-control 'wife' was subordinated to the population-control 'husband.'" 391.

107. According to Gordon, "Between 1965 and 1976 the annual U.S. appropriation for 'population-assistance' grew from $2 million to $248 million. By the mid-1960s, U.S. government experts considered population control the best hope for economic development in the Third World." *Woman's Body, Woman's Rights*, 396.

108. Jean Sharpe, "The Birth Controllers," in *Seizing Our Bodies*, ed. Dreifus, 57–72, 66.

109. Discourse on contraceptives in early postwar America often focused on its utility for securing ideological norms. During the 40s, contraceptives were advocated by professionals and social critics as "an effective weapon in creating a strong people . . . to defend our way of life." Quoted in Sharpe, "The Birth Controllers," 65. Advocacy for contraceptives diminished right after World War II, when women were enjoined to bear numerous children to offset, by sheer numbers, the threat of communism overtaking the United States. As more contraceptive techniques became available during the 50s, however, experts promoted them as a way to heighten married couples' sexual fulfillment, thus ensuring more stable marriages. *Homeward Bound*, 149–151.

110. Quoted in Gordon, *Woman's Body, Woman's Rights*, 395.

111. See the documents written by Black Panther women against birth control in Philip Foner, ed., *The Black Panthers Speak* (Philadelphia, J. B. Lippincott, 1970). A counterview, however, was offered by the Black Women's Liberation Group of New York, which argued that, although it might be true that birth control was part of a program of genocide against black people, being forced to raise children in poverty was also genocidal. "Like, the Vietnamese have decided to fight genocide, the South American poor are beginning to fight back, and the African poor will fight back, too. Poor black women in the United States have to fight back, too. Poor black women in the United States have to fight back out of our own experience of oppression. Having too many babies stops us from supporting our children, teaching them the truth, or stopping the brainwashing . . . and from fighting black men who still want to use and exploit us." "Statement on Birth Control," *Sisterhood is Powerful*, ed. Morgan, 404–406.

112. Ellen Frankfort, "Vaginal Politics," in *Seizing Our Bodies*, ed. Dreifus, 265, 270.

113. Morgan, "Taking Back Our Bodies," 33; emphasis in original. In the headnote to a revised reprint of this article in a recent collection, Morgan notes that this piece was written in 1974 "at the request of Colorado women, to be the introduction to a self-help health handbook, 'Circle One,' being published by the women's health movement." She continues in the headnote by disclaiming her analysis:

> Such comparisons [between sexism and colonization] are invidious in terms of human suffering—no scale dare weight that, and no analysis, political or otherwise, had better "compare and contrast" that—although such more-oppressed-than-thou approaches are attempted all the time. I was searching for a means of articulating sexism. . . . We resort [to analogies of sexism to colonization] because any conditions of oppression that women share with men

(racism, homophobia, discrimination due to class, age, physical disability, etc.) are always taken more seriously—simply because the oppression affects male human beings, too. For precisely this reason, the colonial analogy itself is insufficient to describe women's predicament. . . . For myself, this essay now stands as an artifact, a brave if superficial first hazarding on the subject.

Despite these disclaimers, Morgan still maintains that "we are not only colonized as women per se but also as members of mixed-gender populations who have been colonized in the traditional sense. Not surprisingly, the latter condition is still taken more seriously than the former." And in her conclusion to this head-note, she muses that the problems with her analysis may have been that they were not taken far enough. Throughout, Morgan relies on biological, corporeal gender as the distinguishing factor between oppressed and oppressor. "On Women as a Colonized People," *The Word of a Woman: Feminist Dispatches 1968–1992* (New York: W. W. Norton, 1992), 74–75.

114. Dreifus, Introduction to *Seizing Our Bodies*, xix.

115. For feminist studies of obstetrical practices see Ann Oakley, *The Captured Womb: A History of the Medical Care of Pregnant Women* (Oxford: Basil Blackwell, 1986); Michelle Stanworth, ed., *Reproductive Technologies: Gender, Motherhood, and Medicine* (Minneapolis: University of Minnesota Press, 1987), especially Rosalind Pollack Petchesky, "Foetal Images: The Power of Visual Culture in the Politics of Reproduction," 57–80; Emily Martin, *The Woman in the Body: A Cultural Analysis of Reproduction* (Boston: Beacon Press, 1987); and Paula Treichler, "Feminism, Medicine, and the Meaning of Childbirth," in *Body/Politics: Women and the Discourses of Science*, ed. Mary Jacobus, Evelyn Fox Keller, and Sally Shuttleworth (New York: Routledge, 1990): 113–138. For a Foucauldian approach to the history of obstetrics, see William Ray Arney, *Power and the Profession of Obstetrics* (Chicago: University of Chicago Press, 1982).

116. Arney, *Power and the Profession of Obstetrics*, 51.

117. Ibid., 59–60.

118. With this development, Arney points out, "obstetricians began to treat the fetus as a second patient." Ibid., 134. The current antichoice rhetoric of the "rights of the fetus" can be traced to the "discovery of the fetus," as Arney terms it. Petchesky notes that it has been through visualization of the fetus in obstetrical technologies that the antichoice movement has been able to mobilize popular sentiment around the idea that the fetus is independent of the mother's body. See "Foetal Images," 61–62.

119. Ann Oakley, "From Walking Wombs to Test-Tube Babies," in Stanworth, ed., *Reproductive Technologies*, 44. Also see Oakley, *The Captured Womb*. According to Petchesky, by 1986 at least one-third of all pregnant women underwent ultrasound monitoring. "Foetal Images," 66.

120. Quoted in Petchesky, "Foetal Images," 68–69.

121. According to Petchesky, while the militarism evident in the *Life* photo-essay may not be "implicit in the origin of the technology (most technologies in a militarized society either begin or end in the military); nor in its focus on reproduction (similar language constructs the 'war on cancer')," it might "correspond to the very culture of medicine and science, its emphasis on visualization as a form of surveillance and 'attack.'" "Foetal Images," 69.

122. Treichler, "Feminism, Medicine, and the Meaning of Childbirth," 133, n. 3. According to Claudia Dreifus, "By virtue of their reproductive functions,

women use medical facilities 25 percent more frequently than their male counterparts." Introduction to *Seizing Our Bodies*, xviii.

123. Colette Price, "The First Self-Help Clinic," in *Feminist Revolution*, ed. Sarachild and Redstockings, 136.

124. Gordon, *Woman's Body, Woman's Rights*, 446.

125. Boston Women's Health Collective, *Our Bodies, Ourselves: A Book by and for Women* (New York: Simon and Schuster, 1971), 1, 2.

126. Boston Women's Health Collective, *Our Bodies, Ourselves*, 4. This song was reprinted in *Sisterhood Songs* 1 (1971): 25.

127. Ellen Willis, Foreword to *Daring to Be Bad*, by Echols, vii, viii.

128. A few titles will serve to indicate this: Juliet Flower MacCannell and Laura Zakarin, eds., *Thinking Bodies* (Stanford, Calif.: Stanford University Press, 1994); Elizabeth Grosz, *Volatile Bodies: Toward a Corporeal Feminism* (Bloomington: Indiana University Press, 1994); Elspeth Probyn, *Sexing the Self: Gendered Positions in Cultural Studies* (London: Routledge, 1993); Susan Bordo, *Unbearable Weight: Feminism, Western Culture, and the Body* (Berkeley: University of California Press, 1993); Judith Butler, *Bodies That Matter: On the Discursive Limits of "Sex"* (New York: Routledge, 1993).

4. Fragging the Chain(s) of Command

1. A Peace Lover, *A Four-Year Bummer* 1, no. 2 (1969): 4. This poem also appeared in two other GI papers that year: *Rough Draft* (August 1969) and *Eyes Left* (September 1969).

2. See Harry W. Haines, "Soldiers Against the War in Vietnam: The Story of *Aboveground*," *Voices from the Underground*, vol. 1, *Insider Histories of the Vietnam Era Underground Press*, ed. Ken Wachsberger (Tempe, Ariz.: Mica Press, 1993), 188.

3. Mike Connell, "Vietnam: A Personal View," *A Four-Year Bummer* 1, no. 2 (1969): 4.

4. Greg Laxer, "For My Still Imprisoned Comrades," *The Bond*, June 30, 1971, 7.

5. David Cortright, *Soldiers in Revolt: The American Military Today* (Garden City, N.Y.: Doubleday, Anchor, 1975), 43.

6. Ibid., 35–39. "Cincinnatus" (a pseudonym for an army officer critical of the military's handling of the war) has noted, "Mutiny became so common that the army was forced to disguise its frequency by talking instead of 'combat refusals.'" *Self-Destruction: The Disintegration and Decay of the United States Army during the Vietnam Era* (New York: Norton, 1981), 156.

7. Elaine Scarry, *The Body in Pain: The Making and Unmaking of the World* (New York: Oxford University Press, 1985), 62.

8. According to James R. Hayes, "desertion, AWOLs, drug use, and even fraggings . . . have long plagued the United States military [but] organized resistance appears to be a uniquely Vietnam-era phenomenon. The social movement characteristics exhibited by the movement, e.g., a sense of group identity and solidarity, consciously articulated ideologies, movement organizations, distinguish it from other more spontaneous and transitory uprisings such as the 'Back Home Movement' in the aftermath of World War II." "The Dialectics of Resistance: An Analysis of the GI Movement," *Journal of Social Issues* 31, no. 4 (1975): 126. The "Back Home Movement" emerged because of troop frustration at the

slow pace of demobilization after World War II; thus, it is a distinctly "peacetime" movement, whereas the GI movement occurred in wartime.

9. Matthew Rinaldi, "The Olive-Drab Rebels: Military Organizing During the Vietnam Era," *Radical America* 8, no. 3 (May-June 1974): 39. One notable exception to this was the Movement for a Democratic Military (MDM), which was interracial and described itself as a "rainbow coalition." MDM framed much of its political agenda around anticolonialist and antiracist activism. Barbara L. Tischler, "Breaking Ranks: GI Antiwar Newspapers and the Culture of Protest," *Vietnam Generation* 2, no. 1 (1990): 31–32.

10. Quoted in James William Gibson, *The Perfect War: The War We Couldn't Lose and How We Did* (New York: Vintage, 1986), 217. Cortright fought a federal court case, *Cortright v. Resor* (325 F. Supp. 797), for the right to unionize soldiers. His book, *Soldiers in Revolt,* is one of the only in-depth studies of the GI Resistance published. More recently Cortright published, with Max Watts, *Left Face: Soldier Unions and Resistance Movements in Modern Armies* Contributions in Military Studies, no. 107 (New York: Greenwood Press, 1991). He has also served as executive director of the antinuclear organization SANE.

11. "Antiwar GIs," *Black Liberator,* July 1969, 3.

12. Quoted in Tischler, "Breaking Ranks," 38. According to Tischler, black activism in the military, although generally ambivalent toward the organized GI Resistance, played a major role in the articulation of GI politics. Exposés of racism in the military and the harassment of black GIs, which tended to be much more severe than that received by white GIs, were regular features in GI newspapers. Such stories and stories about African American activism helped rally soldiers together. But Tischler cautions, "To regard African-American soldiers who opposed the war simply as a part of the larger antiwar movement in which white students, civilians, and military personnel played major roles would be to oversimplify that movement and present an incomplete picture of black resistance and rebellion." Ibid., 33. The main focus of African American GI dissent tended to be racism. Black resistance viewed the war as a manifestation of American racism, not simply as bad military policy, which many white GIs believed. See ibid., 33–39.

13. Introduction to *In the Combat Zone: An Oral History of American Women in Vietnam, 1966–1975,* ed. Kathryn Marshall (Boston: Little, Brown, 1987), 4.

14. Barbara L. Tischler, "Voices of Protest: Women and the GI Antiwar Press," in *Sights on the Sixties,* ed. Barbara L. Tischler (New Brunswick, N.J.: Rutgers University Press, 1992), 204.

15. Quoted in ibid., 206. Tischler quotes from the "Anniston Women's Project Report," *GI News and Discussion Bulletin* 9 (September-October 1971).

16. Tischler, "Voices of Protest," 202.

17. Ibid., 201.

18. Ibid., 205. Here Tischler quotes an article entitled "Bragg Briefs," which was reprinted in a 1971 issue of *GI News and Discussion Bulletin.*

19. Tischler, "Voices of Protest," 205.

20. Ibid., 206.

21. Ibid., 209. Also, according to Cortright, an underground paper appeared briefly in 1970 at Fort Lewis, Washington; called *Yah-Hoh,* it was published by "Hew-Kacaw-Na-Ya," a group of Native American servicemen and women. *Soldiers in Revolt,* 291.

22. Terry H. Anderson, "The GI Movement and the Response from the

Brass," in *Give Peace a Chance: Exploring the Vietnam Antiwar Movement*, ed. Melvin Small and William D. Hoover (Syracuse, N.Y.: Syracuse University Press, 1992), 110.

23. Quoted in Tischler, "Voices of Protest," 208.

24. There is some precedent in the twentieth century for the production of an oppositional-style military press during a time of war. During World War I, after finding a printing press in a nearby deserted town, British troops stationed in Europe produced a satirical paper initially called *The Wipers Times*. The paper was named after the Square at Ypres, in Belgium, where the printing press was found. The paper was later renamed as troops were moved to different encampments (*The Somme-Times, The "New Church" Times, The Kemmel Times*). It featured articles that mimicked typical English newspaper stories in ways that satirized the life of "blighters." The papers also regularly published poems by infantry soldiers; these often involved satirical and ironic reinterpretations of neo-Romantic Edwardian verse and articulate the disillusionment with the mythologies of war often evident in poems by Wilfred Owen and others of the period. These papers, however, were always produced within the legitimacy of the military. Unlike the Vietnam-era GI press, they did not advocate dissent, mutiny, or resistance among troops, and they were often supported by officers. See *The Wipers Times: A Facsimile Reprint of the Trench Magazines—The Wipers Times, The New Church Times, The Kemmel Times, The Somme Times, The B. E. F. Times* (London: Herbert Jenkins, Ltd., 1918). I am grateful to Kim van Alkemade for calling this book to my attention.

25. Hayes, "The Dialectics of Resistance," 132. Also see Cortright, *Soldiers in Revolt*, and Haines, "Soldiers Against the War." The official U.S. military figure on dissident press production during the war is considerably less than the 144 I have cited. Hayes, Cortright, and Haines, however, have carefully documented their figures, through either their involvement in the movement or their access to special collections.

26. Philip D. Beidler has suggested that Vietnam War poetry of veterans and soldiers has "trac[ed]. . . the patterns of [the war's] broader mythic configuring within our life and culture at large." *Re-Writing America: Vietnam Authors in Their Generation* (Athens: University of Georgia Press, 1991), 146.

27. According to Barbara Tischler, contributors to GI underground papers often communicated with each other through poetry. "Breaking Ranks," 25. In the twenty-five different papers I have studied, poetry is by far the predominant form of imaginative expression.

28. Lorrie Smith also argues that poetry's marginality in the American canon and marketplace acts as a space from which to enact subversion; for soldier-poets, she argues, "the periphery can become the site of a truly subversive art that disrupts the cultural and political mainstream but speaks directly to the concerns of common people." "Resistance and Revision in Poetry by Vietnam War Veterans," in *Fourteen Landing Zones: Approaches to Vietnam War Literature*, ed. Philip K. Jason (Iowa City: University of Iowa, 1991), 50.

29. The on-line discussion group V-War List has become an important forum for veterans of the war. In the four years I subscribed to this list, a considerable number of subscribers posted poetic texts to the list. Often, these poems bear witness to a veteran's struggles with post-traumatic stress disorders and served to initiate dialogue among list members about these struggles.

30. For a more comprehensive study of the poetry of Vietnam War veterans, see Vince Gotera, *Radical Visions: Poetry by Vietnam Veterans* (Athens: University of

Georgia Press, 1994). The only book-length study of veterans' poetry, *Radical Visions* focuses primarily on poetry written after the war. While Gotera's study is concerned with mapping out literary formal and thematic typologies of veterans' Vietnam War poetry, my brief account will focus on the discourses of corporeality and the sociopolitical meaning of the poetry published during the war.

31. Charles DeBenedetti, *An American Ordeal: The Antiwar Movement of the Vietnam Era*, assisted by Charles Chatfield, (Syracuse: Syracuse University Press, 1990), makes only scant reference to the Winter Soldiers, and generally limits discussion of soldier activism to the Vietnam Veterans Against the War. Todd Gitlin, *The Sixties: Years of Hope, Days of Rage* (New York: Bantam, 1987), mentions the GI Resistance in passing several times but never offers an account of the movement's history, actions, or organization. Nancy Zaroulis and Gerald Sullivan, *Who Spoke Up?: American Protest Against the War in Vietnam 1963–1975* (Garden City, N.Y.: Doubleday, 1984), devotes a chapter to the Winter Soldiers and refers to soldier activism but offers no account of the GI Resistance as a significant movement in the antiwar effort. Michael Ferber and Staughton Lynd represent GI activism only insofar as it compares to civilian activism: "The full story of GI resistance will have to be told by others, hopefully by those who organized and experienced it. . . . we can only . . . explore the contribution to the GI movement made by the Resistance." See *The Resistance* (Boston: Beacon, 1971), 186.

The most extended study of the GI movement is Cortright's *Soldiers in Revolt*. *GI Resistance: Soldiers and Veterans Against the War*, *Viet Nam Generation* 2, no. 1 (1990) edited by Harry W. Haines, a special issue of *Viet Nam Generation* guest-edited by Haines, is currently the only book-length study in print; it offers important perspectives on the movement as well as an extensively researched listing of GI underground press titles from the period.

32. Mainstream publishing houses during the Vietnam era often published Black Liberationist and Women's Liberationist anthologies, such as *Black Fire* (William Morrow) and *Sisterhood is Powerful* (Vintage). Only since the mid-1980s have major houses published anthologies of Vietnam War soldier-poetry. Anthologies of GI Resistance literature during the war years came out through small press operations usually run by veterans, such as 1st Casualty Press, which published *Winning Hearts and Minds*. This anthology sold so well in its first printing that it was picked up by a major press for one printing, but it has since gone out of print. See Caroline Slocock, "Winning Hearts and Minds: The 1st Casualty Press," *Journal of American Studies* 16, no. 1 (1982): 107–117.

33. Cortright, *Soldiers in Revolt*, 50.

34. Ibid., 51.

35. Haines, "Soldiers Against the War in Vietnam," 182.

36. Ibid., 184.

37. According to Hayes, "There has been no accurate measure of the numerical strength of the movement, and the estimates vary according to the source—the military appears to underestimate while movement sympathizers tend to exaggerate. . . .It is safe to say, however, that the movement represents only a small fraction of GIs." "The Dialectics of Resistance," 126–127. In 1970, the ASU claimed a membership of seven thousand. Robert Sherrill, *Military Justice is to Justice as Military Music is to Music* (New York: Harper and Row, 1970), 158.

38. Rinaldi, "The Olive-Drab Rebels," 30.

39. Cincinnatus [pseud.], *Self-Destruction*, 150.

40. Hayes notes that the Concerned Officers Movement (COM), a group

that "dissociated itself from the more radical GI groups," and the Concerned Graduates of the Military, Naval, and Air Force Academies, a group made up mostly of ex-officers in the San Francisco area, were the exceptions to this generalization. "Dialectics of Resistance," 126.

41. According to Tischler, "Military protest against war arose first in the Army and the Marines, the branches of the Armed Forces most immediately involved in the fighting and the ones that suffered the highest casualties between 1965 and 1967. After the institution of Richard Nixon's 'Vietnamization' plan that relied more heavily on air and sea power, protests spread rapidly to the Navy and Air Force." "Breaking Ranks," 47, n. 3.

42. "Cincinnatus" quotes one source as claiming in 1971 that only 14 percent of military personnel in Vietnam were in combat, compared to more than 24 percent in 1946. *Self-Destruction*, 146.

43. See Gibson, *The Perfect War*, table 6.4, 215. Also see John Helmer, *Bringing the War Home: The American Soldier in Vietnam and After* (New York: Free Press, 1974), and Lisa Hsiao, "Project 100,000: The Great Society's Answer to Military Manpower Needs in Vietnam," *Vietnam Generation* 1, no. 2 (Spring 1989): 14–37.

44. Gibson, *The Perfect War*, 215.

45. "Letter From an A. W. O. L. Soldier," *Negro Digest*, January 1964, 33–36.

46. Ibid., 34.

47. Hayes, "The Dialectics of Resistance," 127.

48. *Where is Vietnam?: American Poets Respond*, ed. Walter Lowenfels (Garden City, N.Y.: Doubleday, Anchor, 1967), 93, 154. In a biographical note, Morgan is quoted as saying at the rally, "I intend to go back and face whatever charges the Marine Corps will bring. . . . I will not serve even one more day as a Marine—in conscience I cannot" (Quoted in ibid., 154).

49. John Morgan, "The Second Coming," in *Where is Vietnam?*, 93–94. Further citations will appear in the text.

50. Ibid., 94–95.

51. The trope of "turning the guns around" evident in GI Resistance poetry resembles similar tropes of subversion in the radical poetry of the 1930s. See poems in *Social Poetry of the 1930s: A Selection*, ed. Jack Salzman and Leo Zanderer (New York: Burt Franklin, 1978).

52. Rinaldi, "The Olive Drab Rebels," 22.

53. Quoted in Tischler, "Breaking Ranks," 35.

54. Zaroulis and Sullivan, *Who Spoke Up?* 88. For their full account of the Fort Hood 3 case, see 86–88.

55. DeBenedetti, *An American Ordeal*, 155.

56. Zaroulis and Sullivan, *Who Spoke Up?*, 40. DeBenedetti never mentions the soldiers of the Fort Hood 3 by name, nor does he describe their political connections. Instead, he sums up the significance of this case by calling it a "breakthrough for antiwar groups, especially the Trotskyist SWP [Socialist Workers Party]. . . . It rejuvenated plans for the August demonstrations. Moreover, the incident demonstrated the leadership of the strong Fifth Avenue Parade Committee in the absence of a cohesive national coalition." *An American Ordeal*, 155.

57. Hayes, "Dialectics of Resistance," 128. According to Cortright, GI oppositional activism prior to 1968 "was limited, confined largely to isolated acts of conscience." *Soldiers in Revolt*, 52.

58. *Veterans Stars and Stripes for Peace*, November/December, 1967 issue; np.

59. Joseph Conlin, *American Anti-War Movements* (Beverly Hills, Calif.: Glencoe Press, 1967), 109, 119–121.

60. Tischler, "Breaking Ranks," 21–22.

61. Harry W. Haines, "Hegemony and GI Resistance," *Vietnam Generation* 2, no. 1 (1990): 4.

62. Quoted in Gibson, *The Perfect War*, 224.

63. The War Resisters League of New York estimates that conscientious objectors numbered about 2,500 during the Gulf War. Military officials, however, claim that only 313 applications for CO status were filed. The military's repression of troop dissent during the war was massive. Army reserve doctor Capt. Yolonda Huet-Vaughn was sentenced to two and a half years in prison for not only refusing orders to serve in the Gulf but also speaking out against the war, which she argued was criminal. The charges of desertion the military filed against her were called "vindictive" by her attorney. Similarly vindictive was the sentencing of Louisiana National Guardsman Robert Pete to six years in prison for attempting to organize a strike at Fort Hood. As of August 1991, 250 resisters in the military have been charged with court-martial offenses, and most have received sentences of at least a year in prison. The military's repressiveness has been matched only by the news media's silence about troop dissent. The evidence suggests that despite the public image, ideological consensus was not totally achieved among the volunteer troops of the war with Iraq.

64. Ernesto Laclau and Chantal Mouffe argue that "if contingency and articulation are possible, this is because no discursive formation is a sutured totality and the transformation of the elements into moments is never complete." Laclau and Mouffe's argument posits that discursive formations are not unified, seamless totalities, but rather they are characterized by the articulation of their elements into regular dispersion. Because the identity of these elements is always achieved through difference and relation, a social formation, such as the U.S. military, necessarily is inscribed with antagonisms and ruptures. It is only by appearing unified, by arresting the flow of difference, that a formation achieves dominance. See *Hegemony and Socialist Strategy: Towards a Radical Democratic Politics* (London: Verso, 1985), 106–114.

65. Compare these sentences with those given white activists Lt. Henry Howe and army doctor Howard Levy. Cortright, *Soldiers in Revolt*, 52.

66. Quoted in Tischler, "Breaking Ranks," 37.

67. Gibson, *The Perfect War*, 211. This last number may be too high, Gibson suggests, but he concludes it is probably more accurate than the Pentagon's numbers, since the Pentagon had more cause to downgrade the extent of rebellion in the ranks and similar high numbers of fraggings were widely reported throughout the military.

68. Hayes, "The Dialectics of Resistance," 130.

69. Lawrence B. Radine, *The Taming of the Troops: Social Control in the United States Army*, Contributions in Sociology, no. 22 (Westport, Conn.: Greenwood, 1977), 12. Radine points out that such "punitive transfers" are illegal. He reasons that the embarrassment caused the military by such illegal actions being brought before a court would have precluded the use of such transfers. He cites no such cases successfully tried, however; furthermore, the chances of a soldier surviving a hazardous combat duty made such cases unlikely. One way GI Resistance newspapers tried to thwart military repression was by publicizing cases of punitive transfer.

70. Tischler, "Breaking Ranks," 47 n. 4.

71. Military courts have been notorious for the severity of the punishment they hand down to individual soldiers convicted of resistance. The courts sentenced privates Dam Amick and Ken Stolte to four years for distributing antiwar literature on base; William Harvey and George Daniels, African-American marines accused of criticizing the war in their barracks, received sentences of six and ten years hard labor respectively. As Matthew Rinaldi notes, repression and court sentences for civilians involved in the GI coffeehouses and other antiwar networks were never as severe. "The Olive-Drab Rebels," 40–41.

72. Cortright and Watts, *Left Face*, 29–31.

73. This latter tactic was primarily deployed by the Trotskyist Young Socialist Alliance, whose members sometimes consented to be drafted in order to organize soldiers. The Fort Jackson Eight incident was one of the YSA's most important successes. See Cortright, *Soldiers in Revolt*, 59.

74. Ibid., 53.

75. Pete Rode, "How Vietnam vets and GIs helped end the war," *Minneapolis Star Tribune*, April 28, 1991, 25A.

76. Haines, "Hegemony and GI Resistance," 4.

77. Quoted and discussed in Rinaldi, "The Olive-Drab Rebels," 18; emphasis added. Metaphors of infestation and disease abound in official studies of troop dissent in the Vietnam War. See also Gunter Lewy's account, quoted previously.

78. Rinaldi, "The Olive-Drab Rebels," 23–24.

79. Lauren Kessler, *The Dissident Press: Alternative Journalism in American History*, Sage CommText Series, vol. 13 (Beverly Hills, Calif.: Sage, 1984), 150–151.

80. Figures comparing incidents of fragging between 1968 and prior years are unavailable because the Pentagon did not keep statistics on fragging until 1969. Gibson, *The Perfect War*, 211.

81. Hayes, "Dialectics of Resistance," 129–131.

82. There is evidence that the Puerto Rican liberation movement, the Chicano movement, and the American Indian Movement (AIM) may have also had some influence in shaping resistance among minority soldiers.

83. Rinaldi, "The Olive-Drab Rebels," 32.

84. Held from January 31 to February 2, 1971, the Winter Soldier hearings were conducted by the Vietnam Veterans Against the War (VVAW). Over one hundred recently returned veterans of the war testified to atrocities and war crimes committed by the U.S. military and confessed their own complicity with or participation in such crimes. It was one of the first of a number of antiwar activities staged in 1971 as President Nixon escalated the Vietnamization program, which was officially intended to turn the war over to the South Vietnamese but actually was calculated to undermine the antiwar movement. At about the same time, Lt. William Calley's trial for the My Lai massacre was drawing to a close. Calley's conviction and life sentence provoked an overwhelming public and government reaction that resulted in his release on parole. The VVAW staged Winter Soldiers and such later actions as Operation Dewey Canyon III as an attempt to dramatize how Calley's crimes were systemic and widespread in the U.S. military's prosecution of the war.

85. John Kerry and Vietnam Veterans Against the War, *The New Soldier*, ed. David Thorne and George Butler (New York: Macmillan, 1971), 24.

86. *Winning Hearts and Minds*, ed. Larry Rottmann, Jan Barry, and Basil T.

Paquet (Brooklyn: 1st Casualty Press, 1972), was not the first anthology of poetry by soldiers of the Vietnam War. In 1968, the official military newspaper *Pacific Stars and Stripes* published an anthology of poems entitled *Boondock Bards* and edited by Forest L. Kimler. The work in this book, however, is decidedly prowar, patriotic, anti-Vietnamese, and antileftist. As Kimler writes in the introduction, "Although no attempt was made to select poems of a similar theme, the underlying mood of all is one of dedication, determination and loneliness. Boondock Bards could, for the most part, have been written by one man—a lonely soldier, sailor, airman or marine who believes that what he is doing is worthwhile." *Boondock Bards* (Tokyo: Pacific Stars and Stripes, 1968), np. As opposed to *Winning Hearts and Minds*, Kimler's anthology contains very few representations of mutilation; the poems are almost uniformly written in rhyme, in meters imitative of folk and pop songs. *Boondock Bards* seems to have been designed as a morale booster for the troops and their families. The poems in *Winning Hearts and Minds* are almost all in free verse, and few rhyme; those that do rhyme tend to imitate folk and pop song meters. Other GI anthologies published during the early 70s include *We Promise One Another: Poems from an Asian War*, comp. Don Luce, John C. Shafer, and Jacquelyn Chagnon (Washington, D.C.: Indochina Mobile Education Project, 1971); *Listen, the War: A Collection of Poetry About the Vietnam War*, ed. Frederick Kiley (Colorado Springs: U.S.A.F. Academy Association of Graduates, 1973); and *Demilitarized Zones: Veterans After Vietnam*, ed. Jan Barry and W. D. Ehrhart (Perkasie, Penn.: East River Anthology, 1976).

87. W. D. Erhart, "Soldier-Poets of the Vietnam War," in *America Rediscovered: Critical Essays on Literature and Film of the Vietnam War*, ed. Owen W. Gilman, Jr., and Lorrie Smith (New York: Garland, 1990), 313.

88. Almost all antiwar anthologies published during Vietnam include statements by the editors on how to use the book in resistance activism. Consider, for example, *A Poetry Reading Against the Vietnam War*, ed. Robert Bly and David Ray (Madison, Minn.: Sixties, 1967). In this collection's preface, "Giving to Johnson What is Johnson's," Bly describes the book's purpose as both memorial to antiwar readings and as a way "to make available material that other colleges may use at their poetry readings" (9). Walter Lowenfels writes that his anthology of antiwar poetry "records a historic shift" away from apolitical work, a shift "that may leave a lasting imprint on our literature"; thus he announces the goal of the book as oppositional to mainstream anthologies. *"Where is Vietnam?"*, xi.

89. *Winning Hearts and Minds: War Poems by Vietnam Veterans*, ed. Rottmann et al., 118–119. Further references will be cited as WHAM in the text.

90. Slocock, "Winning Hearts and Minds," 109–110.

91. These chants are quoted in Gibson, *The Perfect War*, 182.

92. Scarry, *The Body in Pain*, 121–123.

93. Vietnam Veterans Against the War, *The Winter Soldier Investigation: An Inquiry into American War Crimes* (Boston: Beacon, 1972), 1–4. In his statement Crandell also explains how the title of the investigation refers to the winter soldiers of 1776 who stayed on to fight despite harsh conditions because of their care for their country. Crandell quotes Tom Paine's famous words, "These are the times that try men's souls. The summer soldier and the sunshine patriot will in this crisis shrink from the service of his country; but he that stands it now deserves the love and thanks of man and woman." Ibid., 1. Throughout GI Resistance literature analogies are made between the GI Resistance and the revolutionary heroes. In fact, in the antiwar movement generally a common

means of subverting the authority of conservative claims to true patriotism was to invoke models from revolutionary America.

94. Charles C. Moskos, Jr., "The American Combat Soldier in Vietnam," *Journal of Social Issues* 31, no. 4 (1975): 28–29.

95. Kali Tal, "Speaking the Language of Pain: Vietnam War Literature in the Context of a Literature of Trauma," *Fourteen Landing Zones*, ed. Jason, 229.

96. Robert J. Lifton, "Home From the War: The Psychology of Survival," *The Vietnam Reader*, ed. Walter Capps (New York: Routledge, 1992), 60–61. Lifton's study, published as *Home From the War: Vietnam Veterans: Neither Victims Nor Executioners* (1974), has had a profound influence on the study of post-traumatic stress disorders in Vietnam War veterans.

97. Vietnam Veterans, *The Winter Soldier Investigations*, 163–164. Tal relates Rottmann's description of his will to testify to experiences of sexual abuse victims and Holocaust victims. See "Speaking the Language of Pain."

98. Tal suggests that one reason literary critics misread veterans' literature is because of their inability to comprehend the actual events of the war and their insistence on reading war as symbol, metaphor, or image. "Speaking the Language of Pain," 223. Tischler emphasizes the "tell it like it is" ethic as integral to the style of the GI Resistance press. "Breaking Ranks," 24–25, and personal communication, May 7, 1991.

99. The M-16 rifle, for example, routinely jammed. One soldier wrote Congress claiming that out of 250 men in his company, 107 returned from one operation alive. "Practically every one of our dead was found with his [M-16] rifle torn down next to him." Quoted in Gibson, *The Perfect War*, 194. The military insisted that M-16s had no problems and that soldiers failed to clean them properly. Such official responses to GIs' concerns fueled the resistance movement. As Gibson notes, soldiers often "called the M-16s 'Mattels' after the plastic toy guns produced by the Mattel Corporation in the 1950s and 1960s. It was one way of making a joke out of a grim situation. 'If it's Mattel, it's swell,' went the old TV ads." Ibid., 96.

100. Michael Herr coined this phrase to describe the excesses of U.S. military onslaught against the Vietnamese. *Dispatches* (New York: Avon, 1978), 62.

101. "Vietnam: The Thousand Plateaus," in *The 60s Without Apology*, ed. Sohnya Sayres, Anders Stephanson, Stanley Aronowitz, and Fredric Jameson (Minneapolis: University of Minnesota Press, 1984), 145, 146.

102. Ibid., 145.

103. R. Wayne Eisenhart, "You Can't Hack it Little Girl: A Discussion of the Covert Psychological Agenda of Modern Combat Training," *Journal of Social Issues* 31, no. 4 (1975): 17.

104. Ibid., 16. According to Eisenhart, "The means by which the military socialization process forged this link between an individual's sexuality and his military mission was proportional in intensity to the resistance encountered" (15).

105. Ibid., 15.

106. Klaus Theweleit, *Male Fantasies*, vol. 2, *Male Bodies: Psychoanalyzing the White Terror*, trans. Erica Carter and Chris Turner, with Stephen Conway (Minneapolis: University of Minnesota Press, 1989), 164.

107. Ibid., 164.

108. This concept paraphrases Susan Jeffords's argument concerning how Vietnam representations attempt to "remasculinize" American culture, or regain the privileged authority of the masculine that was supposedly lost in the Vietnam

war. See *The Remasculinization of America: Gender and the Vietnam War* (Bloomington: Indiana University Press, 1989).

109. Ronald J. Willis, "Victory," *Gigline* 1, no. 4 (1969): 18.

110. *OM* 1, no. 4 (October 1969): 11.

111. Julia Kristeva, *Powers of Horror: An Essay on Abjection* (New York: Columbia University Press, 1982), 53.

112. A more recent version of this poem revises the second stanza to read: "A brainless, savage flurry/of arms and legs and eyes." W. D. Erhart, *To Those Who Have Gone Home Tired: New and Selected Poems* (New York: Thunder's Mouth Press, 1984), 9. This revision focuses even more attention on the fragmentation of the body by deleting the qualifier "at once" and letting the list of body parts close the poem. And where the early version achieves a certain symmetry with the two tercets, the newer version's asymmetry underscores the dismemberment represented in the final lines.

113. Gibson, *The Perfect War*, 112–128.

114. Ibid., 112–114.

115. Cincinnatus [pseud.], *Self-Destruction*, 94.

116. Georges Bataille has written that the ritual of burial may have arisen as a means of keeping the living from being infected by death. "Death was a sign of violence brought into a world which it could destroy. Although motionless, the dead man had a part in the violence which had struck him down; anything which came too near him was threatened by the destruction which had brought him low. . . . Death is a danger for those left behind. If they have to bury the corpse it is less in order to keep it safe than to keep themselves from its contagion." *Erotism: Death and Sensuality*, trans. Mary Dalwood (San Francisco: City Lights Books, 1986), 46.

117. Cincinnatus [pseud.], *Self-Destruction*, 94.

118. Gibson, *The Perfect War*, 126.

119. D. C. Berry, "The Sun Goes Down," *Saigon Cemetery* (Athens: University of Georgia Press, 1972), 1.

120. Umojo Kwaguvu, "A Vet Raps to a POW," *The Bond*, April 1973, 8. Ground combat troops often expressed animosity toward pilots, who seemed above the gritty reality of the war, and who often endangered U.S. troops by their imprecise bombings. See, for example, Larry Rottmann, "What Kind of War?" in *Winning Hearts and Minds*, 97.

121. John Balaban, "Mau Than," in *Carrying the Darkness: American Indochina—The Poetry of the Vietnam War*, ed. W. D. Ehrhart (New York: Avon, 1985), 11.

122. Homi K. Bhabha, "Postcolonial Authority and Postmodern Guilt," in *Cultural Studies*, ed. Lawrence Grossberg, Cary Nelson, and Paula A. Treichler (New York: Routledge, 1991), 65. Bhabha quotes Freud's "Mourning and Melancholia" (1917).

123. L. Smith, "Resistance and Revision," 50.

124. Quoted in Phillip H. Melling, *Vietnam in American Literature* (Boston: Twayne, 1991), 95. This quote originally appeared in Walsh's "Poetic Representation of Vietnamese Women by American Soldier Poets," *Vietnam and the West*, 2.

125. Dewey Canyon culminated in thousands of veterans returning their military medals to the government. The veterans had planned to return them in body bags but, confronted with a fence authorities had built on the Capitol steps, they threw them over the fence. Photographs of this scene appeared in media through-

out the country. A moving document of Dewey Canyon can be found in Kerry et al., *The New Soldier*.

126. John Balaban, "After Our War," in *Carrying*, 15–16. This poem first appeared in Balaban's book *After Our War* (Pittsburg: University of Pittsburgh Press, 1974), now out of print.

127. Since the late 80s, a number of critical studies have appeared on U.S. imaginative representations of the Vietnam War. For more recent studies of U.S. literature of the Vietnam War that give extensive attention to poetry, see Owen W. Gilman, Jr., and Lorrie Smith, eds., *America Rediscovered: Critical Essays on Literature and Film of the Vietnam War* (New York: Garland, 1990); *Fourteen Landing Zones: Approaches to Vietnam War Literature*, ed. Jason; Philip D. Beidler, *Re-Writing America: Vietnam Authors in Their Generation* (Athens: University of Georgia Press, 1991); and Melling, *Vietnam in American Literature*. The only book-length study of soldier-poetry of the war is Gotera, *Radical Visions*.

128. Philip D. Beidler, *American Literature and the Experience of Vietnam* (Athens: University of Georgia Press, 1982), 75.

129. Jeffrey Walsh, *American War Literature 1914 to Vietnam* (New York: St. Martin's Press, 1982), 204.

130. Adi Wimmer, "The American Idea of National Identity: Patriotism and Poetic Sensibility Before and After Vietnam," *Cultural Legacies of Vietnam: Uses of the Past in the Present*, ed. Richard Morris and Peter Ehrenhaus (Norwood, N.J.: Ablex, 1990), 72; emphasis in original.

131. Cary Nelson, *Repression and Recovery: Modern American Poetry and the Politics of Cultural Memory 1910–1945* (Madison: University of Wisconsin Press, 1989), 37. As Nelson later demonstrates, the virtual extinction of a poet such as H. H. Lewis, known as the "Plowboy Poet," results "partly because his poetry does not generally display the surface indecision and ambivalence that many critics since the 1950s have deemed a transcendent, unquestionable literary and cultural value" (44).

132. Fredric Jameson, *The Political Unconscious: Narrative as Socially Symbolic Act* (Ithaca, N.Y.: Cornell University Press, 1981), 10.

133. Scarry, *The Body in Pain*, 64. Scarry also points out that "this disowning is not necessarily authored (not at any rate exclusively authored) by those who wish to perpetuate war." Her point is that these locutions are structural in a culture's discourse on war, that they are authored not simply by individuals in power but by a more complex set of cultural relations that enable any nation to wage war.

134. Ibid., 65–81.

135. Ibid., 64.

136. Paul Lauter, "Caste, Class, and Canon," in *A Gift of Tongues: Critical Challenges in Contemporary American Poetry*, ed. Marie Harris and Kathleen Aguero (Athens: University of Georgia Press, 1987), 66.

137. Erhart, "Soldier-Poets of the Vietnam War," 313.

138. Tischler, "Breaking Ranks," 24; emphasis in original.

139. In a cartoon by Chuck Mathias, for example, an obese officer is depicted devouring small, naked men as fully dressed and armed soldiers emerge from his anus. Reprinted in Tischler, "Breaking Ranks," 26. The caption notes that the cartoon appeared in many GI papers, but no titles are given.

140. L. Smith, "Resistance and Revision," 53.

Conclusion

1. For more on the politics of literary criticism and canons with respect to antiwar poetry, see Michael Bibby, "'Where is Vietnam?': Antiwar Poetry and the Canon," *College English* 55, no. 2 (1993): 158–178.

2. There are, of course, notable exceptions, but these tend to be thematically exceptional as well. Alicia Ostriker, *Stealing the Language: The Emergence of Women's Poetry in America* (Boston: Beacon Press, 1986), for example, develops a historical-critical survey of women's poetry that recognizes the significance of 60s activism; unlike the studies I am discussing here, however, Ostriker is thematically focused on *women's* poetry. James Mersmann, *Out of the Vietnam Vortex: A Study of Poets and Poetry Against the War* (Lawrence: University Press of Kansas, 1974), similarly, focuses on poetry of the antiwar movement.

3. David Perkins, *A History of Modern Poetry: Modernism and After* (Cambridge: Harvard University Press, Belknap Press, 1987), 348.

4. Paul Breslin, *The Psycho-Political Muse: American Poetry since the Fifties* (Chicago: University of Chicago Press, 1987), 7.

5. For examples, see ibid., 204–205, 208–209.

6. For example, see Charles Altieri, *Enlarging the Temple: New Directions in American Poetry during the 1960s* (London: Associated University Presses, 1979), 226.

7. Ibid., 238, 226.

8. Robert von Hallberg, *American Poetry and Culture, 1945–1980* (Cambridge: Harvard University Press, 1985), 140, 146.

9. This is especially evident when he claims, "The only anthologies or critical studies of post–World War II political poetry concern Vietnam poetry." Von Hallberg, *American Poetry and Culture*, 118, 117. In fact, as my study has shown, the Black Liberation and Women's Liberation movements produced a number of politically oriented anthologies. Antiwar anthologies tended to favor established writers working in writing workshops.

10. Ibid., 145.

11. Marcuse, for example, rejected much activist art and insisted that in sophisticated, difficult form lay art's subversive potential. See Carol Becker, "Herbert Marcuse and the Subversive Potential of Art," in *The Subversive Imagination: Artists, Society, and Social Responsibility*, ed. Carol Becker (New York: Routledge, 1994), 113–129. Theodor Adorno argued that the poem's politics must be immanent, and that it must engage its historical contexts only implicitly. "Lyric Poetry and Society," *Telos* 20 (1974): 56–71.

12. Cary Nelson, *Repression and Recovery: Modern American Poetry and the Politics of Cultural Memory, 1910–1945* (Madison: University of Wisconsin Press, 1989), 52.

13. Cary Nelson, *Our Last First Poets: Vision and History in Contemporary American Poetry* (Urbana: University of Illinois Press, 1981), 2.

14. In criticizing antiwar poems of the Vietnam era, Nelson suggests that they fail to transcend their historical moment. "[W]hat above all undoes most Vietnam poems, even the poems which are frankly beautiful and original, is an apparent ignorance of how history has usurped both their language and their form." Later, he exemplifies this with a reading of James Wright's "A Mad Fight Song for William S. Carpenter, 1966," suggesting that Wright's need to footnote the historical context of the poem points to one of its central problems. Nelson's

footnote emphasizes his point: "It is no small matter that some Vietnam poems, particularly those that make use of factual data, have to be published with footnotes to jog the memory; more footnotes will be required with each reprinting. This is particularly true for a poem like Ginsberg's 'Wichita Vortex Sutra.'" Ibid., 4, and 5, n. 6.

15. Nelson, *Repression and Recovery*, 50–51.

16. By teaching anthologies, I mean books marketed by publishers such as Heath, Norton, and others and designed primarily to serve as textbooks in literature courses. For more on this term, see Alan Golding, "A History of American Poetry Anthologies," in *Canons*, ed. Robert von Hallberg (Chicago: University of Chicago Press, 1983, 1984), 279–308.

17. Here I am referring specifically to their antiwar poetry. The 1973 edition of *The Norton Anthology of Modern Poetry*, for example, includes antiwar poems by Bly and Levertov, but the 1988 edition presents only one by Bly and none by Levertov and Ginsberg. Interestingly, the selections of Levertov's poems extend chronologically from her early work of the 50s to poems from 1964 and then skip to poems from 1975, editing out an eleven-year period. Richard Ellman and Robert O'Clair, eds., *The Norton Anthology of Modern Poetry* (New York: Norton, 1973). For more on this, see Bibby, "'Where is Vietnam?'"

18. Nina Baym et al, eds., *The Norton Anthology of American Literature*, 3rd shorter ed. (New York: Norton, 1989), 2407.

19. The Heath anthology includes the following Vietnam-era activist poems: Muriel Rukeyser, "Orpheus" and "Martin Luther King, Malcolm X"; Pedro Pietri, "Puerto Rican Obituary"; Mari Evans, "I am a Black Woman"; Sonia Sanchez, "to blk/record/buyers"; Amiri Baraka, "Ka' Ba," "Black People: This is Our Destiny," and "A Poem Some People Will Have to Understand"; Marge Piercy, "The woman in the ordinary" and "Unlearning to not speak." This list includes poems published in the Vietnam era that addressed specific political struggles of the period. I also noticed significant gaps in the representation of many poets' works from the Vietnam era. The selection of Gwendolyn Brooks's poetry contains none of her Afrocentric work from the late 60s. Although Muriel Rukeyser, Robert Hayden, Robert Lowell, Gary Snyder, Denise Levertov, James Wright, Lawrence Ferlinghetti, and Allen Ginsberg are represented here, and all wrote poems about the Vietnam War, none of these poems are included in the Heath anthology. Even though June Jordan's activist poetry dates from the late 60s, only work published since the late 80s is included. Similarly, Audre Lorde's work is anthologized here only from 1978 on. And while the collection includes a relatively substantial number of Michael Harper's poems, none of his important antiwar cycle, *Debridement*, appears. Activist poetry is much more represented by the 30s and the 80s. A subsection of the modernist section of the anthology, entitled "A Sheaf of Political Poetry in the Modern Period," edited by Cary Nelson, runs over thirty pages and includes nine poets and sixteen poems. Paul Lauter, gen. ed., *The Heath Anthology of American Literature*, 2nd ed., vol. 2 (Lexington, Mass.: D. C. Heath, 1994).

20. Barbara Harlow, *Resistance Literature* (New York: Methuen, 1987), 33.

21. Personal communication wtih Patricia Giggans, July 13, 1995.

Bibliography

Primary Sources

Alta. "Living in a Country at War/1968 Version." *It Ain't Me Babe*, 23 September 1970, 10.

Alhamisi, Ahmed, and Harun Kofi Wangara, eds. *Black Arts: An Anthology of Black Creations*. Detroit: Black Arts, 1969.

Baker, Houston A., Jr., ed. *Black Literature in America*. New York: McGraw-Hill, 1971.

Barba, Sharon, and Laura Chester, eds. *Rising Tides: 20th Century American Women Poets*. New York: Washington Square Press, 1973.

Bass, Ellen, and Florence Howe, eds. *No More Masks!: An Anthology of Poems by Women*. Garden City, N.Y.: Doubleday, Anchor, 1973.

Berry, D. C. *Saigon Cemetery*. Athens: University of Georgia Press, 1972.

Bly, Robert, and David Ray, eds. *A Poetry Reading Against the Vietnam War*. Madison, Minn.: Sixties, 1967.

Brandy French (pseud). "A Womb on Strike." *It Ain't Me Babe*, 4–17 September 1970, 15.

Brooks, Gwendolyn, ed. *A Broadside Treasury*. Detroit: Broadside Press, 1971.

———, ed. *Jump Bad: A New Chicago Anthology*. Detroit: Broadside Press, 1971.

Chapman, Abraham, ed. *Black Voices: An Anthology of Afro-American Literature*. New York: New American Library, Mentor, 1968.

———, ed. *New Black Voices: An Anthology of Contemporary Afro-American Literature*. New York: New American Library, Mentor, 1972.

Coombs, Orde, ed. *We Speak As Liberators: Young Black Poets*. New York: Dodd, Mead, 1970.

Davis, Frank Marshall. *47th Street*. Prairie City, Ill.: Decker Press, 1948.

Ehrhart, W. D., ed. *Carrying the Darkness: American Indochina—The Poetry of the Vietnam War*. New York: Avon, 1985.

———. *To Those Who Have Gone Home Tired: New and Selected Poems*. New York: Thunder's Mouth Press, 1984.

Emory. "On Revolutionary Art." *The Black Panther*, 20 June 1967, 1.

Ericka. "Revolution." *The Black Panther*, 5 October 1968, 14.

Foner, Philip, ed. *The Black Panthers Speak*. Philadelphia: J. B. Lippincott, 1970.

Giggans, Patricia. "Two Poems." *Aphra* 3 (Summer 1972): 32–33.

Gill, Elaine, ed. *Mountain Moving Day: Poems by Women*. Trumansburg, N.Y.: Crossing, 1973.

Gitlin, Todd, ed. *Campfires of the Resistance: Poetry from the Movement*. Indianapolis: Bobbs-Merrill, 1971.

Harper, Michael. *Debridement*. Garden City, N.Y.: Doubleday, 1972, 1973.

Henderson, Stephen, ed. *Understanding the New Black Poetry: Black Speech and Black Music as Poetic References*. New York: William Morrow, 1973.

Herr, Michael. *Dispatches*. New York: Avon, 1978.

Iverson, Lucille, and Kathryn Ruby, eds. *We Become New: Poems by Contemporary American Women*. New York: Bantam, 1975.

Jones, LeRoi. *The Dead Lecturer*. New York: Grove Press, 1964.

Jones, LeRoi, and Larry Neal, eds. *Black Fire: An Anthology of Afro-American Writing*. New York: William Morrow, 1968.

Jordan, June, ed. *Soulscript: Afro-American Poetry*. Garden City, N.Y.: Doubleday, Zenith, 1970.

Kimler, Forest L., ed. *Boondock Bards*. Tokyo: Pacific Stars and Stripes, 1968.

King, Woodie, ed. *Black Spirits: A Festival of New Black Poets in America*. Assisted by Imamu Amiri Baraka. New York: Random House, 1972.

Komunyakaa, Yusef. *Dien Cai Dao*. Middletown, Conn.: Wesleyan University Press, 1988.

Kwaguvu, Umojo. "A Vet Raps to a POW." *The Bond*, April 1973, 8.

Laxer, Greg. "For My Still Imprisoned Comrades." *The Bond*, 30 June 1971, 7.

LeMieux, Dotty. "The war is still on somewhere." *Women*, Fall 1970, 6.

Lowenfels, Walter, ed. *In a Time of Revolution: Poems from Our Third World*. New York: Random House, 1969.

———, ed. *Where is Vietnam?: American Poets Respond*. Garden City, N.Y.: Doubleday, Anchor, 1967.

Major, Clarence, ed. *The New Black Poetry*. New York: International Publishers, 1969.

Morgan, Robin. *Monster*. New York: Vintage, 1972.

———, ed. *Sisterhood is Powerful: An Anthology of Writings from the Women's Liberation Movement*. New York: Random House, 1970.

Murphy, Beatrice, ed. *Ebony Rhythm: An Anthology of Contemporary Negro Verse*. New York: The Exposition Press, 1948.

Neal, Larry. *Black Boogaloo (Notes on Black Liberation)*. San Francisco: Journal of Black Poetry Press, 1969.

———. *Hoodoo Hollerin' Bebop Ghosts*. Washington, D.C.: Howard University Press, 1974.

Nuriddin, Jalal, and Suliaman El Hadi. *The Last Poets: Vibes From the Scribes, Selected Poems*. London: Pluto Press, 1985

A Peace Lover. "Comes the silence." *A Four-Year Bummer* 1, no. 2 (1969): 4.

Plath, Sylvia. *The Collected Poems*. Edited by Ted Hughes. New York: Harper & Row, 1981.

Randall, Dudley, ed. *Black Poetry: A Supplement to Anthologies Which Exclude Black Poets*. Detroit: Broadside Press, 1969.

Rich, Adrienne. *The Fact of a Doorframe: Poems Selected and -New, 1950–1974*. New York: Norton, 1984.

———. *Leaflets: Poems 1965–1968*. New York: Norton, 1969.

———. *On Lies, Secrets, and Silence: Selected Prose 1965–1978*. New York: Norton, 1979.

————. *The Will to Change: Poems 1968–1970*. New York: Norton, 1971.

Robinson, Sandy. "I HAD TO BE TOLD." *Journal of Black Poetry* 16 (Summer 1972): 34.

Rodgers, Carolyn. "My Lai as Related to No. Vietnam Alabama." In *Afro-American Writing: An Anthology of Prose and Poetry*, edited by Richard A. Long and Eugenia W. Collier, 2:776–777. New York: New York University Press, 1972.

Rottmann, Larry, Jan Barry, and Basil T. Paquet, eds. *Winning Hearts and Minds: War Poems by Vietnam Veterans*. Brooklyn: 1st Casualty Press, 1972.

Salzman, Jack, and Leo Zanderer, eds. *Social Poetry of the 1930s: A Selection*. New York: Burt Franklin, 1978.

Segnitz, Barbara, and Carol Rainey, eds. *Psyche: The Feminine Poetic Consciousness*. New York: Dial Press, 1973.

Sexton, Anne. *The Complete Poems*. Boston: Houghton Mifflin, 1981.

————. *Selected Poems of Anne Sexton*. Edited by Diana Wood Middlebrook and Diana Hume George. Boston: Houghton Mifflin, 1988.

Smitherman, Geneva. "The Power of Rap: The Black Idiom and the New Black Poetry." *Twentieth-Century Literature* 19,no. 4 (1973): 259–274.

Stanford, Ann, ed. *The Women Poets in English: An Anthology*. New York: McGraw-Hill, 1972.

Tate, Allen. Preface to *Libretto for the Republic of Liberia*, by Melvin B. Tolson. London: Collier-Macmillan, 1970.

Taylor, Clyde, ed. *Vietnam and Black America: An Anthology of Protest*. Garden City, N.Y.: Doubleday, Anchor, 1973.

Taylor, Prentiss. "Tony." *Journal of Black Poetry* 16 (Summer 1972): 49.

Theodore. "You Are the Black Woman." *Liberator*, March 1969, 13.

Turner, Sherry. "An Overview of the New Black Arts." *Freedomways* 9, no. 2 (1969): 156–163.

Van Devanter, Lynda, and Joan A. Furey, eds. *Visions of War, Dreams of Peace: Writings of Women in the Vietnam War*. New York: Warner, 1991.

Vietnam Veterans Against the War. *The Winter Soldier Investigation: An Inquiry into American War Crimes*. Boston: Beacon, 1972.

Willis, Ronald J. "Victory." *Gigline* 1, no. 4 (1969): 18.

The Wipers Times: A Facsimile Reprint of the Trench Magazines—The Wipers Times, The New Church Times, The Kemmel Times, The Somme Times, The B. E. F. Times. London: Herbert Jenkins, Ltd., 1918.

Selected Secondary Sources

Allen, Robert. *Black Awakening in Capitalist America: An Analytic History*. Trenton, N.J.: Africa World Press, 1990.

Anderson, Terry H. "The GI Movement and the Response from the Brass." In *Give Peace a Chance: Exploring the Vietnam Antiwar Movement*, edited by Melvin Small and William D. Hoover, 93–115. Syracuse, N.Y.: Syracuse University Press, 1992.

"Antiwar GIs." *Black Liberator*, July 1969, 3.

Arney, William Ray. *Power and the Profession of Obstetrics*. Chicago: University of Chicago Press, 1982.

Baker, Houston A., Jr. *Blues, Ideology, and Afro-American Literature: A Vernacular Theory*. Chicago: University of Chicago Press, 1984.

Baraka, Ameer [also known as LeRoi Jones, also known as Amiri Baraka]. "The Black Aesthetic." *Negro Digest*, September 1969), 5–6.

Barbour, Floyd B., ed. *The Black Seventies*. Boston: Porter Sargent, 1970.

Beidler, Philip D. *American Literature and the Experience of Vietnam*. Athens: University of Georgia Press, 1982.

———. *Re-Writing America: Vietnam Authors in Their Generation*. Athens: University of Georgia Press, 1991.

Bhabha, Homi K. "Postcolonial Authority and Postmodern Guilt." In *Cultural Studies*, edited by Lawrence Grossberg, Cary Nelson, and Paula A. Treichler, 56–66. New York: Routledge, 1991.

Bland, Edward. "Racial Bias and Negro Poetry." *Poetry* 63 (March 1944): 328–333.

Bordo, Susan. *Unbearable Weight: Feminism, Western Culture, and the Body*. Berkeley: University of California Press, 1993.

Boston Women's Health Collective. *Our Bodies, Ourselves: A Book by and for Women*. New York: Simon and Schuster, 1971.

Breslin, Paul. *The Psycho-Political Muse: American Poetry since the Fifties*. Chicago: University of Chicago Press, 1987.

Burris, Barbara. "The Fourth World Manifesto." In *Radical Feminism*, edited by Anne Koedt, Ellen Levine, and Anita Rapone, 322–357. New York: New York Times Books, Quadrangle Books, 1973.

Butler, Judith. *Bodies That Matter: On the Discursive Limits of "Sex"*. New York: Routledge, 1993.

———. *Gender Trouble: Feminism and the Subversion of Identity*. New York: Routledge, 1990.

Cabral, Amilcar. *Return to the Source: Selected Speeches*. Edited by Africa Information Service. New York: Monthly Review, 1973.

Carson, Clayborne. *In Struggle: SNCC and the Black Awakening of the 1960s*. Cambridge, Mass.: Harvard University Press, 1981.

Cincinnatus [pseud]. *Self-Destruction: The Disintegration and Decay of the United States Army During the Vietnam Era*. New York: Norton, 1981.

Clausen, Jan. *A Movement of Poets: Thoughts on Poetry and Feminism*. Brooklyn, N.Y.: Long Haul Press, 1982.

Cleaver, Eldridge. *Soul on Ice*. New York: Delta, 1968.

Connell, Mike. "Vietnam: A Personal View." *A Four-Year Bummer* 1, no. 2 (1969): 4.

Cortright, David. *Soldiers in Revolt: The American Military Today*. Garden City, N.Y.: Doubleday, Anchor, 1975.

Daly, Mary. *Gyn/Ecology: The Metaethics of Radical Feminism*. Boston: Beacon Press, 1978.

Damon, Maria. *The Dark End of the Street: Margins in American Vanguard Poetry*. Minneapolis: University of Minnesota Press, 1993.

de Beauvoir, Simone. *The Second Sex*. Translated by H. M. Parshley. New York: Alfred Knopf, 1952; reprint, New York: Vintage, 1974.

DeBenedetti, Charles. *An American Ordeal: The Antiwar Movement of the Vietnam Era*. Assisted by Charles Chatfield. Syracuse, N.Y.: Syracuse University Press, 1990.

de Lauretis, Teresa. *Technologies of Gender: Essays on Theory, Film, and Fiction*. Bloomington: Indiana University Press, 1987.

Dreifus, Claudia, ed. *Seizing Our Bodies: The Politics of Women's Health*. New York: Vintage, 1978.

Du Bois, W.E.B. *The Souls of Black Folk*. 1903. Reprint, New York: Vintage Books, The Library of America, 1990.

Echols, Alice. *Daring to Be Bad: Radical Feminism in America, 1967–1975*. Minneapolis: University of Minnesota Press, 1989.

Ehrenreich, Barbara, and Deirdre English. *Complaints and Disorders: The Sexual Politics of Sickness*. New York: The Feminist Press, 1973.

Ehrhart, W. D. "Soldier-Poets of the Vietnam War." In *America Rediscovered: Critical Essays on Literature and Film of the Vietnam War*, edited by Owen W. Gilman, Jr. and Lorrie Smith, 313–331. New York: Garland, 1990.

Eisenhart, R. Wayne. "You Can't Hack it Little Girl: A Discussion of the Covert Psychological Agenda of Modern Combat Training." *Journal of Social Issues* 31, no. 4 (1975): 13–25.

Evans, Sara. *Personal Politics: The Roots of Women's Liberation in the Civil Rights Movement and the New Left*. New York: Vintage, 1980.

Fanon, Frantz. *Black Skin, White Masks*. Translated by Charles Lam Markmann. New York: Grove Weidenfeld, 1967.

———. *The Wretched of the Earth*. Translated by Constance Farrington. New York: Grove Press, 1968.

Fields, Barbara Jeanne. "Slavery, Race and Ideology in the United States of America." *New Left Review* 180 (1990): 95–118.

Firestone, Shulamith. *The Dialectic of Sex: The Case for Feminist Revolution*. New York: Morrow, 1970.

Foucault, Michel. *The Archaeology of Knowledge*. Translated by A. M. Sheridan Smith. New York: Vintage, 1972.

———. *Discipline and Punish: The Birth of the Prison*. Translated by Alan Sheridan. New York: Vintage, 1979.

———. *The History of Sexuality*. Vol 1, *An Introduction*. Translated by Robert Hurley. New York: Vintage, 1980.

———. *Language, Counter-Memory, Practice: Selected Essays and Interviews*. Edited by Donald F. Bouchard. Translated by Donald F. Bouchard and Sherry Simon. Ithaca, N.Y.: Cornell University Press, 1977.

———. *Power/Knowledge: Selected Interviews and Other Writings 1972–1977*. Edited by Colin Gordon. New York: Pantheon, 1980.

———. "Technologies of the Self." In *Technologies of the Self: A Seminar with Michel Foucault*, edited by Luther H. Martin, Huck Gutman, and Patrick H. Hutton, 16–49. Amherst: University of Massachussetts Press, 1988.

Fuller, Hoyt W. "Towards a Black Aesthetic." In *The Black Aesthetic*, edited by Addison Gayle, Jr., 3–11. Garden City, N.Y.: Doubleday, Anchor, 1971.

Fulton, Len. *The Directory of Little Magazines and Small Presses*. 3rd ed. El Cerrito, Calif.: Dustbooks, 1967.

Gabriel, Michael. "The Astonishing Growth of Small Publishers, 1958–1988." *Journal of Popular Culture* 24 (Winter 1990): 61–68.

Gates, Henry Louis, Jr. "African American Criticism." In *Redrawing the Boundaries: The Transformation of English and American Literary Studies*, edited by Stephen Greenblatt and Giles Gunn, 303–319. New York: Modern Language Association, 1992.

———, ed. *"Race," Writing, and Difference*. Chicago: University of Chicago Press, 1986.

Gayle, Jr., Addison, ed. *The Black Aesthetic*. Garden City, N.Y.: Doubleday, Anchor, 197

Gibson, James William. *The Perfect War: The War We Couldn't Lose and How We Did*. New York: Vintage, 1986.

Gill, Gerald. "From Maternal Pacifisim to Revolutionary Solidarity: African-American Women's Opposition to the Vietnam War." In *Sights on the Sixties*, edited by

Barbara L. Tischler, 177–195. New Brunswick, N.J.: Rutgers University Press, 1992.

Glicksberg, Charles I. "Negro Poets and the American Tradition." *Antioch Review* 6 (1946): 243–253.

Gloster, Hugh M. "Race and the Negro Writer." *Phylon* 11, no. 4 (Winter 1950): 369–371.

Gordon, Linda. *Woman's Body, Woman's Rights: Birth Control in America.* Rev. ed. New York: Penguin, 1990.

Gotera, Vince. *Radical Visions: Poetry by Vietnam Veterans.* Athens: University of Georgia Press, 1994.

Gramsci, Antonio. *The Modern Prince and Other Writings.* Translated by Louis Marks. 1957; reprint, New York: International Publishers, 1987.

Grosz, Elizabeth. *Volatile Bodies: Toward a Corporeal Feminism.* Bloomington: Indiana University Press, 1994.

Haines, Harry W. "Hegemony and GI Resistance." *Viet Nam Generation* 2, no. 1 (1990): 3–7.

Harlow, Barbara. *Resistance Literature.* New York: Methuen, 1987.

Harris, William J. *The Poetry and Poetics of Amiri Baraka: The Jazz Aesthetic.* Columbia: University of Missouri Press, 1985.

Hayes, James R. "The Dialectics of Resistance: An Analysis of the GI Movement." *Journal of Social Issues* 31, no. 4 (1975): 125–139.

Henderson, Stephen. "'Survival Motion': A Study of the Black Writer and the Black Revolution in America." In *The Militant Black Writer in Africa and the United States,* by Mercer Cook and Stephen Henderson, 63–129. Madison: University of Wisconsin Press, 1969.

Hsiao, Lisa. "Project 100,000: The Great Society's Answer to Military Manpower Needs in Vietnam." *Vietnam Generation* 1, no. 2 (1989): 14–37.

James, David E. *Allegories of Cinema: American Film in the Sixties.* Princeton, N.J.: Princeton University Press, 1989.

Jameson, Fredric. "Periodizing the 60s." In *The 60s Without Apology,* edited by Sohnya Sayres, Anders Stephanson, Stanley Aronowitz, and Fredric Jameson, 178–209. Minneapolis: University of Minnesota Press, 1984.

———. *The Political Unconscious: Narrative as Socially Symbolic Act.* Ithaca, N.Y.: Cornell University Press, 1981.

———. *Postmodernism, or the Cultural Logic of Late Capitalism.* Durham, N.C.: Duke University Press, 1990.

Jeffords, Susan. *The Remasculinization of America: Gender and the Vietnam War.* Bloomington: University of Indiana Press, 1989.

Johnson, Abby Arthur, and Ronald Maberry Johnson. *Propaganda and Aesthetics: The Literary Politics of African-American Magazines in the Twentieth Century.* Amherst: University of Massachusetts Press, 1991.

Jones, Beverly, and Judith Brown. "Toward a Female Liberation Movement." In *Voices from Women's Liberation,* compiled and edited by Leslie B. Tanner, 63–129. New York: Signet, 1970.

Jordan, Jennifer. "Cultural Nationalism in the 1960s: Politics and Poetry." In *Race, Politics, and Culture: Critical Essays on the Radicalism of the 1960s,* edited by Adolph Reed, Jr., 29–60. Contributions in Afro-American and African Studies, no. 95. New York: Greenwood, 1986.

Kerry, John, and Vietnam Veterans Against the War. *The New Soldier,* edited by David Thorne and George Butler. New York: Macmillan, 1971.

Kolko, Gabriel. *Anatomy of a War: Vietnam, the United States, and the Modern Histori-cal Experience*. New York: Pantheon, 1985.

Kristeva, Julia. *Powers of Horror: An Essay on Abjection*. New York: Columbia University Press, 1982.

Laclau, Ernesto and Chantal Mouffe. *Hegemony and Socialist Strategy: Towards a Radical Democratic Politics*. London: Verso, 1985.

Malcolm X. *The Autobiography of Malcolm X*. Assisted by Alex Haley. New York: Grove, 1965; New York: Ballantine, 1965, 1973.

————. *February 1965: The Final Speeches*. Edited by Steve Clark. New York: Pathfinder, 1992.

————. *Malcolm X Speaks: Selected Speeches and Statements*. Edited by George Breitman. New York: Pathfinder Press, 1965.

Marable, Manning. *Race, Reform, and Rebellion: The Second Reconstruction in Black America, 1945–1990*. 2d ed. Jackson: University Press of Mississippi, 1991.

Marcuse, Herbert. *Eros and Civilization: A Philosophical Inquiry into Freud*. Boston: Beacon Press, 1966.

————. *One-Dimensional Man: Studies in the Ideology of Advanced Industrial Society*. Boston: Beacon Press, 1964.

Martin, Emily. *The Woman in the Body: A Cultural Analysis of Reproduction*. Boston: Beacon Press, 1987.

Mayer, Milton. "Who Wants to Be White?" *Negro Digest*, December 1949, 41–43.

Mercer, Kobena. "'1968': Periodizing Politics and Identity." In *Cultural Studies*, edited by Lawrence Grossberg, Cary Nelson, and Paula Treichler, 424–438. New York: Routledge, 1992.

Morgan, Robin. "On Women as a Colonized People." In *The Word of a Woman: Feminist Dispatches 1968–1992*, 74–77. New York: W. W. Norton, 1992.

————. "Taking back our bodies." In *The New Woman's Survival Sourcebook*, edited by Kirsten Grimstad, Susan Rennie, Sandra Dzija, and Ann Schroeder, 33. New York: Alfred A. Knopf, 1975.

Neal, Larry. *Visions of a Liberated Future: Black Arts Movement Writings*, edited by Michael Schwartz. New York: Thunder Mouth's Press, 1989.

Nelson, Cary. *Our Last First Poets: Vision and History in Contemporary American Poetry*. Urbana: University of Illinois Press, 1981.

————. *Repression and Recovery: Modern American Poetry and the Politics of Cultural Memory, 1910–1945*. Madison: University of Wisconsin Press, 1989.

Omi, Michael, and Howard Winant. *Racial Formation in the United States: From the 1960s to the 1980s*. New York: Routledge and Kegan Paul, 1986.

Orlen, Michael. "The Umbra Poets' Workshop, 1962–1965: Some Socio-Literary Puzzles." In *Belief vs. Theory in Black American Literary Criticism*, vol. 2 of *Studies in Black American Literature*, edited by Joe Weixlmann and Chester J. Fontenot, 177–224. Greenwood, Fla.: Penkevill Publishing, 1986.

Ostriker, Alicia. *Stealing the Language: The Emergence of Women's Poetry in America*. Boston: Beacon Press, 1986.

Patton, Gwendolyn. "Black People and War." *Liberator*, March 1966, 31.

Perkins, David. *A History of Modern Poetry: Modernism and After*. Cambridge, Mass.: Harvard University Press, Belknap Press, 1987.

Peter X. "BLACK!! Who Me?" *Black Vanguard* 5 (1968): 3.

Pollard, Vicki. "Producing Society's Babies." In *Voices from Women's Liberation*, edited by Leslie B. Tanner, 193–199. New York: Signet, 1970.

Probyn, Elspeth. "This Body Which is Not One: Speaking an Embodied Self." *Hypatia* 6, no. 3 (1991): 111–124.

Public Papers of the Presidents of the United States: Lyndon B. Johnson, 1965. Book 1: January 1 to May 31, 1965. Washington, D.C.: United States Government Printing Office, 1966.

Rabinowitz, Paula. *Labor and Desire: Women's Revolutionary Fiction in Depression America*. Chapel Hill: University of North Carolina Press, 1991.

Rapone, Anita. "The Body is the Role: Sylvia Plath." In *Radical Feminism*, edited by Anne Koedt, Ellen Levine, and Anita Rapone, 407–412. New York: New York Times Books, Quadrangle Books, 1973.

Rapaport, Herman. "Vietnam: The Thousand Plateaus." In *The 60s Without Apology*, edited by Sohnya Sayres, Anders Stephanson, Stanley Aronowitz, and Fredric Jameson, 137–147. Minneapolis: University of Minnesota Press, 1984.

Redding, J. Saunder. "The Negro Writer—Shadow and Substance." *Phylon* 11, no. 4 (1950): 371–373.

Reed, Jr., Adolph. "The 'Black Revolution' and the Reconstitution of Domination." In *Race, Politics, and Culture: Critical Essays on the Radicalism of the 1960s*, 61–95. Contributions in Afro-American and African Studies, no. 95. New York: Greenwood, 1986.

"Rescuing the NAACP." *Freedomways* 7, no. 4 (1967): 286.

Rinaldi, Matthew. "The Olive-Drab Rebels: Military Organizing During the Vietnam Era." *Radical America* 8, no. 3 (1974): 17–52.

Robinson, Paul. *The Freudian Left: Wilhelm Reich, Geza Roheim, Herbert Marcuse*. Ithaca, N.Y. Cornell University Press, 1969; reprint, 1990.

Rodgers, Carolyn. "Black Poetry—Where It's At." *Negro Digest*, September 1969, 7–16.

———. "Uh Nat'chal Thang—The WHOLE TRUTH—US." *Black World*, September 1971, 4–14.

Rosen, Ruth. "The Day They Buried 'Traditional Womanhood': Women and the Politics of Protest." *Vietnam Generation* 1, no. 3/4 (1989): 208–234.

Sarachild, Kathie. "Taking in the Images: A Record in Graphics of the Vietnam Era Soil for Feminism." *Vietnam Generation* 1., no. 3/4 (1989): 235–245.

Sarachild, Kathie, and Redstockings, eds. *Feminist Revolution*. New York: Random House, 1978.

Sartre, Jean-Paul. *Being and Nothingness*. Translated by Hazel E. Barnes. New York: Washington Square Press, 1992.

Scarry, Elaine. *The Body in Pain: The Making and Unmaking of the World*. New York: Oxford University Press, 1985.

Shilling, Chris. *The Body and Social Theory*. London: Sage, 1993.

Smith, David L. "Amiri Baraka and the Black Arts of Black Art." *boundary 2* 15, no. 1/2 (1986/87): 235–254.

Smith, Lorrie. "Resistance and Revision in Poetry by Vietnam War Veterans." In *Fourteen Landing Zones: Approaches to Vietnam War Literature*, edited by Philip K. Jason, 49–66. Iowa City: University of Iowa, 1991.

Swerdlow, Amy. "Motherhood and the Subversion of the Military State: Women Strike for Peace Confronts the House Committee on Un-American Activities." In *Women, Militarism, and War: Essays in History, Politics, and Social Theory*, edited by Jean Bethke Elshtain and Sheila Tobias, 7–28. Savage, Md.: Rowman and Littlefield, 1990.

Synnott, Arthur. *The Body Social: Symbolism, Self and Society*. London: Routledge, 1993.

Tal, Kali. "Speaking the Language of Pain: Vietnam War Literature in the Context of a Literature of Trauma." *Fourteen Landing Zones: Approaches to Vietnam War Literature*, edited by Philip K. Jason, 217–250. Iowa City: University of Iowa Press, 1991.

Tischler, Barbara. "Breaking Ranks: GI Antiwar Newspapers and the Culture of Protest." *Vietnam Generation* 2, no. 1 (1990): 20–50.

———. "Voices of Protest: Women and the GI Antiwar Press." In *Sights on the Sixties*, 197–209. New Brunswick, N.J.: Rutgers University Press, 1992.

Turner, Bryan. *Regulating Bodies: Essays in Medical Sociology*. London: Routledge, 1992.

Van Deburg, William L. *New Day in Babylon: The Black Power Movement and American Culture, 1965–1975*. Chicago: University of Chicago Press, 1992.

Van Devanter, Lynda. *Home Before Morning: The Story of an Army Nurse in Vietnam*. New York: Warner, 1983.

von Hallberg, Robert. *American Poetry and Culture, 1945–1980*. Cambridge, Mass.: Harvard University Press, 1985.

Walker, Margaret. "New Poets." *Phylon* 11, no. 4 (1950): 345–354.

Walsh, Jeffrey. *American War Literature, 1914 to Vietnam*. New York: St. Martin's Press, 1982.

"The War in Vietnam." *Freedomways*, Spring 1965, 224.

White, Walter. "Has Science Conquered the Color Line?" *Negro Digest*, December 1949, 37–40.

Zald, Anne E., and Cathy Seitz Whitaker. "The Underground Press of the Vietnam Era: An Annotated Bibliography." In *Voices from the Underground*, vol. 2 of *A Directory of Sources and Resources on the Vietnam Era Underground Press*, edited by Ken Wachsberger, 1–38. Tempe, Ariz.: Mica Press, 1993.

Zaroulis, Nancy, and Gerald Sullivan. *Who Spoke Up?: American Protest Against the War in Vietnam, 1963–1975*. Garden City, N.Y.: Doubleday, 1984.

Index

About the Author

Michael Bibby teaches in the English Department at Shippensburg University in Pennsylvania. He is the editor of *The Viet Nam War and Postmodernity*, and is currently working on a collection of essays on postpunk gothic subculture.